100 THINGS
MINNESOTA FANS
SHOULD KNOW & DO
BEFORE THEY DIE

100 THINGS
MINNESOTA FANS
SHOULD KNOW & DO
BEFORE THEY DIE

Brian Murphy

TRIUMPH
BOOKS

Library of Congress Cataloging-in-Publication Data

Names: Murphy, Brian, 1971 November 06– author.
Title: 100 things Minnesota fans should know & do before they die / Brian Murphy.
Other titles: One hundred things Minnesota fans should know and do before they die
Description: Chicago, Illinois : Triumph Books LLC, [2017]
Identifiers: LCCN 2017003418 | ISBN 9781629373317
Subjects: LCSH: University of Minnesota—History. | University of Minnesota—Miscellanea. | Minnesota—History.
Classification: LCC LD3348 .M87 2017 | DDC 378.009776/579—dc23
LC record available at https://lccn.loc.gov/2017003418

This book is available in quantity at special discounts for your group or organization. For further information, contact:
Triumph Books LLC
814 North Franklin Street
Chicago, Illinois 60610
(312) 337-0747
www.triumphbooks.com

Printed in U.S.A.
ISBN: 978-1-62937-331-7
Design by Patricia Frey

Photos courtesy of the University of Minnesota unless otherwise indicated

For Megan, Claire, and Ethan,
my lighthouse in the storm

Contents

Foreword

Personally, I believe that any good fortune that I've had in hockey or business is the direct result of attending the University of Minnesota. Those were the best four years of my life because they prepared me to become an NHLer and a person who could succeed in business.

As well as this, my wife and I were able to forge friendships that are very strong and still exist today.

All the work that I put into sports and education at the U resulted in better development for me as an athlete and businessman.

I feel that fundraising allows me to give U of M student-athletes an opportunity to improve their lives. I think it's an effective way for me to repay a debt to the U for providing the platform it did for my life in sports and business.

—Lou Nanne
U.S. Hockey Hall of Fame Member
and Former Minnesota North Star

Acknowledgments

I am grateful to author Ross Bernstein for recommending me for this project. Thanks also to Triumph editor Michelle Bruton for guiding this first-time author to the finish line.

Hat tip to Jeff Keiser in Gophers athletics for story tips and for steering me to valuable books and research materials.

Special thanks to University of Minnesota archivist Erik Moore, whose generosity and patience opened a treasure trove of artifacts, photographs, and documents that brought these subjects and moments to life.

Thank you Lou Nanne for your contribution and wisdom, Stew Thornley for your deep research, and *Pioneer Press* columnist Charley Walters for your bottomless well of telephone numbers.

1 Herbie

They flocked by the thousands to the old church on the hill on a sweltering summer day to say goodbye to the man who turned the Gophers into a championship destination and a team of shaggy-haired college kids into heroes during that bygone winter when America badly needed them.

A lone bagpiper played while a soloist sang the "Battle Hymn of the Republic" as 33 honorary pall bearers raised their hockey sticks in unison. Vintage World War II aircraft flew over Saint Paul Cathedral and the capital city skyline, their whirring propellers piercing the somberness before disappearing over the Mississippi River.

The aging men who wore the Maroon and Gold or Red, White, and Blue in their youth choked back tears as the casket bearing their coach, their mentor, their friend was carried down the sun-scorched steps and into a hearse for a private burial.

Herbert Paul Brooks earned fame as the hard-nosed head coach who defeated the mighty Soviets to win Olympic gold in the 1980 "Miracle on Ice." He was feted at the White House, glorified by Hollywood, and stalked by corporate titans for inspiration on the lecture circuit.

But Brooks always considered himself a lunch-pail guy from St. Paul's hardscrabble East Side, an Episcopalian who called himself a "back-door Catholic." He would rather drink light beer from a can than sip Cabernet out of stemware.

The iconoclast undoubtedly would have been tickled to see casually dressed laborers and clock punchers rubbing shoulders

1

with politicians and hockey glitterati in designer shades and suits celebrating his life inside such a resplendent house of worship.

Attending the funeral were 19 of the 20 players Brooks coached on the U.S. Olympic team. He was the last to take credit and the first among them to go.

"It's the one reunion that nobody wanted to go to," said Buzz Schneider.

Brooks turned 66 less than a week before he was killed midday August 11, 2003, driving back to his suburban St. Paul home after playing in a charity golf outing for the U.S. Hockey Hall of Fame in northern Minnesota.

Brooks was ejected from his Toyota minivan when he swerved and lost control on southbound Interstate 35, about 20 miles from his front door. He was not wearing a seatbelt, according to Minnesota state police.

Unrivaled as a transformative hockey coach, sharp-elbowed innovator, and restless intellect, Brooks figured to have one more big play to make, which made the pain from his untimely death cut bone deep. His vagabond career started at the University of Minnesota in 1972 and included layovers in Switzerland, New York City, Minnesota, France, and Pittsburgh before a 2002 encore with Team USA that closed the circle on Brooks' professional life.

"America's Coach" was more than a taskmaster in a track suit with a whistle between his lips.

He was married for 39 years to his indefatigable wife, Patti; dad to son Danny and daughter Kelly; grandfather of five; David's and Gayle's big brother. His closest friends were Minnesota hockey royalty, from the late John Mariucci, Glen Sonmor, Warren Strelow, and Wendell Anderson to John Mayasich, Lou Nanne, John Harrington, and Tom Vannelli.

Most, however, knew him simply as "Herbie." The guy who returned to his East Side barber for haircuts, hobnobbed with the

In seven seasons at Minnesota, Herb Brooks won three national titles among four Frozen Four appearances and coached five All-Americans and 23 future NHL players—all before becoming an international celebrity when he lead Team USA to an Olympic gold medal in the 1980 "Miracle on Ice."
University of Minnesota Archives

regulars at Vogel's Lounge on Payne Avenue, and once spent two weeks helping an old friend clear brush because the tree trimmer's workers bailed on a major landscaping project.

"I'm sure he was the greatest coach ever," eulogized Bill Butters, Brooks' first Gophers captain. "But he was a father figure, a man of integrity, a man of character, and a man of passion."

People were drawn to Brooks' everyman quality and his sardonic wit, which could leave dinner companions in stitches and the press eating out of his hands.

Even his players chuckled at his barbed-wire "Herbisms."

"You're playing worse every day and right now you're playing like next month!" he would bark from behind the bench.

Flying to Nagano for the 1998 Winter Olympics, Brooks was seated next to a woman who started breastfeeding her infant.

"I hope you're not offended, sir, but it's the only thing that will stop his ears from popping," she said.

"I'm not offended but all these years I've just been chewing gum," Brooks quipped.

One night Brooks was waiting for a table at a Philadelphia restaurant when he spotted a picture of former President Jimmy Carter.

"He called me three times in two days a few years ago but I haven't heard from him since."

Hockey made Brooks a global celebrity, but his passion for the sport matured on the tiny 10-by-20-foot rink his father built alongside the family duplex near Lake Phalen.

Born August 5, 1937, Brooks was the oldest of three children raised by a tough Irishman and frugal Swede. Herb Sr. sold insurance and coached junior hockey. Pauline was a proofreader at a local publishing house and a summer lifeguard.

Brooks played forward and first base for the hockey and baseball teams at St. Paul Johnson High School. In 1954–55 he helped lead the Governors to a 26–1–2 record and state hockey championship. Brooks was a swift skater and fierce competitor with a sneaky playmaker's touch. He scored two goals in the title game in vanquishing Minneapolis Southwest 3–1.

He dreamed of becoming a fighter pilot, but color blindness prevented him from attending the Air Force Academy. Brooks had a scholarship offer to Michigan, but his father leaned on him to walk on at Minnesota, which was coached by Mariucci, in those days one of the few Americans with an NHL pedigree.

"He was one of the fastest, if not the fastest, players in college hockey in that era," Mariucci said.

Brooks scored 18 goals among 45 points for the Gophers from 1957–59 and graduated in 1961 with a degree in psychology, which he leveraged to diabolical effect willing his 1980 team to victory.

The U.S. Olympic team recruited Brooks to play in 1960 at Squaw Valley, California. The Soviet Union emerged during the early days of the Cold War as the dominant force in international hockey, having mastered the free-flowing and creative style Brooks counterattacked 20 years later. The United States was an afterthought behind the Soviets and traditional powers Canada and Czechoslovakia.

Just days before the Opening Ceremony, U.S. coach Jack Riley convinced 1956 Olympian Bill Cleary to rejoin the team. Cleary agreed on the condition that baby brother Bob Cleary come too. Brooks was the odd man out.

The team photo had already been taken. So Cleary's head was pasted over Brooks' body. It was humiliating.

Still, Brooks could not look away as the Americans upset the Soviets and roared into the gold-medal game against the Czechs on February 28, 1960. That Sunday afternoon Brooks and his father watched at home on the family's black-and-white television.

The Cleary brothers starred in Team USA's 9–4 victory. When the game ended, Herb Sr. glanced at his son and said, "Well, I guess the coach cut the right guy."

Later in life Brooks turned his father's stinging rebuke into a punch line, but the snub ignited a competitive fire that burned until the day he died.

Brooks played at the 1964 and '68 Olympics and captained the 1970 U.S. national team. He met Patti in December 1963 after breaking his arm in a semipro game in St. Paul. She was an emergency room nurse who helped treat the dashing young player. They were engaged three months later and married in September 1964.

The NHL, still dominated by Canadians, remained skeptical of Americans, although Brooks had to think twice before turning down a chance to sign with the Detroit Red Wings.

"I don't think I was good enough to make it," he said.

So Brooks followed his father into the insurance business and had a lucrative job as an underwriter for W.A. Lang in St. Paul when Sonmor hired him in 1968 to coach the Gophers' freshman team.

"I knew he would make a great coach, even back then," Sonmor wrote. "He just had that special quality that made him a winner. He was so intelligent, too. He had an ability to see everything that was going on around him and then was able to pick out what was really important. His players maybe didn't love him but they respected him and went to war for him."

Brooks was also tenaciously self-righteous.

When athletic director Marsh Ryman told him there was not enough money to fly Sonmor's assistant coaches with the Gophers to the 1971 NCAA championships in Syracuse, N.Y., Brooks quit on the spot and founded a junior franchise to coach, the St. Paul Vulcans.

"I've never seen anyone carry things as far as he would for a principle," Sonmor recalled. "I said, 'Herbie, why do you always have to tilt at windmills?'"

In February 1972, Sonmor left Minnesota to coach the Fighting Saints of the fledging World Hockey Association. Interim coach Ken Yackel was the first choice of new athletic director Paul Giel but he turned down the job.

"The day I came to the university, I found myself without a hockey coach," Giel said. "It's no secret I tried to convince Yack to stay on but it's also no secret that Herb Brooks was the only other man for the job in my mind."

The expansion Atlanta Flames wooed Brooks for an NHL assistant coaching job. Sonmor offered him the position of assistant general manager of the Fighting Saints.

"I decided my first love is coaching. This is what I want to do, particularly at my alma mater," Brooks said at his introductory news conference. "I believe in the hockey players at this school and I only hope I can [make] the University of Minnesota hockey team the most desirable team to play for in the country."

Brooks, 34, became the youngest college hockey coach in the United States, inheriting a team that had finished last in the Western Collegiate Hockey Association, with an average attendance of just 2,500 at 6,800-seat Williams Arena.

One of the first things he did was design a new jersey with the distinctive "M" on the front, which the team has worn in varying styles for 45 years. His mantra was simple: "Work hard, believe in the guy next to you, and everything will fall into place."

Giel showed his commitment to Brooks by awarding the hockey program six full scholarships rather than the partials his predecessors were forced to ration.

"When Paul told me I would have enough scholarship money and better facilities I was able to get the players necessary to do the job," Brooks told the St. Paul Pioneer Press in 1980.

The Gophers climbed to third place in 1972–73. The next season they were national champions after defeating Michigan Tech.

A "Brooks for Governor" banner flew at MSP International Airport when the Gophers returned from Boston on March 17, 1974, armed with the school's first hockey title and unbridled confidence.

"That was probably the most satisfying coaching period that I ever had in my life," Brooks recalled.

Minnesota won two more championships in 1976 and '79 while advancing to four Frozen Fours in Brooks' seven years at the helm. He coached five All-Americans and 23 players who went on to play in the NHL, finishing with a record of 167–97–18.

And he did it all with Minnesotans, refusing to recruit outside the state while his competitors combed North America and titled the ice by acquiring older, more experienced Canadians and junior stars. Brooks was a disciple of Mariucci's closed-ranks philosophy, which endeared both men to Minnesota's parochial hockey fans.

"John believed in Minnesota kids and gave them a chance," Brooks recalled in a 1979 interview with the Pioneer Press. "He could have been like other college coaches and done the bulk of his recruiting in Canada. But John was different. John cared."

On the ice, Brooks was notoriously strict with his players, and he was aloof to them off it. Captains, superstars, or checkers, it didn't matter. They would pass him in hallways without eliciting so much as a nod from their coach.

"Traumatic was the best way to describe playing for him," goalie Steve Janaszak recalled to author Wayne Coffey in *Boys of Winter: The Untold Story of a Coach, a Dream and the 1980 U.S. Olympic Team.*

Brooks was intolerant of lackadaisical effort in practice and games. He would call out stars in front of teammates to deliver his global message, then circle back to the victim, embrace him in private, and quietly whisper encouragement—classic tear-'em-down, build-'em-up tactics.

Floaters were punished by having to skate "Herbies," back-and-forth sprints from goal line to blue line, red line, the far blue line, and the opposite goal line.

"We used to say if Herbie did this to a dog, the Humane Society would throw him in jail," Don Micheletti, a Gophers winger from 1976 to '80, said in an interview with author Ross Bernstein. "But it taught us to keep pushing each other as teammates and to be in shape that third period so we could win."

One year, after the Gophers were swept at Michigan Tech, Brooks was so upset he canceled the team's charter flight and booked a seven-hour bus ride home from the Upper Peninsula. The Huskies tended to bring out his ire.

In March 1979, with Minnesota en route to its third national championship, Brooks went ballistic in the dressing room after the

Gophers surrendered three third-period goals in a 5–3 WCHA playoff win over Michigan Tech.

He hurled a case of soda pop across the room and shattered a blackboard. Afterward he unloaded to the media, touching raw cultural nerves to scold his team while threatening to quit.

"Talk, talk, I'm sick of talking to these fucking players! This game is still won by hungry people," he fumed. "I'm not going to go to bed with these cake-eaters anymore. This is a working man's game, not a game for some god-blessed rich kids from the suburbs. After this season is over, the University of Minnesota can have this job."

Headlines raged about Brooks' possible resignation, and he was forced to walk back his comments the following day. However, it was evident the end was near.

In 1977, Minneapolis *Star Tribune* columnist Sid Hartman reported Brooks had decided to resign and enter private business. A November announcement was delayed. Then Brooks changed his mind.

In the fall of 1978, Nanne, then general manager of the North Stars, offered Brooks a two-year contract to coach Minnesota's NHL team. Brooks agreed. A news conference was scheduled. Then Brooks demanded a three-year contract. Nanne balked. The deal fell through.

Giel, Minnesota's athletic director, granted Brooks a leave of absence for 1979–80 so the three-time NCAA champion could coach the 1980 U.S. Olympic team. The plan was for assistant coach Brad Buetow to fill in as head coach that season so Brooks could return in the fall of 1980.

No one, not even a supremely confident Brooks, could have predicted the magical upset and geopolitical earthquake that erupted at Lake Placid.

The U.S. hockey team, average age 22, had been embarrassed 10–2 by the Soviets a month earlier in an exhibition game but would take down the CCCP's Big Red Machine 4–3 on that unforgettable Friday, February 22, 1980. Two days later, the Americans defeated Finland 4–2 to finish undefeated on the world stage.

Twelve Minnesotans, including seven who played for Brooks with the Gophers, won gold medals—the first for the United States since Brooks was cut from the 1960 team, and America's last men's Olympic hockey championship.

Brooks, who sequestered his players and commandeered media attention during the tournament, became a deity overnight.

There were the New York Rangers negotiating a coaching contract with his agent during the Games. There were Herb and Patti chatting with Jimmy and Rosalyn Carter in the White House the day after winning the gold medal. Endorsement deals poured in.

The world was Brooks' oyster. His days in Dinkytown were numbered. On April 9, 1980, he resigned as Gophers hockey coach and gave a series of exit interviews that were neither overly sentimental nor introspective.

"The common denominator of all the guys who played throughout my seven years was that they were really competitive, very hungry, very focused and mentally tough—to go along with whatever talent they had. I think that really carried us," he told the *Pioneer Press*.

Brooks rejected offers from the Rangers and Los Angeles Kings and decided to burnish his pro credentials in Davos, Switzerland. In 1981, Brooks returned from overseas and did sign on with the Rangers. He led New York to its best finish in 10 years, but his teams failed to gain traction. He was fired in January 1985.

Three months later, Giel tried to lure Brooks back to Minnesota but was spurned. Instead, Brooks took over the overlooked program at St. Cloud State. He lasted one season before Nanne finally brought Herbie back to the Twin Cities.

However, the 1987–88 North Stars were an injury-ravaged, dysfunctional disaster. Nanne resigned in the middle of the season to pursue a business career; Brooks fell out with the new front office and was fired after a last-place finish.

His name surfaced whenever there was an NHL opening, but nothing ever materialized. Brooks had soured on the clutch-and-grab style that was suffocating the league, even writing Commissioner Gary Bettman to encourage rule changes to loosen up the game—many of which would be implemented after his death.

He scouted for the Penguins and briefly returned to coaching when Pittsburgh GM Craig Patrick, his Olympic assistant coach, hired him midseason 1995–96 to resuscitate a moribund team. Despite a second-round playoff ouster, Patrick wanted Brooks back the following season, but he could not strike a long-term deal with the bankrupt franchise.

Brooks shocked the international hockey community when he returned to the Olympics in 1998, not to coach the United States but unheralded France. That also was the first year NHL players participated. The French finished 11th out of 14 teams.

Four years later, the Winter Games returned to U.S. soil and USA Hockey attempted to rekindle the magic of Lake Placid, hiring Brooks to coach the peewees of 1980 in Salt Lake City.

Team USA responded well to Brooks' tactics in a compressed tournament. He led the Americans to a silver medal after losing 5–2 to Canada in one of the most exhilarating gold medal games in history. Eighteen months later, he was dead.

Brooks' fatal accident shocked the hockey world and blasted a hole in the heart of St. Paul, where Herbie lived his entire life. His memorial was covered by the local media like a state funeral.

More than 2,500 mourners paid their respects at Saint Paul Cathedral. Another 10,000 attended a public service at Mariucci

Arena, where hang the three NCAA championship banners he helped win. None of his successors matched that success. Buetow and Doug Woog failed to win any. Current coach Don Lucia had two national titles to his name as of 2016.

At the opulent Saint Paul Hotel downtown, a wall of fame in the swanky bar offers a history lesson inside. A mosaic of black-and-white photos of famous Minnesotans such as Judy Garland, Charles Schulz, Hubert Humphrey, and F. Scott Fitzgerald includes dates of their birth and death, and a line describing their legacy.

Under Brooks' mug reads: JUST A GUY FROM THE EAST SIDE.

If only.

The legend of the 1980 Olympic team grows as time marches on. Kurt Russell portrayed Brooks to a T, from his clipped cadence and hurried gait to the bark in the old coach's bite, in the 2004 movie *Miracle*, introducing the "Miracle on Ice" to a new generation.

The unexpected joy those long-ago boys of winter engendered also provoked unabashed patriotism during a dark time in U.S. history.

Hostages were being held captive in Iran and the U.S. government was impotent to do anything about it. Gas prices, unemployment rates, and interest rates soared. Inflation raged. The Soviet Union had invaded Afghanistan, and Carter would eventually boycott the 1980 Summer Games in Moscow. Americans were disillusioned and angry.

But along came Brooks' team of relatively unknown amateurs from Minnesota, Wisconsin, Michigan, and Massachusetts, who accomplished over two weeks in upstate New York what no one thought they could, in the only way possible—no favors asked, none given.

"You were born to be hockey players," Brooks told his team in the locker room before they played the Soviets. "You were meant to be here tonight. This is your time. No go out there and take it!"

Team USA marched onto the ice at what would be renamed Herb Brooks Arena and together they skated into history.

"Most miracles are dreams made manifest," Rev. John Malone eulogized at Brooks' funeral. "Herbie had a dream. The players had a dream. If we could all dream...and do our best, we could make this a better world. It's within our reach; it's within God's reach."

2 Murray Warmath

Minnesota's last Rose Bowl–winning coach was initially rejected for a local hero who never came home and a Buckeye who struggled for mediocrity.

Murray Warmath was skeptical of Dinkytown in 1950 when he interviewed for the Gophers' football coaching vacancy after legendary Bernie Bierman had resigned.

It was a token gesture by athletic director Ike Armstrong, who acquiesced to Army coach Earl Blaik's recommendation that Minnesota give his young line coach a chance. The "M" Club was courting Bud Wilkinson, the Minneapolis native and former Gopher who had just won his first national championship at Oklahoma.

"I wasn't sure that was the place for me," Warmath recalled. "There was snow up to my waist and it was freezing. [Paul] Giel was on the freshman team then. If I had known how good he was, I would've pushed for the job."

Wilkinson stayed put. The Gophers hired Wes Fesler. And Warmath went to Mississippi State.

In January 1954, Fesler was out after winning just 10 of 27 games. Warmath threw his hat back in. The small-town Southerner was an outlier among four other candidates, each of whom had Minnesota ties.

Minneapolis Star columnist Charles Johnson wrote of Warmath's 10–6–3 record in two years at Mississippi State, "Not good enough to have the man in the street cheering for him as soon as he moves to Minnesota."

But Warmath beat them all out to earn the job and a $15,000-per-year contract that was one of Minnesota's greatest athletic investments.

He ruled by fear and was harsh in his critiques of players, pugnacious in a suit and tie, stalking the sidelines with a headset over a backward baseball cap. But Warmath made the Gophers winners. Over and above being one of the sport's most successful coaches, he was at the forefront of college football integration.

He led the Gophers to a 7–2 record his first year in 1954, a team that featured All-American halfback Bob McNamara and quarterback Gino Cappelletti.

Six years later, Minnesota defeated No. 1 Iowa, finished 8–1, and was named unanimous national champion. The Gophers lost the Rose Bowl to Washington, but returned to Pasadena in 1962 and routed UCLA 21–3.

Sandy Stephens was named Rose Bowl MVP and became the first black quarterback to earn All-America honors.

Warmath seemed an unlikely leader of social change. He grew up in tiny Humboldt, Tennessee, (population: 3,000) and played football at Tennessee. He was teammates with Beattie Feathers and played against Paul "Bear" Bryant from Alabama.

Besides heading Mississippi State, Warmath was also an assistant coach at his alma mater for defensive guru General Robert Neyland.

But in 1959, Warmath named Stephens, a sophomore, his starting quarterback—the first black signal caller in Big Ten history. Three straight losing seasons had exacerbated racial tensions.

Warmath was hanged in effigy outside Territorial Hall, where players lived. He was unbowed. In the early 1960s, Warmath recruited Judge Dickson, Bobby Bell, Carl Eller, Bill Munsey, Aaron Brown, Ezell Jones, Charlie Sanders, and McKinley Boston.

Minnesota for Minnesota Boys, raged one headline.

"Someone very high in the administration came to me in those early years and said, 'Coach, how many black players do you have now?'" Warmath recalled. "I said, 'I never counted, but if I had two or three more like these young men, we would be really good.' He was trying to tell me I had enough black players, and I was saying, 'Take a hike.'"

The old ball coach became an accidental civil rights leader. He earned the respect of former Grambling coach Eddie Robinson, who became an unabashed Gophers fan for breaking down color barriers in college football.

"Murray Warmath said, 'We are going to win with these players,' and that's what we did," said Bell. "As players we got together and said we knew we couldn't mess up. If we mess up, we're going to set ourselves back how many years? And we're going to disappoint our coach on top of it. We would never do that. That team had no problems, and we played as a team."

Warmath's 1967 team shared the Big Ten championships with Purdue and Indiana with an 8-2 record. It was Minnesota's last piece of a conference title.

The "Autumn Warrior" compiled a record of 86–78–7 in 18 seasons at Minnesota before resigning in 1971 following several seasons of mediocrity. But it was a 1962 victory stolen by controversy that haunted Warmath until his death at age 98 in March 2011.

Murray Warmath, Minnesota's last Rose Bowl–winning coach in 1962, helped integrate college football as one of the first Big Ten coaches to recruit in the Jim Crow South. University of Minnesota Archives

The game between No. 3 Wisconsin and No. 5 Minnesota in Madison was the last between the border rivals with a Big Ten championship on the line.

The Gophers were leading 9–7 late in the fourth quarter when a phantom roughing-the-passer penalty on Eller led to Warmath's ejection and extended the Badgers' game-winning touchdown drive.

"I still wake up in a cold sweat over that," Warmath said 20 years later. "For two or three years after that, I kept punching myself saying, 'It didn't happen.' They took a championship and Rose Bowl trip away from a group of players and coaches. It was a nightmare."

Warmath was the 1960 National Coach of the Year and in 1968 was elected president of the American Football Coaches Association. He was the 1991 recipient of the General Robert Neyland Trophy, named after his former mentor to celebrate contributions to intercollegiate athletics.

Warmath coached 10 All-Americans. Three of his former Gophers players—Bell, Eller, and Sanders—are members of the Pro Football Hall of Fame.

Warmath worked as a color commentator alongside Ray Christensen on Gophers radio broadcasts. In 1978, he was hired by Vikings coach Bud Grant to run the defensive line.

"I've never gotten over the urge to coach," he said. "It's in my blood. It's what I like to do."

After two years back on the field, Warmath moved into the Vikings' front office, where he was a college scout until 1990, finally retiring after 65 years as a player and coach in the game.

Warmath remained a fixture at Gophers games. Former players flocked to him, no longer nervous underlings but as peers drawn to his warmth and ceaseless passion for football.

"In February of my freshman year my dad died of a massive, sudden heart attack," Bob Stein told an interviewer. "I hadn't played a lick, and I wasn't a superstar recruit or anything. But he went to the funeral and had all the assistants with him.

"I didn't think of it at the time, but that showed class."

3 Bronko Nagurski

Uttering his name evokes images of European immigrants grinding their way to a better life in New World fields and factories, of leather helmets, broken noses, and black-and-white snapshots in the cold November mud.

Bronislav "Bronko" Nagurski is a cornerstone of American sports and entertainment in the early 20th century.

He was a pioneering two-way player at Minnesota whose name is forever linked to stars who win the Bronko Nagurski Trophy as college football's best defensive player. He helped legitimize the nascent National Football League before leveraging his name and brawn into a successful career as a professional wrestler.

Nobody in football had ever seen anything like Nagurski when he arrived in 1927. Standing 6'2" and weighing 225 pounds, he was an unyoked ox during an era when few players eclipsed six feet or 200 pounds. He wore a size-8 helmet. No player has been fitted for a larger NFL championship ring than Nagurski's size 19½.

Gophers coach Clarence Spears loved to tell the tale of his recruiting trip to International Falls on the Minnesota–Canada border and spotting Nagurski plowing his family farm. Spears asked for directions to another town. Nagurski lifted his plow and used it to point where it was. Or so the story goes.

Bronislav "Bronko" Nagurski was the only consensus All-American to earn the honor at two different positions in 1929. The Gophers won 18 of 24 games during his three-year career.
University of Minnesota Archives

Nagurski, the youngest of four children born to Ukrainian immigrants, was born in Rainy River, Ontario, but grew up working in his father's grocery store and farm in International Falls.

At Minnesota he played tackle on defense and fullback on offense. Nagurski was a mover of men, capable of powering through two blockers to take down ball carriers while bulldozing running lanes for Minnesota's single-wing formation.

In 1929, Nagurski became the only consensus All-American to earn the honor at two different positions in the same year. The Gophers won 18 of 24 games during Nagurski's three-year career. None of their four losses was by more than two points.

"There is no use in my trying to dig up a new greatest thrill," Nagurski told an interviewer in 1958. "Mine will always be that Wisconsin game at Madison in 1928."

Nagurski was suffering with two broken ribs and two fractured vertebrae and wore a steel corset for protection when the Gophers (5–2) visited the border-rival Badgers (7–0–1) on November 24, 1928.

In the third quarter, he recovered a fumble at the Wisconsin 17-yard line, which ultimately led to Nagurski's touchdown run— the game's only score.

Later in the fourth quarter, with the Badgers driving inside Minnesota's 10-yard line, Nagurski chased down quarterback Bo Cuisinier and tackled him for a loss on third down and then knocked down Cuisinier's fourth-down pass to end the threat.

Nagurski teamed with Red Grange playing for Chicago coach George Halas, leading the Bears to three NFL championships in 1932, '33, and 1943, when he came out of retirement to fill out Halas' World War II–depleted roster.

A contract dispute with Halas in 1938 prompted Nagurski to quit football for wrestling. Nagurski won four heavyweight wrestling championships before retiring back home to International Falls.

Nagurski opened a filling station in town and used his muscle to maintain a loyal customer base. It wasn't the friendly service or cheap gas that kept them coming back, according to local legend.

Nagurski screwed his customers' gas caps so tight after fill-ups they had no choice but to drive back to his station because Bronko was the only one strong enough to open them.

Bruce Smith

Football heir. Game changer. Heisman winner. Hollywood minute. Navy pilot. NFL player. Would-be Saint.

Bruce Smith was born to be a Gopher, according to legend. He left an indelible footprint in Dinkytown at the dawn of World War II. However, his star-crossed life was cut short by a disease that failed to crush his spirit.

Minnesota's only Heisman Trophy recipient was the school's first athlete to have his number (54) retired in 1977. Smith captained the 1940 and '41 national championship teams as a triple-threat halfback in the waning days of the single-wing formation.

He grew up in Faribault, Minnesota, son of Lucius Smith, who played two ragtime seasons at tackle and kicker for the Gophers. In 1910, Minnesota and Michigan, two undefeated teams vying for the national championship, clashed in Ann Arbor.

Injuries on defense forced the elder Smith to substitute at unfamiliar positions, which the Wolverines exploited by running the winning play over him in a 6–0 loss. Crestfallen, Smith supposedly vowed afterward that someday he would have a son who would play for Minnesota and avenge that painful loss.

Lucius Smith, who became an attorney in Faribault, always denied the proclamation.

"How would I know at age 19 or 20 that I'd have a son who would do so well against Michigan?" he told an interviewer in 1975. "I'm not that great a prophet."

No matter. It was baked in to family lore when Bruce Smith followed his collegiate trail.

Thirty years later, the old man was among 64,000 fans who shoehorned into Memorial Stadium to watch Bruce battle

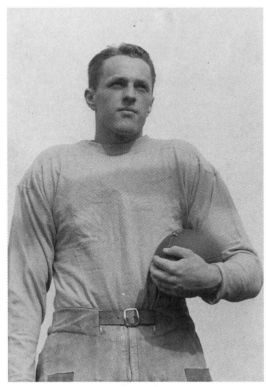

Bruce Smith was Minnesota's only Heisman Trophy winner in 1941. The All-American halfback and World War II Navy pilot had his life story glamorized by Hollywood's film, Smith of Minnesota.
University of Minnesota Archives

Michigan and its star halfback, Tom Harmon, with another unde-feated season at stake.

It was November 9, 1940, and the then-record crowd was drenched by rain that turned the field into a muddy mess. It was the front of a storm system that unleashed what became known as the "Armistice Day Blizzard," which raked the upper Midwest with snow, wind, and plummeting temperatures.

The two-day storm was blamed for the deaths of 145 people—including 49 Minnesotans, according to the Minnesota Climatology Office.

The Gophers trailed 6–0 late in the fourth quarter when Bob Papprath intercepted a Wolverines' pass in the end zone, setting up Minnesota at its 20-yard line.

On the first play of the drive, Smith took a reverse handoff, hydroplaned through seven Michigan defenders, and scored his third game-winning touchdown of the season to help secure Minnesota's fourth national title under coach Bernie Bierman.

Smith's dashing touchdowns made him a hero in Minnesota, where Gophers fans climbed trees and telephone poles to watch his exploits.

But his star turn against Harmon, the 1940 Heisman winner, made him a household name across the country. His guile and guts in 1941 propelled him to further greatness.

In the season's penultimate game at Iowa, Smith was not in the lineup because of a knee injury.

The Gophers were undefeated again and vying for their second straight national championship. However, the underdog Hawkeyes quickly went up 7–0 and confidently stacked their defensive line knowing they did not have to contend with Smith.

Smith harangued Bierman on the sideline to put him in the game. Desperate for a spark, the coach obliged. Smith's first play was a 39-yard completion to Bill Garnaas. Another downfield strike to Garnaas set up a touchdown run.

On the next possession, Smith led a 93-yard scoring drive and Minnesota never trailed again. The Gophers managed just two first downs without Smith. They finished with 24 as Smith ran or threw for all of their touchdowns in a 34–13 win.

"It would be difficult to find another occasion when one player so completely turned a game around from probable defeat to overwhelming victory as Smith did on that Iowa field," wrote *Minneapolis Tribune* columnist Dick Cullum.

Smith beat out Notre Dame's Angelo Bertelli for the 1941 Heisman. No other Gopher has been anointed the best player in college football.

He received his trophy in New York on December 9, 1941— just two days after Japan's sneak attack on Pearl Harbor.

"In the Far East they may think Americans are soft, but I have plenty of evidence in black and blue to prove otherwise," Smith told reporters. "I think that in this emergency the value of football to a nation will be demonstrated."

He cut such a dashing figure with his wavy blond hair that Columbia Pictures signed Smith to star as himself in *Smith of Minnesota*, a movie about a small-town family whose son becomes an All-American halfback.

Warren Ashe played the cynical Hollywood screenwriter dispatched to Faribault to chronicle Smith's college career who eventually is won over by the admiration for the town's prodigal son, portrayed by Smith.

Smith was in the U.S. Navy when the movie premiered in 1942. He was enlisted for three years, initially as a pilot at the Great Lakes Naval Station in Chicago, where he also played football. Later he trained pilots in California.

Smith resumed his football career in 1945 and played four seasons with the NFL's Green Bay Packers and Los Angeles Rams.

In 1947 he almost died after suffering a ruptured kidney playing against the Bears. Smith retired at age 29 and settled back home in Faribault with his wife, Gloria, a former fashion model from Philadelphia, and their four children.

He ran a sporting goods store in Northfield, worked as a distributor for Hamm's Beer, and sold power mowers.

Smith was a devout Catholic and humble man, never one to command attention or regale audiences with tales of his glorious football life, according to his daughter, June. In the late 1960s, Smith was diagnosed with cancer.

Father William Cantwell, assistant pastor of St. Lawrence Church in Minneapolis, regularly visited patients at St. Barnabas Hospital in Minneapolis. He befriended Smith, whose body had withered to 90 pounds and was racked with pain. Cantwell marveled

Gophers Retired Football Numbers

Player	Number
Paul Giel	10
Sandy Stephens	15
Bruce Smith	54
Bronko Nagurski	72
Bobby Bell	78

at his new friend's grace in facing his terminal disease and the kindness he showed comforting fellow patients—right up to his death.

It was weeks before Cantwell learned Smith had even played football, never mind that he was one of the best college running backs of his era.

Smith died on August 26, 1967. He was 47.

For years Cantwell campaigned unsuccessfully to have Smith sainted.

"Because he lived a life of heroic value and because of the way he died, Smith deserves to be canonized," Cantwell told the Catholic News Service in 1978. "He was a Christian optimist with the guts and courage of an All-American."

Smith was buried at Fort Snelling Cemetery in St. Paul.

On September 29, 1970, demonstrations against the Vietnam War, the civil rights struggle, and generational culture clashes were shaking the pillars of American society.

That night, 80-year-old Lucius Smith presented Bruce's Heisman Trophy to the University of Minnesota, his voice cracking with emotion as he lionized his late son and framed his boy's triumphs in nostalgia.

"My memory tells me that the days of 1940 and 1941 were great days in Minnesota. Members of all political parties and of all religious faiths gave up their differences and found themselves in happy agreement that Minnesota was the greatest in football.

"How nice it would be if we could quit talking about beads, bombs, and long hair and once more find ourselves in happy agreement, not only that the miniskirt is here to stay, but also that once again Minnesota is the greatest in football."

5 On to Pittsburgh

Minnesota played its first football game in 1882, but the Gophers did not truly arrive as a program until 1934. To be exact, it was October 20, 1934.

The United States was in the throes of the Great Depression. German carpenter Bruno Hauptmann was in the second day of a hunger strike in a New York jail after proclaiming his innocence in the kidnapping and murder of the infant son of aviation hero Colonel Charles Lindbergh.

And the epicenter of college football and the sporting press was in Pittsburgh for the clash between the Gophers and Panthers, two undefeated teams vying for the mythical national championship.

Bernie Bierman returned to his alma mater after coaching Tulane to the 1931 Rose Bowl. By his third season, Bierman had assembled an offensive juggernaut by the modest standards of the era.

Led by All-Americans Francis "Pug" Lund, Bill Bevan, and Butch Larson, the Gophers averaged 33.7 points, using a power running attack to account for 295 of their 325 average yards per game.

Eight different players rushed for touchdowns led by Stan Koska's nine, including four in one game.

Minnesota trounced North Dakota and Nebraska, outscoring its first two opponents by an aggregate of 76–12. A bye week allowed Bierman and athletic director Frank McCormick to scout Pittsburgh's October 13 home game against powerful USC. The Panthers pounded the Trojans 20–6.

Pittsburgh sought revenge for its 7–3 loss to the Gophers in 1933—its only loss of the season. The Panthers had outscored their three opponents 73–18 to set up the East–West showcase.

The Gophers departed Union Station in Minneapolis two days before the game, cheered on by 2,000 fans. They arrived at 9:30 AM Friday morning, checking in to their hotel outside of campus, which was covered by "'Beat Minnesota' placards," according to newspaper accounts.

Minnesota was installed as a 5–4 favorite. The game was scheduled to be broadcast nationally on radio. Columnists from across the country descended on Pittsburgh, including Grantland Rice, who predicted, "Minnesota by a shade, with more power and more experience, in a hammering, battering, low-scoring jamboree."

More than 65,000 fans packed the stadium on a sun-splashed afternoon. The Panthers jumped out to a 7–0 lead, which they carried into the fourth quarter.

Perhaps it was nerves or the two-week layoff, but the Gophers looked sluggish. *Minneapolis Tribune* columnist Charles Barton was hazed in the press box by his colleagues.

"So that's the great Minnesota football team we've been hearing so much about, eh? They're just a bunch of mugs who think they can play football. Where's all those powerhouse and deceptions plays we've read about?"

Finally, early in the fourth quarter, the Gophers answered with a 22-yard touchdown run by Julius Alfonse to tie the game. The defense forced Pittsburgh to punt and Minnesota quickly drove inside the Panthers' 20-yard line. And the tricks came out of the bag.

Minnesota that season ran a series of plays called buck laterals, but never one as intricate as the fourth-down sleight of hand that doomed the Panthers.

Fullback Stan Kostka took the snap from center. He faked a rush up the middle and pitched to Glen Seidel, who lateraled to Lund, the halfback. Lund swept wide right to evade two defenders before throwing on the run down the right side to Bob Tenner, who hauled it in over his shoulder at the 10-yard line and scampered untouched into the end zone.

"We'd never used it before in a game," Bierman said years later.

The Panthers never recovered as Minnesota skulked out of town with a 13–7 victory.

The headline in the next day's *Minneapolis Tribune* read: FURIOUS GOPHER FINISH SMASHES PITT LINE AND U.S. TITLE HOPES IN 13–7 WIN.

The Gophers' train pulled into downtown Minneapolis Sunday afternoon to a delirious throng. Cars seven-deep jammed Hennepin and Nicollet avenues.

The Gophers ran the table, defeating Iowa 48–12; shutting out Michigan (34–0), Indiana (30–0), and Wisconsin (34–0); and whipping Chicago (35–7) en route to a perfect 8–0 season and the program's first national championship. Pittsburgh finished 8–1.

Four decades later, Bierman was asked to name his favorite Gophers team. He did not hesitate.

"Football is a better game in some ways today," he told an interviewer in the early 1970s. "There are more boys to choose from and statistics prove that they have gotten bigger from one decade to the next. But I have not seen a team anywhere—in person, on film, on television—that is better than my 1934 team."

6 "We Want the Pig!"

Change was coursing through the country November 5, 1960, when college football's dominant teams clashed at Memorial Stadium in a game that validated the Gophers' last national championship, vested Murray Warmath in Minnesota, and quietly made civil rights history.

In three days, 43-year-old John F. Kennedy would be elected president by a razor-thin margin over Richard M. Nixon, opening a "New Frontier" in White House leadership, policymaking, and style before an assassin martyred him three years later.

The Twin Cities was poised to become a big-league sports market. The relocated Washington Senators baseball club and expansion Vikings of the NFL were scheduled to begin play in 1961.

But on this overcast Saturday afternoon, the nation's athletic attention was focused on the University of Minnesota. A stadium-record crowd of 65,610 watched the Gophers rally from a three-point halftime deficit for a 27–10 victory over archrival Iowa and cheered wildly as triumphant players carried Warmath and the Floyd of Rosedale trophy off the field.

Fans also witnessed a moment much more significant than the game, a landmark feat that was barely acknowledged at the time but has resonated for decades.

Here were two nationally ranked teams being commanded by African American quarterbacks: Sandy Stephens of Minnesota and Iowa's Wilburn Hollis.

This was four years before Congress passed the Civil Rights Act desegregating the Jim Crow South, where college football remained an all-white endeavor until 1967. Alabama coaching icon Bear

Bryant did not recruit his first black player until 1971. It was 1968 before an African American, Marlin Briscoe of the AFL's Denver Broncos, quarterbacked a professional game.

Warmath and Iowa coach Forest Evashevski were pioneers in racial integration. Stephens and Hollis were among seven African Americans in uniform that day. There was nary a headline about the milestone in Iowa or Minnesota newspapers or *Sports Illustrated* leading up to the battle between No. 1–ranked Iowa and No. 3 Minnesota.

"The funny thing about it is that, in that era, most of us didn't think about that," Hollis told the Minneapolis *Star Tribune* in a 2012 interview. "We didn't think about the significance of what we were going through. It never struck me as to how significant it was until I started getting calls years later."

Hollis heard from Briscoe and Warren Moon about how that 1960 game at Memorial Stadium inspired them to pursue their quarterback dreams.

"They said, 'Hey, you guys are the ones who made us believe we could do what we wanted to do,'" Hollis said. "You don't think about that at the time. And I didn't know they were thinking about us. It sure made me have a second thought. Knowing that I, or Sandy Stephens, had that influence? That is so rewarding."

On the field that day, Stephens and Hollis played secondary roles in a game marred by turnovers and dominated by Gophers 245-pound guard Tom Brown, who went on to win the Outland Trophy as the country's best interior lineman. The win was the apex that season for a sneaky Minnesota team that was dismissed by preseason prognosticators.

Warmath entered his seventh year in Minnesota tainted by three straight losing seasons, including a last-place Big Ten finish in 1959. The Gophers had lost five conference games by a total of 32 points and were embarrassed by Iowa 33–0.

Warmath was hanged in effigy on campus. A group of Minneapolis businessmen raised $35,000 and offered to buy out the two remaining years of his contract. No news service ranked the Gophers before the season. The outlook for 1960 was bleak after the team lost a preseason game 19–7 to an alumni squad.

But a season-opening 26–14 road win over Nebraska was a confidence booster. The Gophers responded with four straight Big Ten wins, including shutouts over Indiana, Northwestern, and Michigan. After blowing out Kansas State 48–7 Minnesota prepared to host undefeated Iowa.

Both teams were 6–0. The Gophers had the best defense in the conference, allowing just 3.3 points and 229 yards per game. The Hawkeyes were 1½-point favorites. The hype was massive for the day as the national press descended on Minneapolis for the show.

Scalpers were getting $100 for tickets between the 20-yard lines, about $800 in 2016 dollars. Hotels were sold out within a 20-mile radius. More than 30 radio stations in Minnesota, Iowa, and the Dakotas were wired to broadcast the game, which was televised in the Twin Cities by an independent station.

"I've never been connected with a more important game either as a coach or as a player," Warmath told reporters.

Iowa led 10–7 early in the third quarter after spoon-feeding the Gophers a touchdown. Center Bill Van Buren sailed a snap over punter John Calhoun's head and Minnesota took possession at the Hawkeyes' 14-yard line. Bill Munsey grabbed a pitch from Stephens and scored from seven yards out.

The second half was all Minnesota. Stephens culminated a 12-play, 81-yard drive with a one-yard scoring plunge. Fullback Roger Hagberg caught three third-down passes from third-string quarterback "Smokey" Joe Salem to set up the touchdown.

In the fourth quarter, Hagberg gashed Iowa's defense for a 42-yard touchdown run. He finished with 103 yards on 15 carries.

Salem capped the scoring with a one-yard quarterback sneak after the Gophers recovered the last of Iowa's five turnovers.

As the clock ticked down, the crowd started chanting, "We Want the Pig! We Want the Pig!" Gophers captain Greg Larson seized the rivalry trophy and sat with it in a jubilant Minnesota locker room.

"This is the greatest moment of my life!" he said. "Nothing's even close."

The teams combined for eight giveaways in a punishing game. Brown was a tackling and blocking force. Iowa was held to just 198 total yards. Gophers tackle Bobby Bell lost part of a tooth in one collision and ended up swallowing it.

"It's not easy to digest," he deadpanned.

Warmath, who was almost run out of town the previous year, basked in the afterglow of his signature victory.

"We've never played a better game or a better team," he said. "We made more mistakes than we have made in any game this year but we beat a great team."

The Gophers were the consensus No. 1 team in the wire service polls, but they almost blew it with a major letdown the following week against lowly Purdue. The Boilermakers carried a 2–4–1 record into Memorial Stadium but waltzed out with a 23–14 upset.

The loss plunged Minnesota to fourth in the rankings while Iowa vaulted back to No. 1. The Gophers responded to a must-win at Wisconsin with a convincing 26–7 victory over the Badgers in the season finale to earn enough first-place votes in the final AP and UPI polls to secure their seventh national championship and punch their first-ever ticket to the Rose Bowl.

7 From the Cellar to the Penthouse

Herb Brooks returned to his alma mater in 1972 with a spackling knife and motivational mantras to rebuild the downtrodden men's hockey program, foreshadowing the no-nonsense coaching style that would make him an Olympic icon.

"Work hard, believe in the guy next to you, and everything will fall into place," was among them.

Despite John Mariucci's coaching legacy and John Mayasich's scoring brilliance, the Gophers had never won a national championship and hockey remained a marginal sport on campus behind football and basketball. Outgoing coach Glen Sonmor only had two and a half full scholarships to offer before athletic director Paul Giel in 1971 increased the total to six.

Minnesota was coming off a 8–24, last-place finish in the Western Collegiate Hockey Association when Brooks arrived. He improved their standing to sixth in his first season behind the bench. Still, not much was expected of the Gophers in 1973–74.

In October, the ice-making plant at Williams Arena shut down, forcing the Gophers to practice at whatever municipal rinks were available. They opened the season 0–4–1 and were heading nowhere.

When their home was fixed Minnesota went on a tear, posting a 22–11–6 record after their winless start—including a 13–1–2 finish at Williams Arena. A nine-game unbeaten streak propelled them through the WCHA playoffs and into the national tournament.

"It kind of took the whole Twin Cities and our team as much by surprise, not so much that we won, but the fact we got into position to win," recalled forward Rob Harris.

Respect would have to be earned.

Brad Shelstad, Minnesota's last goaltending captain, was snubbed in All-America voting, losing out to Michigan's Robbie Moore. Adding insult to injury, a Boston newspaper referred to him as "Ben Shetland" when the Gophers arrived for the Frozen Four at venerable Boston Garden.

"When it comes down to it, I'd rather be on a national championship team than be an All-American," Shelstad told reporters.

Shelstad would have the last laugh.

In the semifinals against hometown Boston University, the top seed out of the East, the Gophers roared out to a 3–0 lead. However, the Terriers clawed back to eventually tie the game 4–4.

With 44 seconds remaining, Dick Spannbauer was penalized for hooking, leaving Minnesota shorthanded for the rest of the third period.

Brooks sent out Mike Polich to check Boston University center Peter Marzo, who already had two goals. Polich poke checked Marzo at the Terriers' blue line, jumped into the offensive zone, and unloaded a 35-foot slap shot that beat All-American goalie Ed Walsh with 13 seconds remaining to secure a dramatic 5–4 victory.

There was little celebrating, however. The Gophers were upset about their haphazard play and blowing a three-goal lead.

"That was the worst performance for our team in a month," Brooks said. "And it was Mike's worst game in longer than that. I was on him the whole game. He was just lugging the puck and not doing anything with it. That goal was his only shot of the game."

Added forward John Harris: "How can you not be motivated for the national tournament? But we weren't."

The win earned Minnesota a title clash with WCHA regular-season champion Michigan Tech, which was ranked No. 1 in the country.

It was Minnesota's fifth national championship game. The previous four ended in defeat.

Brooks cut the tension when he walked into the team meal before the game and said, "Ok, gentlemen, this will be the last time you'll have to put up with my clichés."

The Gophers took a 2–0 lead on goals by John Sheridan and John Perpich. Rob Harris bagged the game-winner 4:45 into the third period and Phil Pippen added an empty-netter as Minnesota secured a historic 4–2 win.

Nineteen Minnesotans accounted for the school's first hockey national championship, the first all-American roster to win a national championship since Boston College in 1949.

The most valuable player of the tournament was Shelstad, the forsaken goalie who played his finest hockey when it mattered most.

"It's hard to say this is a bigger thrill than winning the state high school tournament was, but it's equal," Shelstad said. "This says something for Minnesota high school hockey and all of our kid programs. We have no All-Americans. But we're all Americans."

A banner reading BROOKS FOR GOVERNOR flew at MSP airport when fans greeted the Gophers when they returned from Boston March 17.

"People laughed a few weeks ago when I called this a team of destiny," Brooks said. "But here we are. I still find the whole thing hard to believe but we did it, with 19 Minnesota kids."

The first of Minnesota's five national championships also started a streak of three straight WCHA playoff titles and Frozen Four appearances.

A dynasty was born.

Spitting Mad

The mid-1970s was the NHL's brawn-and-brawling era as the sport tripled in size by expanding into non-traditional hockey markets aroused by the game's violence along with its speed and skill.

Hard-nosed teams like the Philadelphia Flyers, a.k.a. the "Broad Street Bullies," won back-to-back Stanley Cups. Hollywood icon Paul Newman starred in the cult classic *Slap Shot* as the player-coach who led his band of marauders to a minor league championship.

Against that backdrop, the Minnesota Gophers crashed the 1976 Frozen Four in Denver by defeating Michigan State in an unforgettable triple-overtime thriller to win the Western Collegiate Hockey Association playoff title.

They had the worst record among the finalists after finishing third in the WCHA regular season. Top defenseman Joe Micheletti missed significant time with a knee injury. Minnesota never won more than five straight but also never lost more than two consecutive games.

"Nobody expected us to be there so there was no pressure on us," Micheletti said.

Michigan Tech was back to defend its crown. The Huskies had eliminated the '74 national champions in the 1975 championship game. Minnesota exacted revenge but not before spilling blood during a bench-clearing brawl in the semifinals against East powerhouse Boston University.

The Gophers were tough enough to boast a raucous fan club of prisoners, who were captivated in captivity during the Michigan State game. Goaltender Jeff Tscherne set a school record that still stands with 72 saves in the 7–6 win over the Spartans at East Lansing, Mich.

Minnesota prison sergeant Vince Hamann, watching the game that night with his inmates, was moved to write a letter to coach Herb Brooks "regarding that loud roar from Stillwater."

Brooks posted the letter on the locker-room bulletin board before Minnesota traveled to Denver, according to the *Minneapolis Tribune.*

"If I hadn't been watching the game on an inmate's TV myself I would have thought another riot had just started when Pat [Phippen] scored that winning goal," Hamann wrote. "The noise froze two dozen guards to the floor. You've got to tell the boys they've got to find another way to win at Denver.

"Some of the staff have faced death here and never let it bother them, but after the second overtime they turned off the set and said their hearts couldn't take it. But the inmates loved it, so tell your boys that there are 900 inmates here who are going to be rattling their cells when the next puck drops."

Boston University was 25–3 entering the national tournament. The Terriers were presumptive favorites. They averaged six goals per game, boasted a wicked power play, and deployed skilled players at both ends of the ice.

"All that stuff in the papers about how Boston is the best team? Shit, we're going to shove that down their throats," Gophers rightwinger Warren Miller told reporters before the March 26, 1976, game. "We'll win it. People say we're pushovers but we'll show 'em, especially those preppies from out East."

Tensions exploded on the ice in the opening minute of the second semifinal. Minnesota defenseman Russ Anderson was penalized for cross-checking. A half-minute later, the Terriers' leading scorer Terry Meagher was banished for slashing.

The penalty box at Denver University arena back then was an undivided area adjacent to the Gophers' bench. What happened next was disputed, but the result was mayhem.

Meagher was heckled and claimed Minnesota trainer Gary Smith spit at him. Smith countered that Meagher taunted him with his stick and the trainer grabbed it before Meagher spit on him.

Anderson jumped out of the penalty box. Suddenly the benches emptied and a brawl erupted. It took 15 minutes for officials to break up the fights. They huddled with NCAA officials. The power brokers assessed a bench minor to Minnesota and game misconducts to Anderson and Meagher, who were also banished from the tournament.

"He spit on me and when some of our players looked like they might go after him he reached around and shoved his stick toward them, but it hit me," Smith said afterward. "Words are one thing, but spitting shows no class. He reached in with his stick and hit me with it like a spear. I grabbed it and pulled it away, but all hell broke loose then."

Meagher said the Gophers trash-talked his Canadian heritage when he was escorted to the penalty box.

"When I spit down at them, it was my way of offsetting their verbal abuse at me. It was just a reflex," he said. "I made a mistake, yes. It's something I'm going to have to live with. [Smith] was right there. He spit back at me. It turned into a nationalistic thing. I lost my head."

Terriers coach Jack Parker was incensed at losing his best player barely one minute into an elimination game, and blamed Brooks for instigating the brawl.

"There's no doubt in my mind that Minnesota planned to do this at the start of the game," Parker fumed. "That's a helluva trade—a 30-goal scorer for a defenseman."

Brooks dismissed Parker's charges of premeditation as "immature" and "sour grapes."

The incident would spawn an NCAA investigation. It also sparked the Gophers. Tom Vannelli, Mark Lambert, and Tom

Younghans scored third-period goals for a 4–2 win that catapulted them into the national championship game against Michigan Tech—and made an unlikely hero out of a forgotten goaltender.

Tom Mohr was a walk-on who did not make varsity until his senior year and only played seven games in 1975–76. He joked he was "semi-retired" playing behind starter Tscherne and Steve Janaszak.

The Huskies were the dominant team of the West. They had eight players who stood over 6'2" and outscored their WCHA opponents by 33 goals. They jumped on Minnesota for three first-period goals and were poised to win their second consecutive national title.

During the intermission, Tscherne complained of an upset stomach and headache. So Brooks replaced him with Mohr. The Gophers closed ranks around their inexperienced netminder and played tight defense, limiting the Huskies to just three second-period shots. They also erased the three-goal deficit. It was 4–4 entering the third period.

Phippen, the savior against Michigan State, scored the game-winner 2:48 into the third. Miller added an empty-netter with 30 seconds remaining. Anderson, who was suspended for his role in the Boston University brawl, was standing in the front row behind the Michigan Tech net and celebrated Miller's goal by pounding on the Plexiglas.

He pounded so hard a pane of glass tumbled onto the ice, causing a delay.

"I guess it was the only way I could get into the game," Anderson quipped to reporters.

Mohr allowed only one goal in two periods of relief, making dramatic stops on Jim Mayer and Mike Zuke during Minnesota's comeback.

"My thought was, 'Stop that biscuit; go for it all,'" Mohr said.

Vannelli was involved in five of Minnesota's six goals against Michigan Tech and earned NCAA Championship Most Valuable Player honors. He finished the season with 26 goals and a team-leading 69 points.

The Gophers had no superstar scorer and no Canadians on their roster, and they won it all with a third-string goaltender. Their 14 losses were the most among the school's five national championship teams.

"We've been the underdog for a long time, but we've got heart," Brooks said. "You spot the No. 1–ranked team in the country three goals and come back to win 6–4, that's just a classic."

The day after their victory, the Gophers were welcomed back with a rally at Williams Arena. Phippen, the captain, crystallized the season.

"They called us shabby. They called us inconsistent. Now they call us NCAA champions," he told the crowd.

That offseason the NCAA summoned Brooks to testify at a hearing about Minnesota's brawl with Boston University. Flanked by athletic director Paul Giel and a university attorney, Brooks told the panel he did not instigate the fight.

In November 1976, the NCAA cleared Brooks of any wrongdoing, though he remained bitter about the incident.

"It's been sort of trying," he told the *Tribune*. "I've been accused of premeditation and slandered by those Boston people. Basically I was guilty until proven innocent, because the Boston coach and their people were carrying it on to such an extent."

Four years later, ironically, Brooks coached several players from both teams to an Olympic gold medal in the "Miracle on Ice" at Lake Placid, New York.

9 End of an Era

By the end of the 1970s, the Gophers were college hockey's dominant program, a hunted rival led by a candid head coach who willingly sewed the bull's-eye on his team's back.

Herb Brooks had won the school's first two national championships in 1974 and '76, but Colorado College upset Minnesota in the 1978 Western Collegiate Hockey Association playoffs, a bitter loss that only emboldened him.

At the team's season-ending banquet, Brooks declared, "Next year, we're going all the way. We will win it all."

Brooks' confidence grew over the summer. Athletic director Paul Giel consulted with him about a fall advertising campaign to bolster Gophers season tickets.

"I asked Herb what he wanted to say in the ads," Giel told the *Minneapolis Star Tribune*. "'We're going to win it all,' Herb said. 'It's OK to say that.'

"I prevailed on him to say we 'can' go all the way, not that we will. But you know Herbie," Giel added. "He doesn't mince words."

Brooks' coaching colleagues at Minnesota laughed at such public recklessness.

"They said I was hurting myself, that I should give myself an out, with 'if' and a 'but,'" he recalled. "But I don't subscribe to that theory."

The gauntlet had been thrown down for a special season that turned out to be Brooks' last at Minnesota. No one had an inkling 1978–79 would mark the end of a magical era.

No Gophers team had won more games (32) or scored more goals (239). 168,458 fans attended games at Williams Arena that season.

Three players reached or eclipsed 30 goals—Steve Christoff (38), Don Micheletti (36), and Eric Strobel (30). Freshman winger Neal Broten had points in his final 17 games, and his 50 assists surpassed the great John Mayasich's single-season record.

Senior captain Bill Baker set a then–school record for points by a defenseman, with 12 goals and 42 assists. Goalie Steve Janaszak played all but four games and finished with a 3.23 goals-against average. Freshman defenseman Mike Ramsey started the season on junior varsity and ended up on the NCAA all-tournament team.

"And we struggled. Can you believe that?" Strobel recounted.

Brooks' braggadocio coupled with an early-season slump caused stress that invited boos at Williams Arena.

However, from November 24 through January 6, the Gophers won 11 of 12 games. They finished 18–3–1 at home.

"The last dozen games or so they put on their hard hats, carried their lunch pail, and did an honest day's work," Brooks said. "It all paid off."

Not without one final hiccup.

Minnesota defeated Michigan Tech 5–3 in the first round of the WCHA playoffs, but Brooks was so upset by how they allowed three goals in the final nine minutes he shattered a blackboard and hurled a case of canned pop across the dressing room after the game and unloaded to the media.

"Talk, talk. I'm sick of talking to these fucking players! This game is still won by hungry people," he fumed. "I'm not going to go to bed with these cake-eaters anymore. This is a working man's game, not a game for some god-blessed rich kids from the suburbs. After this season is over, the University of Minnesota can have this job."

The following day, after the Gophers downed Michigan Tech 6–1 to punch their ticket back to the Frozen Four, Brooks walked back his resignation outburst.

"That was my mouth acting up," he said. "My only problem is I heard Johnny Paycheck singing "Take This Job and Shove It" on the way to the game and it stuck in my mind afterward."

Unbeknownst to Brooks, who was preparing for a furlough to coach the 1980 U.S. Olympic team, his time in Minnesota was already running out. There was one more mountain to climb.

Gophers fans flocked to Detroit's Olympia Stadium, turning it into Williams Arena east. A 4–3 semifinal victory over New Hampshire set up a championship showdown against archrival North Dakota, the seventh game the teams played that season.

The No. 1–ranked Fighting Sioux dressed 13 Canadians, which Minnesota fans mocked with banners boasting about the Gophers' homegrown talent.

Look, Ma, No Canadians

All Minnesotans vs. 14 Canadians, 7 Minnesotans, and 1 North Dakotan

The All-American Team

The parochialism added to the tension of a tightly contested title game.

The Gophers took an early 3–1 lead on goals by Christoff, Baker, and John Meredith. North Dakota pulled within one goal midway through the second period.

Less than three minutes into the third, it happened—one of the most dramatic, picturesque goals in Gophers history.

Broten cut left over the Fighting Sioux zone and avoided defenseman Bill Himmelright's hip check. Goalie Bob Iwabuchi raced out to poke the puck away. But Broten dived ahead and chipped it over the sprawled goaltender into the net for the eventual game-winning goal.

Gophers 4, Fighting Sioux 3.

Janaszak won tournament MVP honors. For the third time in six seasons, the Gophers won a national championship with an all-Minnesota roster.

And Brooks fulfilled his prediction.

"I put the most pressure on any team ever by saying they could win it all," he said. "Some people laughed, said you should make peace with your hockey club. But then I say a lot of things other coaches don't say."

Brooks was scheduled to take a leave of absence in 1979–80 to coach the U.S. Olympic team. Brad Buetow would fill in. Brooks brought eight Gophers players with him to Lake Placid—Baker, Broten, Christoff, Janaszak, Ramsey, Strobel, Phil Verchota, and Rob McClanahan.

All won gold medals in the "Miracle on Ice," which changed American hockey forever and affected Minnesota's championship program for decades.

Brooks never returned to Dinkytown. After his Olympics mastery, he coached in Switzerland before being hired by the NHL's New York Rangers.

It took the Gophers 23 years to win another NCAA hockey championship.

10 Mychal Thompson

Mychal Thompson could have turned pro in 1977, and who would have blamed him?

The Gophers were stuck in NCAA purgatory after former coach Bill Musselman was rapped for more than 100 rule violations. He dashed for an ABA coaching job in 1975 and left successor Jim Dutcher to muddle through the fallout.

Sanctions included a two-year national television and NCAA tournament ban just as Thompson was emerging as the best big

Gophers Retired Men's Basketball Numbers

Player	Number
Lou Hudson	14
Charley Mencel	30
Trent Tucker	32
Whitey Skoog	41
Mychal Thompson	43
Kevin McHale	44
Jim Brewer	52
Dick Garmaker	53

man in college basketball. The Buffalo Braves plopped a $1.2 million contract in front of Thompson before his senior season.

He said thanks, but no thanks.

"He told me all along that he was coming back to school," Dutcher told the *Washington Post* in 1978. "When you turn down a million bucks because of a loyalty to a school, that says a lot about you."

Thompson still had plenty to say.

The 6'10" Bahaman was the country's best player in 1977–78, concluding a monster four-year career in Minnesota in which he was one of the school's most productive scorers.

"Mychal by far was the best player that's ever played for Minnesota," said former teammate Flip Saunders.

Thompson's 25.9 points-per-game average as a sophomore in 1975–76 remains a school record. A smooth-shooting, fluid-moving big man, he also posted top-10 scoring averages as a junior and senior.

"I don't have any regrets about anything," Thompson said during his senior year. "I never thought about what would have happened if I had gone pro, because I never really planned to [at the time] anyway."

Thompson's NBA moment came in 1979. The Portland Trail Blazers drafted him No. 1 overall, making Thompson the

Gophers in the Basketball Hall of Fame

Player	Year inducted
John Kundla	1995
Kevin McHale	1999

only Gophers player to earn that distinction. He also was the first foreign-born player taken with the top pick.

During his 12-year pro career, Thompson also played for the San Antonio Spurs and Los Angeles Lakers.

The Lakers traded for Thompson in 1987 to back up future Hall of Fame center Kareem-Abdul Jabbar and defend former Gophers teammate Kevin McHale, the star power forward of the Boston Celtics—the Lakers' archrival of the 1980s.

He was part of the Showtime Lakers, whose roster boasted four No. 1 overall picks—Jabbar, Thompson, Magic Johnson, and James Worthy. Thompson was accustomed to being surrounded by top-shelf talent.

He shared the floor at Williams Arena with four future NBA draft picks—McHale, Steve Lingenfelter, Ray Williams, and Mark Landsberger.

Thompson and his wife, Julie, have three sons who followed in the old man's athletic footsteps.

His oldest son, Mychel, played for the Cleveland Cavaliers. Middle son Klay is a guard who helped lead the Golden State Warriors to the 2015 NBA championship and subsequent trip to the Finals. Youngest son Trayce plays baseball for the Los Angeles Dodgers.

Thompson remains a folk hero in his native Bahamas. In 2015, a street outside the Queen Elizabeth Sports Centre in the capital of Nassau was renamed Mychal Thompson Boulevard in his honor.

"I'm a citizen of the Bahamas, but I feel like I'm as much an American as I am a Bahamian and this country has been so good to me," Thompson told WCCO-TV that year. "It's not perfect; there's no perfect place on earth. Everybody has little issues they've got to work out, but in America you have the right to work them out, they give you the opportunity to work out your differences here, you can talk out your differences.

"So that's why when I see citizens of this country put this country down and rip America, I say, that's okay—you can criticize our country—but you have the realize this is the sweetest place in the world to live."

11 "Defeat Is Worse Than Death, Because You Have to Live with Defeat"

The mantra scrawled above the shower door inside the Gophers men's basketball locker room offered a glimpse inside Bill Musselman's consciousness.

He was one of Minnesota's most revered and reviled coaches, a fierce competitor on the court whose sharp wit was countered by thin skin. Musselman was a study in conflict during a four-year reign that jolted a dormant program to life in the early 1970s like a live wire arcing in a thunderstorm.

He was the savior who delivered a Big Ten championship his inaugural season before absconding for the pros four years later under a cloud of controversy.

He was the domineering scapegoat for the infamous 1972 bench-clearing brawl with Ohio State, a vicious episode that touched a raw nerve amongst national sports fans and media and haunted Musselman the rest of his career.

Musselman was a master defensive tactician with a drill sergeant's thirst for discipline and an unabashed showman whose ear for entertainment made home games at Williams Arena the hottest ticket in the Twin Cities.

"This area will support a winner better than any other in the country," he boasted during the heyday. "I'm not surprised by our attendance. Even though I had heard Minnesota was not a basketball area, I assumed that if we won we would bring in the people."

Musselman won early and often. He went 18–7 and 11–3 in conference in 1971–72 to lead the Gophers to their first outright Big Ten championship in 53 years (they shared the title in 1937) and their first ever NCAA tournament.

The 31-year-old was Minnesota's third choice behind Penn's Dick Harker, who went elsewhere, and Murray (Kentucky) State's Cal Luther, who accepted the job in the spring of 1971 but promptly resigned after getting cold feet and opting to stay where he was.

The selection committee reportedly asked Musselman how long it would take to transform Minnesota into a winner.

"We'll win right off," he declared. "I don't believe in rebuilding years."

Musselman was the fourth Gophers coach in five years but he injected an energy and authoritative presence unaccustomed at Minnesota. The program was spinning its wheels when the brash, young leader from tiny Ashland (Ohio) College made a fast break to the Big Ten.

Musselman amassed an eye-popping .845 winning percentage (109–20) at Ashland. His defensively stout teams qualified for the NCAA tournament four times. In 1968–69, Ashland set an NCAA record for defense, allowing 33.9 points per game. Musselman outlined his coaching principles in a book titled *33.9 Defense*.

At his introductory news conference at Minnesota in June 1971, Musselman outlined three goals:

1. Win the Big Ten.
2. Lead the country in team defense.
3. Win national championships.

He accomplished the first two his initial season.

"The University of Minnesota basketball program was not dying when Musselman took over," St. Paul *Pioneer Press* writer Patrick Reusse wrote in January 1973. "It was already dead."

The Gophers drew 7,202 fans per game before Musselman's arrival. They averaged 16,004 in his four seasons. One night they shoehorned 19,121 into The Barn, which must have given the fire marshal heart palpitations.

Home games were sold out before the season started.

Their starting lineup was known as the "Iron Five," which reflected Musselman's hard-nosed rebounding and defensive scheme.

Clyde Turner led the team with 18.6 points per game. Jim Brewer, Dave Winfield, Bob Nix, and Keith Young rounded out the lineup. Winfield went on to have a Hall-of-Fame baseball career. Brewer was a three-time team MVP who was the second overall pick of the Cleveland Cavaliers in 1973 and had a nine-year NBA career.

Fans of that era might not remember the details of certain games, but those who attended under Musselman's watch at Williams Arena would never forget the roaring pregame warm-up, when the Minnesota Rouser shook the rafters.

Fans would call the ticket office for sold-out games just for permission to watch warm-ups. Some who had tickets would watch the 20-minute spectacle and leave before tip-off, thoroughly entertained.

It was basketball under the big top. There were jugglers and a unicyclist, rapid-fire passing and rhythmic dribbling, a 12-man symphony of ball-handling synchronized to the spine-tingling crescendo of the theme song from the sci-fi thriller *2001: A Space Odyssey* and the Harlem Globetrotters' anthem, "Sweet Georgia Brown."

"When you went up on the floor," former point guard Flip Saunders told the Minneapolis *Star Tribune* in 2015, "you were more worried about the pregame than you were about playing Indiana, Michigan, and those other teams."

Errorless rehearsals were drilled at practices the day before games. The routine had to be perfected or players would have to start again.

"We were not allowed out of the arena until we had it perfect," Saunders recalled.

Musselman scripted the routine while at Ashland. He recruited George Schauer, later known as "Crazy George," simply because he could juggle three basketballs, and brought him to Minnesota.

"He was the best salesman I've ever known," Schauer told the *Star Tribune*. "He was the master of hyperbole. The guy could sell salt water to the ocean. He could sell milk to a dairy farmer."

The Gophers became so popular an auxiliary market was hatched for overflow crowds. Tickets were sold to the adjacent hockey rink so fans could watch games on closed-circuit TV.

Visiting coaches griped that the routine worked the crowd into a dangerous lather.

"It motivates my players," Musselman told reporters. "If 'Sweet Georgia Brown' is provocative of bad feeling, someone should suggest a sweeter melody."

The warm-up routine became a lightning rod for criticism when Minnesota and Ohio State clashed on January 25, 1972, at Williams Arena in a pivotal game in the tight Big Ten race.

With the Buckeyes leading 50–44 late in the second half of a rugged game, Ohio State's Luke Witte was fouled hard by Clyde Turner on a put-back and crashed to the floor. Corky Taylor leaned over Witte to supposedly help him up but instead kneed him in the groin.

Players emptied from both benches. Fans rushed the floor. Ron Behagen kicked Witte in the head. Three Ohio State players were hospitalized, including Witte, who suffered serious head and neck injuries. After the chaos ended, officials suspended the game and declared the Buckeyes victors.

The Big Ten suspended Taylor and Behagen for the rest of the season, a move the players challenged unsuccessfully in court as the conference race was scrambled the final six weeks of the season.

Buckeyes coach Fred Taylor was furious. A *Sports Illustrated* article critical of Musselman's tactics described a postgame scene in which Minnesota athletic director Paul Giel approached Taylor in the visitor's locker room to apologize for his basketball team's unchained aggression.

"I knew it would be emotional," Giel told Taylor. "But I had no idea it would be like this."

"It was bush," Taylor howled. "I've never seen anything like it. But what do you expect from a bush outfit?"

Musselman defended his team, but was deeply wounded by the affair.

"Winning is very important to me. I do not take defeat very well," he said years later. "But I know that I don't animalize my players. I deal with them on a personal basis. I felt as badly about the fight with Ohio State as anyone. But I remained confident in my players."

The Gophers finished one game ahead of Ohio State in the Big Ten.

"When he told us after the Ohio State fight we would still win the Big Ten championship, everyone laughed at him," recalled Winfield. "But he wasn't laughing."

Minnesota lost 70–56 to Florida State in the first round of the NCAA tournament.

The following season, Musselman led the Gophers to a school-record 21 wins against five defeats. But they slipped to 10–4 in the Big Ten, finishing one game behind champion Indiana.

In March 1973, Musselman interviewed for the Florida Gators head coaching job.

"I'm not anxious to leave Minnesota but I would if I don't feel I'm being appreciated," he told reporters.

Florida offered him $21,000 per year; Minnesota was paying him $19,000. Giel was managing a $275,000 budget deficit at the time while Florida was promising Musselman an unlimited recruiting budget after Tommy Bartlett had resigned.

Musselman stayed in Minnesota, which matched Florida's offer. But tensions between Musselman and Giel intensified the next two years.

The NCAA announced in 1975 it was investigating Minnesota for more than 100 recruiting violations without naming Musselman or the basketball program; however, the governing body clearly had them in its sights.

In summer 1975 Musselman interviewed with the San Diego Conquistadors of the American Basketball Association, and on July 23 he sat down with *Pioneer Press* sports columnist Don Riley.

"Look, I love coaching colleges. That's all I've ever thought about," he said. "I had a dream one day of winning more college games than Adolph Rupp. I think Bobby Knight, who's the same age, and myself can do it. But I want to be completely happy. And I want security for my family, like anyone else.

"The day may come when the challenge of pro basketball would be greater—more fun. And the day could come when the financial stability of a pro contract would attract me."

It came six days later.

San Diego signed Musselman to a three-year contract for $50,000 per season. He walked away with three years left on his Minnesota deal. He had a 69–32 record (41–8 at Williams Arena) and .683 winning percentage that remains the highest in school history.

He refused to cooperate with NCAA investigators.

"I feel I have a very clear conscience," Musselman said in San Diego. "The investigation is of the university, not of a single individual, and I am no longer a member of the University of Minnesota."

In November, the Sails folded after just 11 games. Musselman became a coaching vagabond over the next quarter century, including two brief stints with the NBA's Cleveland Cavaliers, never spending more than three years in the same job.

He eventually returned to Minnesota in 1988, hired to coach the expansion Minnesota Timberwolves in the NBA. Musselman was coming off three consecutive championships in the Continental Basketball Association.

He went 22–60 in the Timberwolves' inaugural season and improved to 29–53 the following season. However, Musselman was fired in April 1991. It took six years for the Timberwolves to surpass 29 wins in a season.

Musselman suffered a stroke on October 30, 1999, shortly after coaching the Portland Trail Blazers in a preseason game against Phoenix. He was an assistant to head coach Mike Dunleavy, who had been ejected. Six months later, Musselman was hospitalized with more health problems.

He died of heart and kidney failure on May 5, 2000, at age 59, at the Mayo Clinic in Rochester, Minnesota.

Among Musselman's assistant coaches who became NBA head coaches were his son, Eric (Sacramento, Golden State), Sidney Lowe (Minnesota, Memphis), Sam Mitchell (Toronto, Minnesota), Scott Brooks (Oklahoma City, Washington), Tom Thibodeau (Chicago, Minnesota), and Tyrone Corbin (Utah, Sacramento).

Musselman's competitiveness was legendary. But he also betrayed a sense of fair play later in his career.

Charley Rosen was a rookie head coach for the CBA's Savannah Spirits. He recalled being in a close game against Musselman's Tampa Bay Thrillers.

"Late in the fourth quarter, one of the refs called three charging fouls on my best player, Cedric Henderson, and the Thrillers eventually won on a buzzer-beating shot by the late 'Fast' Eddie Jordan," Rosen wrote in a 2003 first-person article about the CBA for ESPN.com.

"Instead of celebrating his victory, Bill followed the refs off the court to their locker room, screaming that they had 'screwed Charley out of the win.' He continued to kick and pound his fists on the closed locker room door, raging for another 10 minutes."

"Muss," I said when he'd cooled down. "What are you doing?"

"If I can't win a game fairly, then I'd rather lose," Musselman answered.

"He walked a few steps away," Rosen wrote, "then turned, smiled tightly, and said, 'Don't worry, Charley, I'll get over it.'"

12 The Brawl

A wicked Alberta Clipper plunged the Twin Cities into a deep freeze on January 25, 1972, just as the sports scene was heating up on a memorable Tuesday for hockey fans and a bloody night college basketball would rather forget.

The 25th NHL All-Star Game was played at the Met Center, the North Stars' home arena in suburban Bloomington.

Bobby Orr of the Boston Bruins was the league's premier superstar and reigning Norris Trophy defenseman, a smooth-skating dynamo who handled the puck like a magician and checked like a moose.

He earned game MVP honors with an outstanding defensive performance. Orr also assisted on Bruins teammate Phil Esposito's game-winning, power-play goal with 44 seconds remaining as the East Division roared back from a two-goal deficit for an exhilarating 3–2 victory over the West.

Meanwhile, 15 icy miles to the north, Williams Arena crackled with electricity. Another sellout crowd was insulated from eight inches of fresh snow on the ground and an air temperature of minus-13. The first-place Gophers basketball team was playing host to Ohio State in a pivotal Big Ten clash between the conference's hottest, most talented teams.

Minnesota (9–3), ranked No. 16, had won four straight games, the No. 6–ranked Buckeyes three in a row. Ohio State boasted the conference's most prolific offense, averaging 80.5 points per game. The Gophers had the stingiest defense, holding opponents to 56.5 points a contest.

The showdown was a seminal moment for first-year Gophers coach Bill Musselman. The brash, 31-year-old defensive mastermind had arrived in town seven months earlier, the third choice of a selection committee banking on a rebuilding project.

The Gophers had not won an outright Big Ten championship since 1919. Musselman, who transformed tiny Ashland College into a perennial NCAA tournament participant, vowed to win immediately. This was the Ohio native's first game against the Buckeyes. The Gophers were undefeated in the Big Ten and trailed Ohio State by one game.

"I would trade a year of my life for a win tomorrow," Musselman told Minnesota media before the game. "I've had teams play in the college division playoffs. And those were mighty important. But this one is more important because it could lead to a Big Ten championship."

The game became Musselman's lifelong albatross.

Tip-off was 8:00 PM, but the show, as always, started an hour earlier. Fans packed the lower bowl and upper deck to watch the Gophers' 15-minute warm-up, their rhythmic dribbling and precise ball-handling routine synchronized to the Harlem Globetrotters' "Sweet Georgia Brown" and the orchestral theme to *2001: A Space Odyssey.*

Fans today would hardly bat an eye at the theatrics but in 1972 visiting coaches griped the unique ritual worked Williams Arena into a dangerous lather, which was Musselman's purpose in creating a home-court advantage. He had brought the practice with him from Ashland.

The Buckeyes were booed lustily when they took the court. The crowd of 17,775 smelled blood, and they got plenty.

Ohio State's 7'0" center Luke Witte was the fulcrum from which its offense pivoted. The Gophers' game plan was to defend Witte physically, a task that primarily fell to forwards Ron Behagen, Jim Brewer, and Corky Taylor.

Game officials Orlando Palesse, Tony Torterello, and George "Red" Strauthers called a tight first half that passed without incident, although tensions increased as the teams exited the court at halftime.

Gophers guard Bob Nix passed in front of Witte, his left arm raised in a clenched-fist salute, according a *Sports Illustrated* story about the game. Witte elbowed Nix's fist aside and clipped Nix in the jaw.

"Our kids were really upset at halftime," Musselman said.

The Buckeyes trailed 32–31 with 11:25 to play in the second half and used an 8–1 run to build a 40–32 lead with 4:45 remaining. Behagen had already fouled out. Minnesota lost momentum and its grip.

"As long as Minnesota was in the game, nothing happened," OSU all-conference guard Alan Hornyak told reporters afterward. "But once we got out in front eight points, [Clyde] Turner, Jim Brewer and others on the Minnesota team just seemed to lose their head and explode. In all of the years I've been in sports, I've never seen such poor sportsmanship."

As Ohio State expanded its lead, officials halted the game because fans littered the court with debris.

With 36 seconds remaining, Witte was driving for a layup when he was knocked to the floor by Turner, who was whistled for a flagrant foul and ejected. Taylor walked over Witte, who was lying flat on his back, and extended his hand to help pull him to his feet.

In the same motion, Taylor kneed Witte in the groin. The Ohio State big man crumpled back to the floor. The benches emptied. And 15 minutes of mayhem ensued with players colliding in a maelstrom of haymakers and wild chases.

Behagen ran over and stomped Witte on the head as he lay prone. Fans rushed the court and joined the fray. Several Gophers reserves, including forward Dave Winfield, who went on to have a Hall of Fame baseball career, chased after Ohio State backup Mark Wagar.

Winfield jumped on top of Wagar and punched him in the face and head. Wagar managed to escape only to be pushed to the floor by one fan and punched in the chin by another.

Strauthers, one of the game officials, ended up with a black eye trying to separate players. Later that week he recounted to an Ohio newspaper that he sensed trouble before the game started.

"It was the worst situation ever," he said. "Things get rough in Minnesota. They throw rocks, bottles...everything. There were only three policemen to handle the crowd of 17,000. We told them before the game they should have ample protection but they told us they never had any problems and didn't expect any."

Order was eventually restored. There were 36 seconds remaining in the game. Ohio State was winning 50–44. Gophers athletic director Paul Giel, fearful of a riot, grabbed the public-address microphone and over a chorus of boos declared the game a forfeit.

"I am not going to prolong this because anything I say would add to your emotions," Giel told the crowd. "No matter what your feelings are, the game is over and Ohio State has won 50–44."

Witte was carried off on a stretcher. He and Wagar, bloodied and seriously injured, were taken to a Minneapolis hospital. Recriminations spewed out of the locker rooms during post-game interviews.

Taylor accused Witte of trying to spit on him before he kneed the Buckeyes center.

OSU coach Fred Taylor blamed Musselman's warm-up for fueling a hysterically hostile environment.

"If the pregame drill is so important to Minnesota's well-being, why doesn't [Musselman] take it on the road? Think about that for a minute," Taylor hissed. "It was bush. I've never seen anything like it. But what do you expect from a bush outfit?"

Musselman blamed the officials for losing control of the game.

"It was a highly emotional game," he said. "With three officials on the floor, you would think they could prevent an occurrence of this type."

Strauthers, the official, blamed both teams.

"It seemed that Brewer, Turner, and other Minnesota players wanted to outmuscle Witte," he said. "They were competing on every rebound. They would get on Witte. But Witte isn't an angel, either. He got his licks in, too."

Big Ten commissioner Wayne Duke, who was in attendance, said, "In all of my years in sports, I've never seen anything like this develop. It was most embarrassing."

In the following morning's *Minneapolis Tribune*, coverage of the brawl shared the front page under a banner headline about President Nixon's secret peace offering to Hanoi to withdraw U.S. troops from Vietnam.

Wagar was treated for lacerations over his left eyebrow. Witte suffered a concussion and needed stitches to close gashes over his eyebrow and chin. Both players spent the night in the hospital.

Witte denied spitting at Taylor. With a thick bandage covering his right eye, Witte told reporters upon returning to Columbus his recollections of the night ended the moment Taylor attacked him.

"After he kicked me in the groin, I passed out. I don't remember anything until I came to in the emergency room at the hospital. I've been told I sat up a couple times in the locker room after the game but I don't remember it," he said.

Ohio governor John Gilligan called the brawl a "public mugging," dumping kerosene on a smoldering story that stirred headlines and a national debate about sportsmanship.

Big Ten officials reviewed television coverage and game films for two days before suspending Behagen and Taylor for the rest of the season.

Sports Illustrated followed up with a scathing report by author William F. Reed, titled "An Ugly Affair in Minneapolis." Reed accused the Gophers' overly aggressive defense and Musselman's malevolence for inciting the brawl, ultimately laying blame at the coach's feet.

Musselman absorbed the criticism to protect his team but admitted privately over the years he was deeply hurt by accusations he fostered thuggish play.

"It has always been amazing to me that some people, especially Fred Taylor, blamed our pregame warm-up," Musselman told the St. Paul *Pioneer Press* in 1995. "That was a harmless thing that brought nothing but fun and excitement to the game. Maybe we were too physical. Maybe they were, although I still believe the officials should have put a stop to that if it was true. But the warm-up drill should never have been blamed. That was ridiculous."

The Buckeyes, without Witte in the lineup, lost to Iowa in their next game and never recovered that season. The Gophers went on to win the Big Ten championship but were eliminated in the first round of the NCAA tournament by Florida State.

A remorseful Taylor expressed regret about kneeing Witte.

"I lost my head," he said a day after the fracas. "Regardless of what Witte did to me, I shouldn't have kneed him. I don't know if it was the tension of the game or the crowd that keyed me. I thought Witte was going to spit on me, and it upset me. There is no excuse for what I did but you wouldn't call Witte's play one of a sportsman."

For years, Taylor could not escape negative publicity or his association with one of the ugliest episodes in college basketball history. He was forever linked to Witte, his victim.

Eventually, Taylor and Witte became pen pals. In 2003, more than three decades after their clash, Witte flew to the Twin Cities to meet his bygone nemesis. By then he was a minister in Charlotte, N.C.

"Regardless of how ugly a situation may have been or escalated into, we're human," Witte told the *Star Tribune* in 2012. "On the other side, being human, we have the chance to reconcile."

Witte stayed at Taylor's suburban Minneapolis home for two days. Together, they watched a video of the brawl. After several minutes of silence, they started a conversation, one that eventually built a friendship with Turner and Taylor that lasted nine years until Taylor's death from cancer in 2012.

"We all had different ideas of what went on," Witte said. "But it was so neat for the three of us, at least, to have that situation, where there was time to talk it through, to heal, on both sides.... It's so neat for me to be able to call Clyde and Corky my friend."

13 Take In "The Barn"

Nine decades of basketball and cultural history have unspooled inside the cramped and crusty confines of Minnesota's crown jewel sporting venue, where electricity is measured in decibels more so than voltage.

Nothing rivals the unique Williams Arena, from its raised court and fans' over-the-back proximity to the reverberating din that thunders down from its confining rafters and the random nooks where wayward rats and roaches roam.

Christened in 1928 by none other than the father of basketball, Dr. James Naismith, "The Barn," as it is affectionately known, is the fourth-oldest Division I facility in the country. Only Northeastern's Matthews Arena (1910) in Boston; Fordham's Rose Hill Gymnasium (1925) in the Bronx, New York; and Penn's Paelstra (1927) in Philadelphia have played host longer.

"I spent many hours by myself in Williams Arena just shooting, and loved it," former All-American forward Kevin McHale once said. "It is funny how you can get a peaceful feeling in a huge building like that all by yourself. There is nothing else like it. It feels like home."

Shaquille O'Neal, John Wooden, Magic Johnson, Mychal Thompson, and George Mikan all played at Williams Arena. Stokely Carmichael of the Black Panthers spoke there. So did the Dalai Lama.

Adolph Rupp, the deity of Kentucky basketball, celebrated his third of four national championships in 1951. Forty-six Minnesota high school basketball championships were decided under its arched roof.

Blood was spilled on the hardwood in 1972 and recriminations between Minnesota and Ohio State echoed for years after the conference rivals clashed in one of the ugliest brawls in sports history.

Twenty-nine years later the Dalai Lama delivered his message of compassion and peace to 9,000 congregants, sitting in a wingback chair on the free throw line mere feet from where Gophers forward Corky Taylor kneed Buckeyes center Luke Witte in the groin to ignite the mayhem.

The Gophers clinched their 1972 and '82 Big Ten championships at home. They sullied later achievements, too. Banners celebrating Minnesota's national tournament berths in 1994 and 1995 and the 1997 Final Four were taken down and scrubbed from history as NCAA punishment for an academic fraud scandal.

In October 2002, Minnesotans bid a tearful goodbye to beloved Democratic senator Paul Wellstone during a memorial service that drew 20,000 supporters and mourners, including political heavyweights such as former President Bill Clinton, the Reverend Jesse Jackson, and former Vice President Walter Mondale, who unsuccessfully ran for Wellstone's vacant seat.

Williams Arena hosted the NCAA hockey title games in 1958 and '66, the 1988 women's volleyball final, and the 1990 men's gymnastics championship.

Once, while coaching the Gophers in the 1980s, Jim Dutcher discovered a hard-luck student manager living there out of sight, out of mind.

"He had a cot back in one of the storage rooms. We told him that he was going to have to find another place to stay," Dutcher told the St. Paul *Pioneer Press*.

From 1950 until 1971, Williams Arena boasted the largest capacity of any collegiate basketball venue in the country at 18,025. But that proved pliable.

On February 28, 1955, the Gophers battled Iowa for Big Ten supremacy and a record 20,176 fans shoehorned themselves into The Barn to watch a 72–70 loss to the Hawkeyes.

Fire marshals would have no more of fans sitting on laps or in the aisles. When the arena was renovated in 1992 capacity was reduced to 14,321. Five years later, 21 barn lofts above the second deck were built, offering luxury amenities and a bird's-eye view of the court. Those 304 seats pushed capacity to its contemporary 14,625.

"We could always make it better, but the atmosphere, the raised floor—it's kind of what college basketball is all about," said Scott Ellison, Minnesota's assistant athletic director for facilities, once told the Pioneer Press.

"When you think of Williams Arena, you think of college basketball. Even if you put a small crowd in there for a non-conference game, it still is a pretty electric environment. Put a small crowd in the Target Center, that's what it is—a small crowd."

Try selling the aesthetics to Jud Heathcote.

The gravelly Michigan State coach was no fan of the racket, the subterranean visitor's locker room, and especially the raised floor, which can hydroplane an unsuspecting player diving for a loose into a pit of folding chairs or photographers.

Heathcote wrote that Williams Arena was "devised by the village idiot or the town drunk." He called the raised floor "a joke for college basketball. If I had a bomb, I'd blow it up."

Forgive old Jud. He compiled a .607 winning percentage over 20 years with the Spartans but was a mere 7–12 at The Barn. After his 1978–79 Spartans clinched the Big Ten title at Williams Arena, the Gophers' band played the Michigan State fight song and gave the team a standing ovation. Led by Magic Johnson, that team won the NCAA championship.

"That wouldn't have happened very many places," Heathcote grudgingly told the Minneapolis *Star Tribune* in 2003.

Crumbling infrastructure and building code violations left Williams Arena at death's door several times. Athletic officials considered moving Gophers games to the State Fairgrounds, St. Paul Civic Center, and Met Center...even the Metrodome.

The Barn has outlasted them all.

A university press release touted it as "a marvel of engineering construction" when the University Fieldhouse opened February 4, 1928—exactly one month before Herbert Hoover was sworn in as the 31st president. The towering brick-and-steel structure at the corner of Fourth Street and University Avenue became the largest indoor college sporting facility in the United States.

Three supporting arches rise 104 feet in the air. The stadium walls are 52 feet high. More than 3,100 tons of steel and 3.5 million bricks encompassed the original 126,000 square feet. General contractor Madsen Construction Co. of Minneapolis built the arena in just nine months starting in May 1927.

Total cost was $650,000, with $200,000 coming from athletic ticket revenue and the balance from tax-exempt state bonds.

Gophers basketball debuted in 1896 at the university armory. The team moved in 1925 to the downtown Minneapolis armory but had to schedule practices around military maneuvers. Both were dingy afterthoughts, renowned more for their standard four walls and roof than any charm.

The multipurpose fieldhouse featured a dirt floor beneath the removable court for the football team to practice, two tennis courts, two jumping pits, a 220-yard circular track, and a batting cage for the baseball team that bisected the building.

Dave MacMillan was in the middle of his second season as Minnesota's basketball coach when the "marvel" opened.

"The new fieldhouse means everything to basketball," he said. "We can use it when we want to and it is much better lighted than the armory downtown."

Dr. Naismith, who devised the game of basketball in 1891 to tame an unruly class at the Springfield, Mass., YMCA, was invited to the opening to serve as honorary referee. Before tossing up the ball to start the game between the Gophers and Ohio State, he delivered a speech to the sellout crowd.

"I wish to congratulate the University of Minnesota on its splendid equipment, not only for basketball, but for the care of the health and development of the students. I assure you that I shall follow the fortunes of your basketball team with more interest and enthusiasm for this personal contact with your institution."

Fans were treated to an original Barn burner. The Buckeyes won 42–40 in double overtime when center Van Heyde sank a one-handed shot at the buzzer. Minnesota guard Mally Nydahl led the Gophers with 14 points.

The Gophers won their first Big Ten championship under MacMillan in 1937. A decade later a $1 million renovation added a 6,800-seat hockey arena and permanent ice plant separated by a wall from the basketball court, which was raised in 1950.

The thought was to improve sightlines for fans and create a natural buffer between spectators and the court. It also left players looking through ankles and knees at the action. Most coaches opt to stand or sit on the court in front of the recessed bench.

The remodel was completed by March 4, 1950, when the field-house was dedicated as Williams Arena during halftime of a 60–54 loss to Wisconsin. It was named after Dr. Henry L. Williams, Minnesota's football coach from 1900 to 1921.

Williams Arena went largely unchanged for 40 years. It did not age well. In 1980 the university deemed the building hazardous and vowed to relocate games unless the state helped fund major renovations.

"It's a good old gentleman of a building, but Williams Arena is potentially an unsafe building, too," said then–university president Peter Magrath.

There was no backup power source, no sprinkler system, no emergency lighting, and only 18 exits. Concession stands still had wooden doors and ceilings. The fire marshal was on a rampage. Smoking was finally banned in 1980.

A $2 million update provided a bandage. Still, in 1986 president Ken Keller labeled Williams Arena "the worst in the nation." Three years later athletic director Rick Bay proposed demolishing the building and replacing it with a modern dual-purpose arena for basketball and hockey.

The blowback from fans was fierce. They were not interested in something new, shiny, and sterile. They wanted their cozy confines preserved.

"There's a feel to the arena that's very important to the people who watch the games there," said late Gophers broadcaster Ray Christensen.

Athletic officials listened, then leveraged. A $41 million renovation was approved to put the women's Sports Pavilion to house volleyball where the old hockey rink sat and build Mariucci Arena across the street.

That project replaced lower-level bleachers with 6,100 chair-back seats, widened aisles, upgraded the ticket lobby, expanded the locker rooms, and widened concourses. To satisfy modern building and fire codes, capacity was reduced to 14,321.

Incredibly, the original court survived it all.

In the late 2000s, facilities manager Michael Dale decided it was time to replace the warped, pockmarked hardwood. When they pulled up the panels he was shocked at what was discovered.

"We saw under the tiles that it was made by a company that has ceased to exist since the 1940s," Dale told the *Star Tribune*. "We had 80 years of history on one court."

Eighty-plus years and counting.

14 Mr. Everything

Legend-in-a-vacuum Paul Giel was a dynamic tailback who thrived in the mediocrity between Minnesota coaching icons Bernie Bierman and Murray Warmath.

The two-time Heisman Trophy runner-up punctuated a bygone era of two-way players and multisport iconoclasts. He eschewed a pro football career for a chance to pitch in the big leagues.

Giel also flexed his fundraising muscle in the early 1970s to rescue a Gophers athletic department that was drowning in red ink before resigning in the wake of one too many scandals.

Giel's turbulent departure in 1988 hardly diminished what he accomplished on the diamond and gridiron or what he meant to fans and the countless coaches and athletes who fed off his energy and passion for Gophers sports. And his sharp wit and self-deprecating humor made him catnip to sportswriters.

"Hey, let's face it," Giel told a St. Paul *Pioneer Press* columnist in 1991. "As a pitcher I wound up with a slider that didn't slide. I had a fastball that you could hang Monday's wash on and a curve you could hit with a walking stick."

Giel's repertoire allowed him to pitch 102 games, 91 in relief. He won 11 games and lost nine, and posted a 5.39 earned run average in a six year major league career with the New York/San Francisco Giants, Pittsburgh Pirates, Minnesota Twins, and Kansas City Athletics.

For the Gophers Giel was 10–4 with 133 strikeouts in 128 Big Ten innings, posting a microscopic 0.42 ERA in 1952. But his football feats made him a household name.

His scholarship only covered athletics, so Giel worked in a brewery to earn money for room and board.

Recruited by Bierman out of Winona, Minnesota, Giel played three years for the Grey Eagle's successor, Wes Fesler. He scored 35 touchdowns and combined for 5,094 passing and rushing yards as a passing halfback. So valuable was Giel, he accounted for 212 of Minnesota's 443 points over three seasons in which the Gophers only won 10 of 27 games.

Giel fretted platoon football would ruin him. Instead it made him a star. He could punt. He could tackle. He could defend passes.

In a 1953 upset of Michigan, Giel completed 13-of-18 passes for 169 yards, ran for another 112, and handled the ball a Big Ten–record 57 out of 73 snaps in a 22–0 blowout. He also led the team in tackles and had two interceptions.

In 1952, he finished six votes behind Billy Vessels of Oklahoma in the Heisman balloting. A year later he was second to Notre Dame halfback Johnny Lattner.

Giel never betrayed bitterness.

"They are both great players. They deserve every honor they got. For a slow-footed guy from Winona just to be in the picture with them was a thrill," he said.

Giel ended his Minnesota football career with 2,188 rushing yards and 1,922 passing, which earned him an induction into the College Football Hall of Fame.

His star power drew interest from the NFL's Chicago Bears and the Winnipeg Blue Bombers of the Canadian Football League. All but a handful of major league baseball teams were intrigued by Giel.

During one of his Heisman visits to New York, he was spotted kibitzing with Yogi Berra at Toots Shor's famous restaurant. The Tigers invited him to Briggs Stadium in Detroit for a tryout.

In June 1954, Giel signed with the Giants for a team-record $60,000 bonus and was slotted on the big-league roster as a

Nicknamed "Mr. Everything," Paul Giel was a two-time All-American halfback and Heisman Trophy runner-up who eschewed a pro football career to pitch six years in Major League Baseball. University of Minnesota Archives

so-called "bonus baby," which tethered him to New York for two years.

Drafted to discourage wealthy teams like the Yankees from signing prospects and stashing them in their minor league systems, many bonus babies languished on the bench and struggled to develop.

Giel debuted July 10, 1954, against the Pittsburgh Pirates and struck out the first three batters he faced—George O'Donnell, Gair Allie, and Vic Janowicz. He only pitched 3⅓ innings the rest of the season as the Giants won the National League pennant.

Giel watched in the dugout as the Giants swept the heavily favored Cleveland Indians in the World Series.

Over the years he pitched sporadically for the Giants, following them to San Francisco in 1958. Giel was waived the following season. Claimed by the Pirates, he knocked around with the Twins and Athletics before retiring from baseball in 1961.

The NFL's expansion Minnesota Vikings hired Giel to be their business manager. In 1963, he became sports director at WCCO radio in Minneapolis and resigned eight years later to become Minnesota's athletic director.

Giel inherited a downtrodden department that was $500,000 in debt, and spent 17 years turning the deficit into a surplus. He rejuvenated the men's and women's programs and leveraged relationships with deep-pocketed boosters to rehabilitate facilities and pack venues for games.

But the men's basketball program was sanctioned under Giel's watch for a series of recruiting scandals in the 1970s. Allegations of sexual misconduct in the mid-1980s and a pay-to-play scheme in 1988 ultimately led university president Richard Sauer to fire Giel.

"All an athletic director can do is make sure, to the best of his ability, that all your people know the rules," Giel told the *Chicago Tribune* at the time. "It did seem that every time I turned around there was a problem.

"What I won't miss about this job is being held accountable for the actions of others you can't control, or someone saying, 'You should have known or could have known.'"

During Giel's tenure Minnesota won three national hockey championships, three men's gymnastics titles, three Big Ten baseball flags, and two men's basketball Big Ten championships.

Among the successful coaches Giel hired were Lou Holtz (football), Herb Brooks (hockey) and Clem Haskins (men's basketball).

The Gophers football program retired his No. 10 uniform and named an award in his honor given annually to the student-athlete "who exemplifies unselfishness and concern about the U of M both on and off the field."

Giel died of a heart attack in 2002 at age 70.

His storied athletic career earned Giel the nickname "Mr. Everything," but he remained a humble caretaker of the university he loved and the legacy he left behind.

"How can I take myself seriously when my wife Nancy greeted me in the kitchen after I returned from the big [College] Hall of Fame dinner in New York and before I could tell her who I sat next to, she told me to take out the garbage?"

15 The Grey Eagle

Simple, predictable, single-wing football was the prevailing scheme of Bernie Bierman's prolific, stoic, and historic reign at Minnesota, an unrecognizable offense paralleled with today's multiple-formation passing attacks.

Bierman relied on speed and power but was inherently boring, a fundamentalist in blocking and tackling, a master organizer and tactician who preached discipline honed from serving in two world wars.

Yet he was masterful.

Beauty was in the eye of beholders who packed Memorial Stadium over 16 seasons as Bierman choreographed victories and championships unmatched since the "Grey Eagle" flew his nest in 1950:

- Five national championships from 1934–41
- Five undefeated seasons
- Seven Big Ten championships
- A 93–35–6 record
- Fourteen All-Americans
- One heck of a nice fella

"Underneath that glassy, chilly exterior was a man of warmth, tenderness, and compassion," wrote St. Paul *Pioneer Press* columnist Don Riley.

"The Grey Eagle" Bernie Bierman was a three-sport star at Minnesota before World War I. As head football coach for 16 seasons, he led the Gophers to five national championships, including five undefeated seasons, from 1934 to '41.
University of Minnesota Archives

Bierman accomplished greatness without an ounce of negative energy expended or venom spewed at a flawed player, erroneous official, or misguided fan. Motivating through fear or psychological gamesmanship was counterproductive to Bierman, who commanded the respect of his players by treating them like men and demanding likewise.

Fiery pep talks were not his style.

"I never made an emotional speech in my life," he admitted.

Bierman was born March 11, 1894, on a farm near Springfield, Minnesota. His parents were German pioneers. A bone infection forced the young man to use crutches when he was not bedridden.

He recovered to play football at Litchfield High School before becoming a three-sport athlete for the Gophers in track, basketball, and football. An All-American halfback, he captained the undefeated 1915 Big Ten championship team. He graduated the following year from the school of business.

He was settling into a coaching career at Butte (Montana) High School when World War I beckoned. Bierman enlisted in the U.S. Marine Corps and fought in Europe before returning stateside and becoming head coach at Montana University.

Stints at Tulane and Mississippi State followed before Bierman's alma mater brought him home again in 1932, the start of the "Golden Era" for Minnesota.

Led by All-American halfback Pug Lund, the Gophers finished 8–0 and won their first national title in 1934, traveling to Pittsburgh to defeat the Panthers in an undefeated East–West showdown that was breathlessly chronicled by the national press.

"They were my favorite team," Bierman said. "It could do anything you'd want a team to do."

Minnesota quickly became a dynasty, winning four more national championships before World War II. The Gophers went 16–0 in 1940 and '41 as Bierman compiled a 63–12–5 record over the span. They outscored opponents 1,597–466 and yielded 20 or more points just twice in 10 years.

Among Bierman's All-Americans were College Football Hall of Famers Lund, Ed Widseth, Dick Wildung, Clayton Tonnemaker, Sonny Franck, Bruce Smith, and Leo Nomellini.

Progressive blocking, smashing off-tackle runs, and buck-laterals—a series of handoffs and pitches off a single snap—constituted Bierman's single wing. He ran it relentlessly behind an unbalanced offensive line. Bierman was chastised for scripting an unimaginative offense, but remained unbowed.

"If I found that four or five plays were doing the job, we stuck with them," he said. "Still, we probably had more plays than our opponents. I always figured that ball control with good execution is the best thing you can have."

He was a perfectionist who was one of the best at eliminating flaws in his players and exploiting them in opponents.

"I'd put him up there with Pop Warner, Knute Rockne, Frank Leahy," Nomellini said about football's coaching innovators. "He was one of the best teachers I've ever known. He always maintained a sense of humor. Bernie's teams weren't fancy but they were sound—and knew what to expect."

On December 7, 1941, Japanese planes attacked the U.S. naval base at Pearl Harbor, Hawaii. The next day, the former Marine major re-enlisted for three years.

Bierman coached at the Navy's PreFlight School at Iowa State, where pilots were trained for missions in the Pacific theater. His assistants with the Seahawks included future Oklahoma head coaches Jim Tatum and Bud Wilkinson.

Bierman returned to Minnesota in 1945 and coached six more seasons, although he failed to win another Big Ten championship and resigned in 1950 after finishing 1–7–1.

For years, Minnesota eschewed athletic scholarships while its competitors continually poached in-state athletes with offers of free education, boarding, and job opportunities. Studies showed Minnesota recruited less of the state's athletes proportionally than general students.

Bierman changed that in 1949.

"We were, of course, one of the first schools in the Big Ten to have jobs at $50 per month for the football players," he recalled in the 1970s. "Ohio State quickly developed a jobs program, too. Years ago our players needed $50 to eat; now they need $50 to make car payments."

Bierman was elected to the College Football Hall of Fame in 1955 and retired to Laguna Hills, California. He died March 8, 1977. He was 82. The Bierman Field Athletic Building on campus was named after him.

"I was always in awe of him," said Paul Giel, Minnesota's athletic director from 1971 to '86. "You had the impression he was cold and distant and impersonal. That was not true at all. In fact, he was quite shy in many respects. But he was an interesting conversationalist on just about any topic."

Especially his beloved football.

Two years before Bierman died he told an interviewer he realized the power and allure of the forward pass, which he had shunned for his more brawny running game.

"You see the trend among the kids playing on the streets or in back lots. Now they throw the ball," he said. "I can understand why coaches do this. They are interested in making the game spectacular for the fans, and I don't blame them."

16 Jerry Kill

For Jerry Kill, it was exit snarling.

The beloved coach who toiled for five years rebuilding the Gophers' moribund football program to respectability on and off the field before retiring because of health issues was livid January 4, 2017, and took to the airwaves to disavow the university, declaring he "won't be stepping foot" back on campus.

It was the morning after athletic director Mark Coyle fired Kill's longtime friend, colleague, and successor, Tracy Claeys, who had just won nine games and scored a Holiday Bowl upset in his first full season as Gophers head coach.

During a blunt half-hour interview on 1500ESPN radio, Kill said Claeys was the convenient fall guy for a sexual assault investigation that led to the suspension of 10 players and, subsequently, a brief player boycott before the Holiday Bowl. Claeys tweeted support for his players, putting himself at odds with Coyle and school president Eric Kaler.

Kill especially took issue with Coyle's assertion during a news conference that he was looking for a head coach who will graduate student-athletes "with class and integrity."

"I would say that the program has been run in a first-class manner," said Kill, the Gophers' head coach from 2011 to '15. "I don't think there's anybody in the country that would argue that, anybody who knows me or knows the assistant coaches. I believe when you make a statement like that, you need to go back. Mark wasn't there when it started....And look how far it's come.

"It didn't come by him. He hasn't been there. It came by a lot of people. They're not building that new facility because of him. There's been a lot of work that's gone into that by a lot of people. So, to call people out like that, I think you've got to know them. I think the [football] guys said he might've come to one practice. The players don't know the guy, the coaches don't know the guy. Yet, he'd call people out like that. I don't think that's professional."

Kill never worked for Coyle, who was hired in June 2016. Kill resigned in October 2015 because of issues related to his epilepsy. Claeys succeeded Kill on an interim basis before being named head coach before the 2016 season.

"Let me tell you something, that program right now is better— a lot better—than when I came in," Kill told 1500ESPN. "There's no question about that. It's a lot better....Beyond what you think of the administration, or what you think of something else, those coaches care about the kids. That's why they coach. Every one of them wants the program to continue to progress and get better. Nobody wants to let it go down the tube. But we put a lot of years into that thing. It wore my ass out."

Jerry Kill earned 2014 Big Ten Coach of the Year honors and led the Gophers to their first New Year's Day bowl in 53 years before epileptic seizures forced him to retire from head coaching a year later. AP Images

In December 2016, Kill returned to coaching after a 14-month hiatus, becoming offensive coordinator at Rutgers, another Big Ten school. His anger at Minnesota was raw.

"I won't be stepping foot back to the stadium and I won't be stepping back at the university," Kill said. "My wife and I, we will not. We gave our best to the state of Minnesota and we'll always come to Minnesota. My daughter is there and we love Minnesota, and I'll go to every [pro] baseball game and pro football game and anything else. But I will not ever be in that stadium or that complex. They're building a new complex, and we had a lot to do with that, but I won't ever see it."

Kill's angry public breakup with Minnesota stood in stark contrast to his emotional farewell on October 28, 2015, when Kill gathered his team together for the final time.

In three days the Gophers would face No. 15 Michigan in a pivotal prime-time game at TCF Bank Stadium. At stake were the Little Brown Jug and Big Ten relevance for struggling Minnesota. Players had no idea they were losing their master, the reigning conference coach of the year, the man who already had defeated cancer and was courageously fighting epilepsy as a national spokesman for those devastated by the disease.

Seizures and insomnia were ravaging Kill's brain and body. They were more frequent and intense. He slacked off going to church. He stopped exercising and wasn't eating right. Kill tried willing himself to continue, but after three decades stalking sidelines he knew his head coaching career was finished.

"Last night when I walked off the practice field...I felt like a part of me died," Kill recounted in his 2016 book *Chasing Dreams: Living My Life One Yard at a Time.*

Kill's life no longer depended on football. His family depended on his making the right decision.

With tears in his eyes, Kill told the Gophers he was resigning, less than a year after leading Minnesota to its first New Year's Day bowl in 53 years and just as "Jerrysota" was making the moribund program a feel-good story again.

"I've given every ounce that I have for 32 years to the game of football," Kill said, his voice cracking, during a hastily called news conference at the stadium. "I ain't done anything else; that's the scary part."

During the team's bye the previous week Kill had suffered seizures at home on consecutive nights. They were the latest in a series of debilitating episodes that overshadowed his work as the Gophers' fiery and folksy coach. There was a sobering collapse on the sideline during his second game with the program in September 2011. Other serious seizures forced him to miss half of the 2013 season.

"This is no way to live," Kill finally admitted to his wife, Rebecca. "We can't keep doing this."

Heartbreaking as Kill's resignation was to Gophers players and loyalists, there was a sense of gratitude and relief.

Not just for his positive influence on the program, including a Citrus Bowl and fundraising power that helped build the $166 million state-of-the-art Athletes Village. But Kill decided to embrace quality of life over continued health crises and an $8 million paycheck.

"The ability to advance our program and join the national stage and all of those competitive advantages have put Minnesota football on the map that it wasn't before," said president Kaler.

"He is the right person for Gopher football. I'm sorry that he is stepping away now. I respect that opinion, that decision. It is in his long-term interest, and I never tried to dissuade him from coming back."

Hired December 10, 2010, Kill finished 29–29 in four-plus seasons with the Gophers, including consecutive eight-win campaigns in 2013 and 2014, only the fifth time since 1906 Minnesota had managed the feat. Overall, Kill was 156–102 (.605

winning percentage) at five schools from Division II to Football Championship Subdivision and the Football Bowl Subdivision.

Kill earned 2014 Big Ten Coach of the Year honors after leading the Gophers to wins over Michigan and Iowa, seizing the Little Brown Jug and Floyd of Rosedale in the same season for the first time since 1967.

"Brick by brick" was Kill's mantra after he inherited a program left in shambles following the disastrous tenure of silver-tongued Tim Brewster, who went 0–10 in trophy games before being fired midway through the 2010 season.

Brewster, who frequently clashed with then–athletic director Joel Maturi, was unable to leverage success despite the 2009 move to TCF Bank Stadium, the $300 million outdoor venue that lured the Gophers back to campus after languishing for 27 years in the sterile Metrodome in downtown Minneapolis. The student section was half empty. Enthusiasm for the program had reached a new low.

Brewster's recruiting chops were impressive. Rivals.com ranked his 2008 class No. 17. But it never translated to success. His teams finished 7–6, 6–7, and 3–9, changing offensive coordinators each season.

Maturi admitted it was a mistake hiring Brewster, a former tight ends coach for the Denver Broncos who had never been a head coach. The brash talker kicked up a stir with premature vows to return the Gophers to the Rose Bowl, where they had not played since 1962.

"You're not following Vince Lombardi here," Maturi told candidates after firing Brewster.

Born August 24, 1961, in Wichita, Kansas, Kill was in seventh grade when he moved 30 miles west to rural Cheney, a farming and cattle-ranching community. "Midwest values," raised Kill and infused him with the self-deprecating, plain-spoken drawl that endeared him to whatever room he commanded.

Kill was renowned for revitalizing teams, but practically anonymous in big-time college football. He was 4–5 in playoff games at Southern Illinois and 0–2 in bowl games with Northern Illinois. His career started at Division II Saginaw Valley (Michigan) State in 1994 and continued at Emporia (Kansas) State before Kill made it to Illinois.

"Jerry Kill is a turnaround artist. He's a fixer, a builder, a renovator, and a repairman," his former Southern Illinois athletic director, Paul Kowalczyk, said in Kill's book.

Kill was shocked at what he discovered at Minnesota.

The program had only two strength coaches, while most Big Ten teams had at least five. One day he received a parking ticket driving to the stadium for practice with a group of recruits. Apparently, there was no designated spot for the head coach. So he parked on the sidewalk.

"Can you imagine that happening at Michigan or Ohio State?" he wrote.

There were also brushfires raging in the classroom. Four players were expelled for various reasons and 22 were on academic probation. Poor academics prompted Minnesota to forfeit three scholarships in 2009 under NCAA sanctions.

"I never knew the academics were as bad as they were," he wrote. "I didn't tell them [the president and athletic director] we were going to the Rose Bowl. I told them we were in deep shit for some time. The toughest thing to change was everything."

Kill cracked down on discipline during his first two years, forcing players who were late to class or meetings to wear T-shirts at practice that read, "I let my teammates down" and "Minnesota Loafers." By the time he left, Minnesota's cumulative grade-point average had increased to 3.0 from 2.4.

Kill's first team finished 3–9 before going 6–7 in 2012 to earn the first of three straight bowl berths. The Gophers were 8–5 each of his last two seasons. The pinnacle was when they went to their first Citrus Bowl in Orlando, Florida.

More than 22,000 Gophers fans traveled to central Florida to bask in the glow of Minnesota's first New Year's Day postseason appearance since that bygone Rose Bowl.

Running back David Cobb set a single-season record with 1,548 yards, which included seven 100-yard games and a pair of 200-yarders to go along with 13 touchdowns. He and tight end Maxx Williams were named All Big Ten. Williams, a sophomore John Mackey Award finalist, caught seven touchdowns and was Minnesota's first academic All-America first-team selection since 1994.

Minnesota lost 33–17 to Missouri in the Citrus Bowl, but optimism ruled as Kill entered his fifth season.

Kill overcame kidney cancer in 2005, when he was first diagnosed with epilepsy. He collapsed on the field coaching a game for Southern Illinois. X-rays revealed spots on his kidneys, which were stage 4 renal cell carcinoma that required surgery to remove part of the organ.

"That one seizure saved my life. Without it happening, they never would have found the cancer," he wrote.

He was seizure-free for almost two years. However, Kill suffered three documented seizures during games with Minnesota, sidelining him for stretches or forcing him to coach from the press box. He wrote that he had up to 20 leading up to the 2015 Michigan game.

"I blame myself," he wrote. "I have always felt that I brought it on myself due to the lack of sleep and lack of taking care of my body. I was married to football. It's what I did."

Kill did not run from his disease. He became an activist. With the Epilepsy Foundation, he and Rebecca led a campaign to make all schools in Minnesota "Seizure Smart," teaching educators and students how to manage crises when their students suffer an episode.

"I have never felt sorry for myself. Never," he wrote. "Sure, I have had bad days and been depressed about my situation, but I have never gone the route of feeling sorry for myself."

17 Paul Molitor

In late summer 1974, Paul Molitor poked his head into the office of grizzled Gophers baseball coach Dick Siebert, aka "the Chief."

The incoming freshman from St. Paul looked like every other 18-year-old of the era—shaggy hair, beard and not a hint of self-awareness.

"Who the heck are you?" Siebert barked.

"I'm Paul Molitor."

"Well, Molitor, before our first practice tomorrow, shave off that beard and get a haircut."

A year later the cleaner-cut freshman infielder debuted for Minnesota and quickly established himself as the cerebral, versatile ballplayer who played 21 major league seasons during a Hall of Fame career.

After leading Cretin-Derham Hall High School to two Minnesota state baseball championships and winning an American Legion title, Molitor was drafted in the 28th round by the St. Louis Cardinals.

He stayed at home and became a first-team All-American with the Gophers in 1976 and '77, the last year Minnesota reached the College World Series. Molitor that year batted .325 with a team-leading 20 stolen bases and 35 runs.

Molitor set school records in runs (112), triples (11), hits (159), home runs (18), total bases (254), RBI (99), and stolen bases. He

Gophers Retired Baseball Numbers

Player	Number
Herb Isakson	5
Paul Molitor	11
Dick Siebert	24
David Chelesnik	26
Dave Winfield	31
Paul Giel	34

was crafty and fearless on the basepaths, traits "the Igniter" would carry into the big leagues.

Longtime Gophers broadcaster Ray Christensen, in his 2002 book *Gopher Tales*, recalled a classic anecdote from Molitor's freshman year during a game against Texas.

Standing on third base against a left-handed pitcher, Molitor whispered to third-base coach George Thomas, "I think I can steal it, okay?"

"Go ahead," said Thomas.

Molitor stole home and trotted to the dugout.

"Siebert, who was blind as a bat," Christensen wrote, "asked what happened. 'Did you get picked off?'"

"No, coach, I stole home," Molitor said.

"Who told you could do that?" Siebert demanded.

"I checked with Coach Thomas," Molitor said.

"Okay, if you get another chance, do it again," the Chief said. So he did.

Molitor never signed with the Cardinals and re-entered the MLB draft in 1977. The Milwaukee Brewers made him the third overall pick.

Molitor played a handful of minor league games before debuting in 1978 with the Brewers as their shortstop. He eventually moved to third base. He played 15 seasons in Milwaukee, setting a

World Series record in 1982 with five hits in a Game 1 victory over St. Louis, which vanquished the Brewers in seven games.

In 1993, Molitor signed with the Toronto Blue Jays as a designated hitter and was World Series Most Valuable Player in helping the Canadian club secure its second consecutive title.

Molitor returned to Minnesota in 1996 and played his final three seasons with the hometown Twins. The seven-time All-Star finished his career with 3,319 hits—tenth all time. Molitor is one of only six players to amass 3,000 hits and 500 stolen bases, including Lou Brock, Ty Cobb, Eddie Collins, Honus Wagner, and Ricky Henderson.

Molitor, whom the Twins hired as their 13th manager in 2014, has remained loyal to Gophers baseball. He donated $250,000 to help renovate Siebert Field while participating in numerous alumni events over the years.

"Paul never got full of himself, said Kevin Carlson, a close friend and former Gophers teammate.

Carlson was a walk-on pitcher struggling to make the junior varsity who felt like he was "on an island by himself" when one day Molitor made it a point to notice his new haircut, according to a 2004 St. Paul *Pioneer Press* profile.

They became lifelong friends. Molitor was an usher at Carlson's 1986 wedding and helped him with charitable work.

"He's always been there for me," Carlson said. "Before his father passed away, I sent Dick a card and said how instrumental Paul has been in my life and how he reached out to me when I was an incoming transfer. I thanked him for raising a kid who had such good qualities."

Gophers baseball coach John Anderson, Molitor's teammate at Minnesota, concurred.

"He never looked down on anybody."

18 Dave Winfield

David Mark Winfield was destined to be linked to Cooperstown whether or not he ever swung a bat.

The future Hall of Famer was born on October 3, 1951, the day Bobby Thompson cracked his pennant-clinching home run—the "shot heard 'round the world"—for the New York Giants.

Raised by his mother, Arline, in a single-family home in St. Paul, Winfield and his older brother Steve played amateur ball in the St. Paul Parks and Recreation league under the tutelage of coach and former Marine Bill Peterson. They won championships at the pee-wee, midget, and American Legion levels, where Dave starred as a pitcher and an infielder.

After earning letters in basketball and baseball at Central High school, Winfield won Big Ten championships in both sports for the Gophers.

He was one of coach Bill Musselman's "Musclemen," a rebounding machine with knee-high socks and an Afro. In 1973, he helped the school win its first conference title in 37 years.

But it was on the baseball diamond that Winfield's star burned brightest as a flame-throwing right-handed pitcher.

He carried the Gophers to the 1973 College World Series championship game by batting .385 with 33 RBIs while compiling a 13–1 record and 2.74 earned run average.

Winfield struck out 14 Oklahoma Sooners in a 1–0 quarter-final victory. Against three-time defending champion Southern California, Winfield dominated the Trojans, fanning 15 while only allowing an infield single through eight innings.

"In my whole career, even facing the big boys in the majors, I have never seen anything like that," said former USC infielder Rich

Dave Winfield, as the only athlete in history to be drafted by four different leagues, had his pick of where (and what) to play after college, but chose Major League Baseball.
University of Minnesota Archives

Dauer, who played 10 major league seasons. "When Dave let go of the ball, it was three feet in front of your face and it seemed like it was going 110 miles an hour."

In the ninth, a potential double play was snuffed on a blown call by the first-base umpire. Minnesota coach Dick Siebert was ejected arguing the play and the Gophers collapsed.

Winfield was chased after allowing three runs and the Trojans rallied for eight to complete the unlikely comeback and retain their national championship. Still, Minnesota's first-team All-American and two-time All–Big Ten pitcher was named the tournament's Most Outstanding Player.

Winfield finished his Gophers career with a 19–4 record, 15 complete games, and 229 strikeouts in 169 innings.

By then, everyone wanted him: the San Diego Padres; the NBA's Atlanta Hawks; the ABA's Utah Stars—even the Vikings, who drafted Winfield though he had never played a down of organized football in his life.

"I stepped from my last collegiate baseball competition to Jack Murphy Stadium in San Diego without a stop in the minor leagues," he told NCAA.com in 2015. "It was more difficult than anyone could imagine because I only pitched until my last year at Minnesota, but the Padres wanted me to play the outfield.

"It was only after a decade of listening, learning, and a lot of coming early to work and staying late that I started to figure things out. But it all added up to experiences that I'll never forget."

Winfield played 22 seasons with the Padres, New York Yankees, California Angels, Toronto Blue Jays, Minnesota Twins, and Cleveland Indians. He collected his 3,000th hit with the Twins in 1993.

Winfield was inducted into the Baseball Hall of Fame in 2001.

19 The Chief

Dick Siebert transformed Gophers baseball from a trifling afterthought to a marquee program that made the upper Midwest a destination for college ballplayers for decades.

A strict fundamentalist who flourished as an All-Star first baseman for Connie Mack's Philadelphia Athletics, Siebert was destined for a calling as a Lutheran minister before seminaries contracted during the Great Depression and professional baseball became his lifeline.

"The Chief" ran a disciplined Gophers program on the diamond, requiring his players to wear suits and ties while traveling, with a ban on facial hair and long locks right through the bawdy 1970s. He earned universal respect by holding stars and scrubs to the same standards, punctuating his legacy with three College World Series championships from 1956 to '64.

"Dick Siebert treats us like men," 1964 captain Dewey Markus once said.

Siebert's three national titles and 12 Big Ten championships highlighted his 31-season tenure, which started in 1948 and ended with his death in December 1978.

The Gophers lost to USC in the 1973 national championship game and reached their final College World Series in 1977. In his final 11 seasons, Minnesota won six Big Ten titles, including three straight (1968–70).

Siebert is one of only five coaches in NCAA Division I history to win three College World Series titles. He finished his career with a record of 754–361–6.

In the 52 years since Minnesota's last national championship, Ohio State in 1966 is the only northern school to win the College World Series.

Siebert build his dynasty recruiting almost exclusively in Minnesota, scouring high school sandlots and American Legion back fields for talent. He coached future major leaguers Jerry Kindall, Paul Giel, Dave Winfield, and Paul Molitor.

His influence on baseball in Minnesota extended beyond wins and losses. Siebert did not become a minister, but he preached his "Gospel of Baseball" in countless seminars and clinics throughout the state.

"This might sound simple, but it started with teaching fundamentals," said 1964 Gophers pitcher Jerry Thomas. "I can attest to this because I played four years of pro ball and wasn't taught one thing that I did not already know from playing for Dick Siebert."

A native of Fall River, Massachusetts, Siebert started playing baseball at St. Paul Concordia High School and continued at

Concordia Junior College. He enrolled at the Concordia Seminary in St. Louis, but in 1932 budget cuts forced second-year students to take a year off.

A Yankees scout who had watched him play seminary ball signed Siebert to a pro contract and the first baseman was dispatched to Dayton, Ohio, in the Class B Central League.

His rookie season, Dayton was losing 3–2 in the ninth inning with a man on second when manager Ducky Holmes called on Siebert to pinch hit, according to the Society for American Baseball Research.

Siebert singled in the tying run. Years later he told a University of Minnesota interviewer, "Had I not hit safely, it could have ended my baseball career right then and there."

After knocking around with the Brooklyn Dodgers, Chicago Cubs, and St. Louis Cardinals farm systems, Siebert became an every day first baseman for the A's in 1938, earning two All-Star appearances over seven seasons.

He retired in 1945 with a .282 career batting average in 1,035 major league games.

Siebert was elected to the College Baseball Hall of Fame and in 1978 was named the Lefty Gomez Award recipient for contributions to the sport.

On April 21, 1979, the University of Minnesota Baseball Stadium was officially renamed Siebert Field.

20 John Anderson

An arm injury ended John Anderson's pitching career in 1975 after just two seasons in Minnesota. So he stuck around for 41 years and made history as a dugout boss.

Anderson capped a milestone 2016 season by leading the Gophers to their 10th regular season Big Ten championship and eclipsing 1,200 victories. His 1,208 wins rank 29th among Division I coaches and 10th among active coaches.

Not that the baseball lifer was counting.

"I've never been a big numbers guy," Anderson told the Minneapolis *Star Tribune* May 3, 2016, after the milestone win over Kansas. "I wouldn't know where [the count] was if people didn't remind me."

Seven times Anderson has been voted Big Ten Coach of the Year, first as a rookie in 1982, then in three straight years from 2002 to '04, and most recently in 2016 after the Gophers posted a 36–22 overall record and 16–7 to claim the conference flag.

The hard-hitting Gophers maintained a top-five batting average in the country and advanced to the final of the College Station Regional. It was a remarkable turnaround from a 21–30 ninth-place finish in 2015, only the second losing season in Anderson's 35 seasons as head coach.

"These guys love playing the game together, and to see the team they've created, that's the rewarding part for me," Anderson said. "I've just had a wonderful year."

After graduating from Nashwauk-Keewatin High School in northern Minnesota, Anderson pitched for legendary Gophers coach Dick Siebert. After injuring his arm, Siebert appointed Anderson student coach in 1976.

The following year, the Gophers reached the College World Series for the last time, led by future MLB Hall of Famer Paul Molitor. Anderson was so valued teammates voted him team MVP.

Anderson became an assistant for George Thomas, who ascended to head coach when Siebert died in December 1978.

After Thomas resigned in 1981, Anderson was named the 13th coach in program history. Twenty-six at the time, he was the youngest head baseball coach in Big Ten history.

Anderson has coached 14 All-Americans, including future big leaguers Dan Wilson, Robb Quinlan, Jack Hannahan, and Glen Perkins.

Anderson's fundraising prowess helped Minnesota build the new Siebert Field, a modern facility with a MondoTurf playing surface. Construction was completed in 2012, and the Gophers opened their new home in 2013.

Lights were added in 2014 as new Siebert Field hosted the program's first night games.

21 Ponder the Wizard of... Dinkytown?

What might have been for Gophers basketball had a blizzard not prevented Frank McCormick from getting to a telephone in April 1948?

John Wooden built an unrivaled dynasty at UCLA in the 1960s and '70s. Seven consecutive national championships were among the 10 the "Wizard of Westwood" delivered in his final 12 seasons as Bruins coach before he retired in 1975.

There was an 88-game winning streak that started in 1971 and ended in 1974. There were four 30–0 seasons and 19 conference championships under Wooden, who compiled a 620–147 record in 27 seasons at UCLA.

Could that have happened in Minnesota? Had Wooden preferred the Midwest over southern California? Did the fact that Minnesota's outgoing coach had another year on his contract muddle the process before the snow started flying?

The truth may be in the eye of the beholder.

At the time Wooden was athletic director, baseball coach, and basketball coach at Indiana Teachers College, which later became Indiana State. Wooden led his basketball team to a 44–15 record in two seasons.

Wooden wrote in his 1988 biography *They Call Me Coach* that he interviewed for coaching vacancies at Minnesota and UCLA in the spring of 1948. Both schools offered him the job.

Wooden told McCormick, the Gophers' athletic director, and UCLA athletic director Wilbur Johns to call him at an appointed date and time, when he would notify them of his decision.

"I had decided to take the Minnesota job except for one problem—the retention of Dave McMillan [sic]," Wooden wrote.

MacMillan resigned as Gophers basketball coach March 1, 1948, after three seasons. He had also coached basketball and baseball at Minnesota from 1927 to '42.

MacMillan still had a year remaining on his contract. Wooden wanted to hire his own assistant coaches. However, McCormick wanted Wooden to retain MacMillan, the man he would be replacing.

That would have been more than awkward.

According to Minneapolis *Star Tribune* columnist Sid Hartman, McCormick sought permission from then–university president Lotus Coffman to negotiate a buyout for MacMillan and increase the basketball budget for Wooden to hire his assistant coaches.

Coffman eventually agreed to the deal. Hartman wrote that McCormick was visiting a friend in South Dakota, where a snow-storm was raging. Phone lines were cut off and McCormick could not call Wooden by the coach's deadline.

"I didn't know of the problem so when Mr. Johns called, right on time, I accepted the UCLA job," Wooden wrote in 1988. "When McCormick finally reached me about an hour later, he told me everything was 'all set.'

"It's too late,' I told him. 'I have already accepted the job at UCLA.' If fate had not intervened, I would have never gone to UCLA."

Minnesota's unfortunate loss was UCLA's epic gain.

Was it that clear-cut?

Sports author Stew Thornley poked holes in Wooden's written account. In a 2010 article, "Minnesota Sports Myths," he questioned the old ball coach's timeline as it related to the upper Midwest weather in April 1948.

"A storm did hit the Dakotas on April 7," Thornley wrote. "McCormick was from South Dakota and still operated a business there, often returning to his home state on weekends. However, this was nearly two weeks before Wooden signed with UCLA, on Tuesday, April 20.

"Wooden, in his autobiography, stated that one of the reasons he refused to renege on his acceptance of the UCLA job was that UCLA had "already released the news of my appointment to the press in Los Angeles."

Thornley points out that Wooden's hiring did not appear in any Los Angeles newspapers until April 21, two weeks after the blizzard at issue.

"While Wooden would most likely stick to the story, the unreliability of the details as he tells it calls into question his overall reliability as a source," Thornley wrote.

Thornley also noted that Wooden, in his book, claimed he was leaving Central High School in South Bend, Indiana, to join the college coaching ranks when, in fact, he was already coaching at Indiana Teachers College.

Perhaps what might have been for Minnesota might never have been at all.

22 Lou Holtz

He talked loudly and carried a big shtick into this football graveyard on that bone-chilling winter's day in December 1983, unleashing an arm's-length rebuilding project that snowed star-crossed Minnesota fans, boosters, and politicians who feted the owlish coach like a pharaoh.

Truth is, Lou Holtz hated cold weather. He had no burning desire to resurrect a sad-sack program so desperate for national recognition university leaders eagerly furnished this Southern carpetbagger his nonbinding ticket out of town.

Minnesota had never experienced anything like L'Affaire Holtz. His meteoric 23-month reign was a marketing godsend that packed the Metrodome and made Gophers football relevant for the first time in two decades.

Maroon-and-Gold mania captured the Twin Cities and swept across the state. Legacy fans dreamed of Rose Bowl parades again and New Year's Day in the southern California sunshine. The newly initiated discovered there was a major college football team in town.

Holtz walked on water…all the way to Notre Dame.

He spent Tuesday, November 26, 1985, deflecting raging rumors he was courting the Fighting Irish job during a news conference in Minneapolis to promote Minnesota's appearance in the Independence Bowl. By Wednesday, he was front and center at a massive media event in South Bend, Indiana, accepting his dream job as jilted Gophers fans fumed.

The biggest shock was that anybody was surprised.

Holtz negotiated an out clause in his five-year contract and told anyone who would listen that Notre Dame was the only college football job worth desertion.

"I've always had a warm spot in my heart for Notre Dame," Holtz said.

Not to surrogates to leak under the cloak of anonymity, but in sit-down interviews with Minnesota reporters.

He spent his introductory news conference in Minneapolis on December 23, 1983, whining about the weather and musing how he had arrived at this way station in his career following an ugly breakup with Arkansas.

Holtz took the Razorbacks to six bowl games in seven seasons and compiled a 37–18–1 record in the cutthroat SEC. A 6–5 finish in 1983 exacerbated a rift with athletic director Frank Broyles, who reportedly was prepared to fire Holtz before the coach caught wind and promptly resigned, raking in an $800,000 contract buyout.

After Holtz cashed out in Fayetteville, Minnesota's search committee was nowhere in its pursuit of a successor for hapless Joe Salem. After the '83 season, Salem resigned following a 1–10 disaster. His 19–35–1 record in five seasons included 17 straight Big Ten losses.

Bobby Ross of Maryland and LaVell Edwards of Brigham Young were solicited for interviews. Both said, "No thanks." The only viable candidate was Vikings assistant coach Les Steckel, who withdrew after his proposed upgrades to the Gophers' dilapidated facilities were stiff-armed.

Search committee chairman Frank Wilderson telephoned Holtz.

"The next thing I know, I'm on my way to Minnesota," Holtz recounted. "I didn't know why; I loathe cold weather. I still do. A woman in Arkansas asked me where I was going to live. I said, 'Indoors.'"

The wind-chill factor was 50 below zero when university president C. Peter Magrath presented Holtz and his wife, Beth, wool hats and scarves during a photo op while declaring it morning in Dinkytown again.

Holtz boasted a college record of 106–53–5 in a career that started at William & Mary and moved on to North Carolina State. After a failed 1976 season with the NFL's New York Jets, Holtz returned to the college ranks when he succeeded Broyles at Arkansas.

His first year with the Razorbacks Holtz finished 11–1, including a shocking 31–6 upset of No. 2–ranked Oklahoma at the 1978 Orange Bowl.

The 21st coach in 101 years of Minnesota football was the most accomplished since Murray Warmath led the Gophers to their only two Rose Bowl appearances in the early 1960s. But Holtz inherited a program that had lost 14 of its last 18 games and had been outscored by an average of 47–16 in 1983, including a nightmarish 84–13 loss to Nebraska at the Metrodome.

"I'm not a miracle worker. It doesn't happen with a magic wand," he said. "You have to have a plan. We will recruit nationally, but we have to have a base and we can't compete in the Big Ten without a base of Minnesota players."

"The No. 1 question is, 'Can we win?' I believe we can."

That belief was pliable.

One day Holtz was driving athletic director Paul Giel to a speaking function. Holtz pulled into the lot and parked up front in a handicap spot.

"Lou, you can't park there; you're not handicapped," Giel told him.

"Paul, there is no one more handicapped than the head football coach at Minnesota," Holtz replied.

Holtz signed a five-year deal for $100,000 annually, the highest base salary in the Big Ten—twice as much as Salem earned. He also made $75,000 annually in radio appearance fees.

At 5'8", 150 pounds, Holtz was all bones and eyeglasses, with a flop of red-blond hair, a lisp, and an evangelist's gift for storytelling that made him a hit on the lecture circuit.

His fame in Arkansas made him a go-to guest for Johnny Carson, who was smitten with Holtz's magic tricks. He had dined with President Reagan.

At his first team meeting with the Gophers, Holtz had players in stitches with his rah-rah mantras, shredded newspaper trick, and three-ball disappearing act. Gophers fans lapped up his irrepressible energy. Governor Rudy Perpich pledged the state's unwavering commitment to promoting Minnesota football.

A Lou Holtz look-alike contest at Dayton's department store in downtown Minneapolis helped drum up season-ticket sales. During the buildup to the 1984 season, 18,000 new season-ticket packages were sold. Football revenue was up $2 million at the end of the fiscal year.

The "Taj Mah Holtz," a $5 million indoor training facility, was green-lit without any of the pushback Steckel experienced.

Holtz's image was everywhere in Minnesota, from grocery bags at Hy-Vee to Big Mac cartons at McDonald's.

"Frankly, that's all you have when you're coming off 1–10," said Gophers ticket manager Ken Buell.

Not everyone was impressed. As the 1984 season dawned, *Sports Illustrated* clucked, "No coach will win again, ever, at Minnesota, where losing is a tradition carved in ice."

Holtz finished 4–7 his initial season, mostly with Salem's leftovers. By 1985, the Gophers were gaining traction.

Quarterback Rickie Foggie was an athletic runner-passer who provided a much-needed offensive spark. Minnesota was No. 20 at midseason before a 23–19 loss to Ohio State knocked them out of the rankings.

The rumors started circulating in November. Gerry Faust was on his way out at Notre Dame. Reports had Holtz meeting with Notre Dame's clergy in Minneapolis and Indiana.

Holtz denied the meetings, but did not run screaming from the speculation. Instead, he embraced it.

"I think I can honestly say this: I wouldn't ever consider leaving Minnesota for any job in the country with the possible exception of Notre Dame," Holtz told St. Paul *Pioneer Press* columnist Charley Walters. "I had that feeling when I came here and I expressed it to the administration."

The Gophers (6–5) were ticketed to play Clemson in the Independence Bowl December 21, just their second postseason appearance since the 1962 Rose Bowl. The timing was terrible for a defection but Holtz, a devout Catholic, was compelled to accept the country's premier college coaching job.

One can argue the temerity of his decision, but not the results. Holtz became a legend in 11 seasons at Notre Dame.

He led the Irish to a 12–0 record in 1988 and a Fiesta Bowl victory that secured the school's first national championship since 1977.

John Gutekunst succeeded Holtz at Minnesota and went 29–37–2 in six-plus seasons, including a 21–14 loss to Tennessee in the 1986 Liberty Bowl.

It took the Gophers another 13 years to reach another bowl game.

23 Sandy Stephens

He was heavily recruited by Ohio State in the late 1950s, but eschewed the Buckeyes for Minnesota after learning coach Woody Hayes refused to start a black quarterback.

Sandford Emory Stephens II was a four-sport athlete from Uniontown, Pennsylvania, and turned down professional baseball to play football for the Gophers. He bulled through racial barriers as the school's first black quarterback and the country's first African American All-American signal caller.

The only Gophers quarterback to win a Rose Bowl arrived in Dinkytown in 1959 from Pennsylvania steel country via Gophers hockey coach John Mariucci. The mayor of a nearby town who served in the Navy with Mariucci had tipped him off about Stephens and another black teammate, Bill Munsey, urging his military buddy to convince Minnesota football coach Murray Warmath to take a look.

Warmath was under pressure to recruit more black players. He also wanted an option quarterback to lead his middling offense. Together, Warmath and Stephens made history on and off the field.

College football programs in the early 1960s remained segregated. Stephens' arrival made Minnesota a destination for black players yearning to escape the Jim Crow South.

After Stephens, Warmath recruited Munsey, Ezell Jones, Judge Dickson, Bobby Bell, Carl Eller, Charley Sanders, and McKinley Boston.

"If Minnesota let Sandy Stephens play quarterback, then we knew we could trust Murray," Jones told the Minneapolis *Star Tribune* in 2000.

As a sophomore, Stephens led Minnesota to an 8–2 record, the 1960 national championship and the school's only Rose Bowl victory in 1962. He earned game MVP honors after scoring a pair of touchdowns and combined on 121 yards from scrimmage in a 21–3 rout of UCLA.

Stephens was the 1961 Big Ten most valuable player and finished fourth in Heisman balloting behind Syracuse's Ernie Davis, the trophy's first black recipient.

"I never saw a guy more dedicated to football or who wanted to win more than Sandy," Warmath once said. "He just loved the game."

In an era of one-platoon football, Stephens also played safety, punted, and returned kicks.

He led the Gophers in total offense and scoring all three years he played, 1959–61. His 160-yard rushing performance in a 1961 victory over Michigan ended with his teammates carrying him off the Memorial Stadium field in triumph.

"The whole experience playing at Minnesota was special to me," Stephens told the St. Paul *Pioneer Press* in 1988. "Winning the national championship in 1960 was the topper. Then came 1961 and the Rose Bowl, being the team MVP and finishing fourth in the Heisman Trophy voting. I couldn't have written a better script."

The Cleveland Browns drafted Stephens in the second round of the 1962 NFL draft while the AFL's New York Titans selected him fifth overall the same year. But racial prejudice remained deep when it came to fielding a black man at the sport's marquee position.

Both teams refused to let Stephens play quarterback, and he never played a snap in either league.

BRIAN MURPHY

The progressive Canadian Football League was more welcoming. The Montreal Alouettes signed him to a three-year, $90,000 contract that included a $25,000 signing bonus.

Stephens played two seasons for Montreal and one for the Toronto Argonauts. He signed with the Vikings in 1964, but his career was derailed by a serious car accident. Stephens signed with the Kansas City Chiefs as a fullback in 1966, but did not play for the eventual Super Bowl I runners-up.

Stephens was inducted into the M Club hall of fame in 1994, the Rose Bowl hall of fame in 1997, and the College Football Hall of Fame in 2011, posthumously. Stephens died of a heart attack in June 2000 at age 59.

"His mantra was always, just give me the opportunity. If I'm not the best, I shouldn't lead the group. But if I'm the best, nothing else should matter," Stephens' sister, Barbara Stephens Foster, told the *Star Tribune* in 2011.

"There was a mantle on his shoulders, and he willingly accepted that. We're grateful that his grandchildren and children will see his legacy continue."

24 Bobby Bell

Bobby Bell's gold watch was still ticking May 14, 2015, as the University of Minnesota graduate collected his degree 56 years after his father presented the timepiece to the teenager as he boarded a plane for Minnesota.

The watch was to help Bell avoid being late for class. He was only late for commencement.

The former Gophers All-American and Kansas City Chiefs Hall of Famer received a standing ovation when he received his park and leisure studies degree, just another 74-year-old posing for pictures and beaming with pride during graduation ceremonies.

That night Bell finally fulfilled the promise he made to his parents in 1959 when he left segregated North Carolina to play football in lily-white Dinkytown, a leap of faith that propelled Bell to greatness on the field and a lifetime waiting to pay it back.

"How many people can say that they've been able to visit with five presidents, travel around the world, know some of the most famous people in the world, have friends like Bob Hope, visit with Johnny Carson, Ed Sullivan?" Bell said.

"That's what I got an opportunity to do because I played football here. Then the rest of my life just took off. That's what Minnesota gave to me."

Bell gave Minnesota three phenomenal seasons as one of college football's most dominant defensive tackles.

He won the 1962 Outland Award as the country's best interior lineman, was voted Big Ten most valuable player that season, and finished third in the Heisman Trophy voting.

The former high school quarterback grew into a 6'4", 230-pound block of granite who ran the 40-yard dash in 4.5 seconds. He converted to defensive lineman as a sophomore, helping lead Minnesota to its last national championship.

Bell also played in consecutive Rose Bowls in 1961 and '62 as the Gophers racked up a 22–6–1 record during his tenure.

Bell was so fast and athletic that Gophers hockey coach John Mariucci begged him to try out even though he had never skated. He did walk on to become Minnesota's first black basketball player.

Drafted in the second round by the Vikings, Bell opted to leave Minnesota 13 credits shy of graduation and sign with the Chiefs of the rival American Football League. Ironically, in January 1970,

Bell helped lead the Chiefs to a 23–7 victory over the Vikings in Super Bowl IV.

By then, Bell was playing linebacker. He played 13 seasons for Kansas City, earning All-Pro honors eight straight years. He was the Chiefs' first inductee into the Pro Football Hall of Fame in 1983.

Bell grew up in Shelby, North Carolina. His father, Pink Lee, picked cotton and chauffeured bosses at the textile mill, according to the *New York Times*. His mother, Zannie, cleaned houses. Education, his parents preached, was the ticket out of segregation.

"My father always said sports and education were things where blacks could compete equally with whites—if given the chance," Bell told the *Times*.

Minnesota coach Murray Warmath was willing to give Bell and other black players that chance. In the late 1950s, Warmath recruited a group that included Sandy Stephens, Judge Dickson, Carl Eller, Bob McNeil, and Bill Munsey.

Warmath asked Bell to switch to the defensive line.

"Coach, I'll play anywhere because I'm not going back to North Carolina," Bell told him.

After retiring from pro football in 1974, he opened Bobby Bell's Bar-b-que in Kansas City and worked the lecture circuit. Over the years, former Gophers teammates like Judge Dickson pestered Bell about fulfilling his 13 credits.

Haunted by his father's wishes, Bell enrolled in Minnesota's Gopher Graduation Program, which helps student athletes schedule and finish course work. Bell became the seventh football player to utilize the scholarship.

Bell completed the work online and picked up his degree three weeks shy of his 75th birthday.

"I just want to encourage all the players who leave here to go back to school and get their degree," he said at graduation. "You still can learn."

25 The Godfather

John Mariucci is the cornerstone of Gophers hockey, the first American to captain an NHL team and a fearless fighter who stood up to opponents on the ice, a protégé under his command, and the cancer that killed him in 1987.

"Maroosh" played 223 games in the NHL with the Chicago Blackhawks from 1940 to '48. After only a dozen, Mariucci's face was a virtual road map of 50 stitches from forehead to chin.

"I'm tired of sewing you up!" Blackhawks trainer Eddie Froelich barked at the rookie forward one day.

"Imagine how I feel!" Mariucci retorted.

During Team USA's game against the Soviet Union at the 1976 world championships in Prague, Lou Nanne became so enraged at Mariucci criticizing him from behind the bench that the right winger charged his coach while the game was going on and the pair slugged it out as teammates and spectators watched in shocked bemusement.

The longtime friends and colleagues were eventually separated and peace was restored. Two years later Nanne, the North Stars general manager, promoted Mariucci from the scouting department to be his assistant.

So many owe so much to the Iron Ranger, who championed Minnesota's interior talent and whose influence on the sport spans seven decades and counting. Mariucci's name adorns the arena that pulsates with energy on Friday and Saturday during the cold, dark nights of winter.

He coached 11 Gophers to All-America honors, guided the United States to its first Olympic medal, helped build the Minnesota

North Stars from scratch, and inspired the prolific careers of men such as Nanne, John Mayasich, Herb Brooks, and Bob Johnson.

"He was the rock on which American hockey has been built," Nanne once said.

The Eveleth, Minnesota, native played offensive and defensive end on Bernie Bierman's 1939 and 1940 football teams. An All-American defenseman on the ice, Mariucci led Minnesota to an undefeated season and its first AAU national championship in 1939–40.

Signed later that year by the Blackhawks, Mariucci quickly became a fan favorite at the old Chicago Stadium. The 5'10", 200-pound winger earned the captain's "C" by defending his teammates with brute force. One fight with Detroit's "Black Jack" Stewart lasted so long the game was delayed a half hour as fans cheered wildly.

Mariucci's playing career ended in 1952 with the minor league Minneapolis Millers. Later that year he was hired to reinvigorate a stagnant Gophers program.

Only 13 players showed up for his first tryout.

"These days you have to beat them away with a stick," Mariucci told an interviewer in 1979. "It's the equivalent of Alabama football."

Mariucci transformed a .500 team into a 23–6 powerhouse his first season, leading the Gophers to the NCAA championship game and earning national Coach of the Year honors. An ardent proponent of homegrown players, Mariucci steadfastly recruited Minnesota players throughout his 15 seasons at the helm.

"This is a state institution and should be represented by Minnesota boys," he declared. "If they're not quite as good as some Canadians, we'll just have to work a little harder, that's all."

Mariucci also threw himself into grassroots development of the state's youth programs. He avidly participated in coaching clinics, attended the opening of hockey facilities in countless cities and

Gophers in Hockey Hall of Fame

Player	Year inducted
John Mariucci	1985
Herb Brooks	2006

towns, helped former players find coaching positions, and even encouraged hockey moms to write city councils to build rinks and develop recreation programs.

"John believed in Minnesota kids and gave them a chance," said Herb Brooks, who walked on to the Gophers team in 1956. "He could have been like other college coaches and done the bulk of his recruiting in Canada. But John was different. John cared."

Mariucci's impact was indelible and everlasting, making the boys' high school hockey tournament and the Maroon-and-Gold program destinations for every Minnesota boy with a stick and skates.

When he started at Minnesota in 1952, attendance at the Minnesota Boys State Hockey tournament was 15,523. When Mariucci left the Gophers in 1966, it was 46,016.

Every year Minnesota's crown jewel sporting event routinely draws more than 130,000 fans over four days to St. Paul's Xcel Energy Center.

In 15 seasons with the Gophers Mariucci compiled a record of 207–142–15, earning a pair of conference titles and four NCAA playoff appearances.

He nurtured talent in the international ranks as well.

In 1956, he led an underdog U.S. team to Cortina d'Apezzo, Italy. Led by 10 Minnesotans, including all-time Gophers leading scorer John Mayasich, Team USA defeated favored Canada, Sweden, and Czechoslovakia to win a silver medal behind the Soviet Union.

In 1967, Mariucci returned to the NHL as a scout for the expansion Minnesota North Stars. Nanne promoted him to be his right-hand man in 1978, a position he held with club until he died.

A charter member of the U.S. Hockey Hall of Fame, Mariucci won the Lester Patrick Award in 1977 for contributions to hockey in the United States. He was inducted into the Hockey Hall of Fame as a builder in 1985, the same year Minnesota renamed the hockey section of Williams Arena after him.

"We'll have to get a broom now and clean this place up since it is named after me," Mariucci quipped.

Quietly, Mariucci was battling a painful form of prostate cancer. His three-year battle against the disease ended when he died March 23, 1987. Six years later, the Gophers' new building opened across Fourth Street from its former home attached to the basketball facility.

Mariucci Arena is an exclusive shrine to the man's legacy, an open-ended gift to the sport that inspired a young Mariucci to lace up a pair of skates on the open range and never stop fighting.

"A man should not be remembered so much for what he's accomplished, but instead for what he's contributed," said Brooks.

26 John Mayasich

John Mayasich was a Minnesota hockey legend before he became a Gophers deity, leaving the smooth-skating, trend-setting American wondering what might have been had he pursued an NHL career.

The son of an Eveleth miner from the state's northern Iron Range and a two-time U.S. Olympian, Mayasich was the only

Gopher to have his (No. 8) jersey retired. He was the first college hockey player credited with using a slap shot.

A powerful skater with deft stick-handling skills, Mayasich could single-handedly kill a penalty by skating through players like pylons.

John Mariucci, the godfather of Gophers hockey and Mayasich's coach at Minnesota, called his prodigy "the Wayne Gretzky of his time."

"John brought college hockey to a new plateau," Mariucci said in the early 1980s. "And today if he were playing pro hockey, he would simply be a bigger, stronger, back-checking Gretzky. The words to describe the boy haven't been invented. When I say he's the best, that's totally inadequate."

Mayasich practically blushed at such a high-minded compliment.

"I don't think Gretzky back checked that much. I don't think I ever did," he said. "The comparison would be being able to see the ice in playmaking and being where the puck would end up. I'm honored that John said that."

Sixty years after last skating for the Gophers, Mayasich still is the school's all-time scoring leader with 144 goals among 298 points—an eye-popping 1.4 goals and three points per-game average. Second is Pat Micheletti, who has 24 fewer goals despite playing 51 more games.

As a senior, Mayasich scored six goals against Winnipeg and tallied eight points against Michigan—records that also still stand.

Gophers fans realized what they had in Mayasich midway through his sophomore season of 1952–53.

Trailing archrival North Dakota 7–1 entering the third period, Minnesota reeled off four straight goals, including two by Mayasich, who finished with a hat trick. Although the Gophers lost that game, their third-period rally was the catalyst for a 10-game winning streak that clinched the Midwest Conference champion-ship and an NCAA tournament berth.

ROTC military obligations prevented Mayasich from turning pro in 1955. Instead he joined forces again with Mariucci, who coached the U.S. national team at the 1956 Winter Olympics in Cortina d'Ampezzo. Mayasich scored a hat trick in a 4–1 victory over the always-dominant Canadians, leading Team USA to a sur-prise silver medal.

Four years later at Squaw Valley, California, Mayasich's strong checking helped thwart the Soviet Union and guide the United States to its first hockey gold medal.

The 10th of 11 Mayasich children, John grew to 6'0", 175 pounds, as a three-sport start at Eveleth High School. He led the Golden Bears to an unprecedented four consecutive undefeated state hockey championships from 1948 to '51.

As a senior he became an icon and statistical touchstone by which all Minnesota boys' high school players are measured. Mayasich scored 15 goals and 18 points in three tournament games—two of the 10 high school records he holds that might never be broken.

"How do you explain that?" he once said about his state tour-nament success. "I guess you can't. Maybe it was the competition we played against back then. But at the time, those were the best teams and players in the state."

The greatest U.S. player of his era, Mayasich eschewed a profes-sional career in the NHL, whose Original Six franchises turned a cold shoulder to Americans.

He earned an education degree from Minnesota. Married with three kids, Mayasich accepted a job at Hubbard Broadcasting in St. Paul, where he worked 40 years as a sales manager, president of radio operations, and head of public relations.

"I probably wish I had given it a try," he said about the NHL. "Had the situation back then been as it is now, I certainly would have felt differently."

Mayasich was referring to the NHL's doubling to 12 teams in 1967 and subsequent expansion that ultimately increased its number of franchises to 30.

"Strictly speaking, John Mayasich was born 10 years too early," said Mariucci. "The opportunity was not good and the pay not much better."

Fire in the Hole...er, Hall!

Cross-country road trips still were in their infancy in 1936 when the Gophers embarked on a journey to Seattle that is forever remembered for their escaping possible tragedy during a layover in Montana.

Coach Bernie Bierman and his two-time defending national champions sought more challenging opponents than the regional nonconference teams of the era. So he scheduled an early-season game against the University of Washington.

It required a four-day train ride that included a stop in at the Florence Hotel in Missoula, Montana, where the Gophers were scheduled to practice en route to Seattle.

About 4:00 AM on September 24, Edward L. Shave, sports editor for the St. Paul *Daily News*, was awakened in his room by the smell of smoke. He opened his door and saw the hallway filled with it. Quickly, he alerted a hotel clerk, who telephoned Bierman, who in turn roused his team.

Coaches and players, most still in their pajamas, escaped to the nearby train station. Within 90 minutes, the four-story hotel was fully engulfed and eventually destroyed, according to newspaper accounts.

Fire officials determined the blaze started in the basement of an adjacent drug store. It caused about $500,000 in damage. About $4,000 worth of personal items and football equipment the Gophers left behind also perished.

"Hardly a Gopher escaped without some loss in the fire," read the story in the *Pioneer Press*. "Many of them lost their shoes, but they were taken to Missoula stores and re-outfitted."

Bierman scheduled a pared-down practice before the shaken Gophers boarded another train for Seattle.

"I'm sorry to hear of the plight of coach Bernie Bierman and his men," Washington coach Jimmy Phelan told the Associated Press. "I hope the fire didn't cause any ill effects. We want the Gophers to be at full strength."

Oh, they were. Minnesota scored a fourth-quarter touchdown to win 14–7, its 25th straight victory. The Gophers extended their winning streak to 28 games before Northwestern upset them 6–0 in Evanston, Illinois, on October 31.

As for the fire, Gophers tackle Louis Midler brought home a souvenir from the Florence Hotel, a candlestick holder. He later donated it to the university. It is on display in the Bierman Building trophy case.

28 Home Cooking

It took a North Dakotan to fulfill Don Lucia's dream of delivering a national championship to Minnesota and end a 23-year title drought in Dinkytown.

Grant Potulny, the only three-time hockey captain in Gophers history, was the only non-Minnesotan on the 2001–02 team. He became a legend April 6, 2002, when the junior center scored the overtime winner against Maine at St. Paul's Xcel Energy Center to clinch Minnesota's first national title since 1979.

The Grand Forks, North Dakota, native came to Minnesota in 1998—the first out-of-state player recruited in 11 years.

"When I came for my first visit here [former assistant coach] John Hill told me the Frozen Four was in St. Paul [in 2002] and how he thought with the players they were bringing in [they] had a chance to be there," Potulny recalled.

"From Day 1 here I've been a Gopher, and I've got that 'M' tattooed on my chest. I'm a Gopher for the rest of my life."

Lucia's hockey journey started in Minnesota, but he took the long way home through Indiana, Alaska, and Colorado.

The son of a high school football coach grew up on the Iron Range and won state hockey championships at Grand Rapids High in 1975 and '76. Lucia played defense at Notre Dame from 1977 to '81 and was team captain as a senior.

Drafted by the Philadelphia Flyers, he eschewed a pro career and planned to become a stockbroker when he was recruited by former Fighting Irish assistant coach Ric Shafer to help build his program at the University of Alaska Fairbanks. As a graduate assistant, Lucia lived in a dormitory, drove the Zamboni, and worked as a janitor during the summer.

After several seasons as Shafer's assistant coach, Colorado College hired Lucia in 1993 to rebuild its moribund program. The Tigers had not had a winning season in 13 years before Lucia led them to three Western Collegiate Hockey Association titles and five straight appearances in the NCAA tournament.

Minnesota hired Lucia in April 1999 after Doug Woog resigned.

"I never envisioned when I was driving my bomb of a car up to Alaska to start my coaching career that I would be the head coach at Minnesota 18 years later," Lucia said. "This is a great job, maybe the best job in college hockey. You only get one shot in life and I want to be part of this."

Three years later, Lucia led the Gophers back to the Frozen Four for the first time since 1989. It was a powerhouse team. Minnesota never lost consecutive games all season.

Senior captains Jordan Leopold and John Pohl were first-team All-Americans. Pohl led the country in scoring with 27 goals among 79 points. He and junior Jeff Taffe led the nation with 14 power-play goals apiece.

Leopold became Minnesota's fourth Hobey Baker Award winner after breaking the single-season record for goals by a defenseman with 20. Senior goaltender Adam Hauser became the WCHA's all-time leader in wins (83) and games (151).

Maine won national championships in 1993 and 1999 under coach Shawn Walsh, but the Black Bears played the 2001–02 season with heavy hearts after he died of cancer on September 24 on the eve of the first practice. Interim coach Tim Whitehead led the Black Bears to an at-large bid to the national tournament.

The Gophers defeated Michigan 3–2 in the semifinals. Maine blew out New Hampshire 7–2. The prelude set up a classic Saturday-night duel for the NCAA crown. A record crowd of 19,324 (mostly) Gophers partisans packed the home arena of the NHL's Minnesota Wild for a game they would never forget.

"Twenty years from now, 40,000 people will swear they were in attendance just like a couple million claim to have been at Woodstock," wrote St. Paul *Pioneer Press* columnist Tom Powers.

The teams traded goals for two periods. Pohl and Keith Ballard scored for the Gophers, Michael Schutte bagged a pair for Maine and Robert Liscak added a third with 4:33 remaining in the third period for a 3–2 lead.

Minnesota pulled Hauser for a sixth skater with 59 seconds remaining and a faceoff in the Maine zone. Pohl won the draw.

A scramble ensued. Matt Koalska dug out the puck and fired a 30-footer past Black Bears goalie Matt Yeats with 53 seconds remaining to set off a wild celebration at the Gophers' bench.

The Gophers carried the play for most of the extra session but Yeats stood tall. Double overtime loomed. Referee Steve Piotrowski called Schutte for tripping Koalska at center ice with about four minutes remaining. Minnesota was 1-for-4 on the power play, but had failed to register a shot during a 72-second two-man advantage earlier in the game.

Leopold wristed a shot from the blue line that was knocked down. Another scramble. Potulny, who was camped out in the slot, swept the puck underneath a sprawled Yeats at 16:58 of overtime.

Potulny was mobbed by his teammates. Xcel Energy Center exploded with joy.

Powers, the St. Paul columnist, compared the roar to the Metrodome reaction to Kirby Puckett's 11th-inning walk-off home run in Game 6 of the 1991 World Series.

Lucia cried on the bench.

"At the start of the year this was all we talked about. It was our time. I'm so proud of our players," he said. "We are all going to remember this day the rest of our lives. It's the most incredible feeling I've ever had."

Potulny was chosen outstanding player of the Frozen Four. He scored three goals in the tournament and finished his career with six goals in four NCAA games. He was joined on the all-tournament team by Pohl and Hauser, who made 42 saves in the clincher and stopped 69 shots in the two games.

"You won it in dramatic fashion," President George W. Bush said during a White House ceremony to honor the 2002 Gophers. "And you had to change your immigration laws to allow somebody from North Dakota to come in to score."

Potulny played 146 games for the Gophers, scoring 68 goals among 116 points, and was renowned for his leadership. He played six minor league seasons before returning to his alma mater in 2009 to become one of Lucia's assistants.

Potulny was behind the Gophers' bench at Boston College November 26, 2016, when Lucia became the eighth NCAA coach to win 700 games.

Still connected after all these years.

29 Shock(ed) the World

A crown on the head comes with a target on one's back, as the 2002–03 Minnesota men's hockey team knows very well.

No one gave the Gophers a chance to repeat as national champions in Buffalo, New York, after they had dramatically won the 2002 title at St. Paul's Xcel Energy Center. Or so the story goes. Nothing galvanizes a team better than reflexive us-against-the-world mantras that rage against disrespect, real or imagined.

To be sure, Minnesota had to grind its way back to the NCAA tournament with a relatively inexperienced roster that lost several key championship cogs. All-Americans Jordan Leopold and John Pohl had graduated along with power-play specialist Jeff Taffe and goalie Adam Hauser.

Moreover, captain Grant Potulny, who scored the overtime winner to vanquish Maine and deliver Minnesota's first NCAA championship in 23 years, broke his ankle in the season opener and was sidelined 22 games. The Gophers stumbled to a 2–7–1 start.

But they also boasted a playmaking magician unlike any freshman who had ever donned a Maroon-and-Gold uniform. Austrian

Thomas Vanek was the first European prospect recruited to the program.

Potulny was a North Dakotan whose heritage became a running joke. President George W. Bush even cracked during the White House ceremony honoring the 2002 national champs that Minnesota had to amend its immigration laws to allow Potulny onto the team.

Blurring the Minnesota–North Dakota border was one thing. But coach Don Lucia's decision to pluck Vanek from overseas raised eyebrows in parochial Minnesota, which proudly points to its all-Minnesota championship teams in the 1970s.

"We were kind of the outsiders, and Tom being a European, that was an even bigger deal," Potulny told the Minneapolis *Star Tribune.* "I never thought about it until Don mentioned that people might not be too happy. I guess I was a little ignorant to it. I didn't understand why. I knew what I could do and that I could help the team, so I hoped I could get people on my side."

Vanek got the people on his side quickly with a breakout season to remember. His 31 goals and 62 points made him the first freshman to lead the Gophers in scoring since Mike Antonovich in 1969–70. He finished one goal shy of John Mayasich's 1951–52 freshman record.

There were a pair of hat tricks not seen since Reggie Bert bagged two in 1995–96. Vanek was as clutch as he was prolific. Seventeen of his goals were scored in the third period or overtime.

The Gophers were 12–6–5 when Potulny, their spiritual leader, returned in mid-January. Led by Vanek's ferocious production, the team went on a 16–2–4 tear, ending its second straight season without suffering consecutive losses.

Junior forward Troy Riddle scored 26 goals among 51 points. Junior defenseman Paul Martin emerged as a second-team All-American after contributing nine goals and 39 points. Sophomore goalie Travis Weber won 18 of his 34 games, posting a pair of shutouts and a 2.50 goals-against average.

Minnesota finished six points behind Colorado College in the Western Collegiate Hockey Association but won the playoff title and surged into the Frozen Four at HSBC Arena, home of the NHL's Sabres.

Michigan was the semifinal opponent. The game went to overtime tied 2–2. Again the Gophers turned to their money player.

At 8:55 of the extra period Vanek had the puck behind the Wolverines' net. He faked to goalie Al Montoya's left and pirouetted around the right post to stuff a wraparound goal between his skates and send the Gophers into the championship game against snakebitten New Hampshire.

"You want your guys to play well, but you also emphasize it's all about winning now," a relieved Lucia said afterward. "Second place is for the birds."

The Gophers had overcome so much to give themselves a chance to become the program's first back-to-back champions and the moment was not lost on them. A sign prominently placed in their dressing room before their final game of the season read: SHOCK THE WORLD.

"We didn't feel that anybody believed we could go back-to-back and that became the statement of the night—'Shock the World,'" recalled Martin. "I think at that point we believed we had a good thing going and could actually make a run at back-to-backs."

The Wildcats, in their seventh Frozen Four, were chasing history, too. New Hampshire was seeking its first national championship. The hunt would continue.

Vanek (who else?) scored the game-winner midway through the third period to snap a 1–1 tie and unleash the floodgates in a 5–1 Minnesota victory.

"Oh, it's unbelievable. It feels so great," Vanek said during the on-ice celebration. "I watched the team last year and had butterflies but this is just unbelievable."

Vanek's star-making performance was the comet tail to his career in Minnesota. The Buffalo Sabres drafted him No. 5 overall in June 2003 and Vanek decided to turn pro.

It was the Gophers' fifth title in 11 championship-game appearances. They also became the first school to win consecutive NCAA championships since Boston University in 1971 and '72.

In the merriment at HSBC Arena, someone updated the sign in the dressing room to reflect the proper verb tense:

Shocked the World.

30 Bob McNamara

No Minnesota alumnus cared as passionately about Gophers athletics or invested more heart and treasure than Bob McNamara, a former football superstar whose energetic philanthropy saved three nonrevenue sports from extinction.

"I have always wanted to do something for the University of Minnesota because it has done so much for me and my brother, Pinky," McNamara told author Jim Bruton in 2009. "Giving back is important to both of us."

Bob and younger brother Pinky McNamara came to Minnesota in the early 1950s from Hastings High School, where older brother grew up idolizing a future Vikings Hall of Fame coach who played for the Gophers in the 1940s.

"When I was playing for Hastings High School, Bud Grant was always my hero," McNamara said. "I have so many great memories playing for the Gophers."

The 1954 All-American halfback/defensive back/kick returner's finest moment came Nov. 13 that year when the Gophers hosted Iowa looking to avenge a 27–0 loss to the Hawkeyes the previous year.

McNamara scored on a 36-yard burst on Minnesota's first possession. After Iowa tied the game, McNamara took the ensuing kickoff at the 11-yard line. He followed his blocks to midfield before a swarm of Hawkeyes descended.

McNamara somehow squirted out of the pileup and went the distance—89 yards for a touchdown that touched off a mad frenzy at Memorial Stadium.

First-year coach Murray Warmath said after the game it was the "greatest example of one man against 11" he had seen in his football life.

The Gophers won 22–20. McNamara played all 60 minutes, rushing for 113 yards from fullback or right halfback in Warmath's split-T formation.

After graduation, he teamed with Grant on the Winnipeg Blue Bombers of the Canadian Football League. McNamara still holds the record for most touchdowns in a CFL game when he scored six on October 13, 1956.

He played two seasons for the American Football League's Denver Broncos before retiring in 1961 and opening a bar/restaurant in Minneapolis with Pinky. From there, the pair dedicated their efforts to fundraising for Gophers athletics.

Bob and his wife, Annette, founded the Golden Gopher Fund in 1973. He also supported five endowed scholarships at Minnesota.

In 2002, Minnesota in a budget crisis announced plans to eliminate the men's and women's golf and men's gymnastics programs. McNamara teamed with fellow donors Harvey McKay and Lou Nanne and raised $2.7 million to save the three teams.

That year the men's golf team won its first and only national championship. Then–Gophers coach Brad James gave McNamara a national championship ring. McNamara responded by endowing four and a half men's golf scholarships.

"I've always been the kind of person where, when I start a project, I like to finish it," McNamara told the Minneapolis *Star Tribune* at the time. "Saving a sport for three years really doesn't mean that much if it's still going to be in danger."

McNamara walked point in fundraising for the Baseline Tennis Center, Siebert Field (baseball), and TCF Bank Stadium. His tireless work in raising capital to build an open-air stadium back on campus earned McNamara a place as one of six honorary captains for the 2009 inaugural game.

The university named the McNamara Academic Center after Bob and Pinky, who died in 2011 after a lengthy struggle with Alzheimer's disease. Bob McNamara died in 2014 at age 82.

"Anyone who knew Bob knew that there was no greater supporter of the university," said former Gophers athletic director Joel Maturi. "Nobody was better at fundraising or cared more about Minnesota than Bob. He will be deeply missed."

Bob and Pinky McNamara played one year together for the Gophers, that 1954 season in which they finished 7–2. They formed a sibling rivalry in the kick-return game.

According to broadcaster Ray Christensen, Warmath had a simple play call for all returns. If it was "1," Bob handed off to Pinky. A "2" had Pinky handing off to Bob.

More often than not "2" was called out for Bob, meaning "1" was truly the loneliest number for Pinky.

One week Pinky approached Warmath about getting the ball more often.

"Maybe next year," Warmath said, "when your brother has graduated."

31 Charlie Sanders

Charlie Sanders left his home in rural North Carolina and the Jim Crow South in 1964 for Minnesota and found himself on another planet.

To be exact, it was Bridgeman's Ice Cream Shop on Fourth Street and 14th Avenue in the heart of Dinkytown.

"I remember walking in the front door, and I remember that I couldn't feel the tension," Sanders told the Minnesota *Daily* in 2007. "That was the greatest experience I had, and I knew I was in the right place."

It was the right place and right time for the Gophers to turn the former defensive end and offensive tackle into a tight end, a position Sanders redefined during his Hall of Fame NFL career with the Detroit Lions. The hardworking, happy-go-lucky locker-room favorite flourished in his new role with the Gophers in 1967 and was a key playmaker on their last Big Ten championship team.

To bulk up he spent the summer of '67 pounding weights and protein shakes, earning the nickname "Banana Malt Sanders" as he packed on 30 pounds. He earned All–Big Ten honors as a senior, helping lead the Gophers to an 8–2 record by catching 21 passes for 276 yards and two touchdowns.

The Lions drafted him in the third round (74th overall) and he quickly changed the dynamic of playing pro tight end, a position known primarily for blocking rather than catching passes. Sanders became the greatest tight end in Detroit history before a knee injury in 1976 ended his career after a decade wearing the Honolulu Blue-and-Silver.

Sanders led the Lions, or was a co-leader in receptions, six times, and he registered 30 or more receptions seven times in addition to amassing at least 500 receiving yards in six different seasons. Sanders was selected to seven Pro Bowls, was a two-time All-Pro (1970–71), and was named to the NFL's All-Decade Team of the 1970s.

It took more than 30 years for the Pro Football Hall of Fame to call in 2007. Sanders became the sixth Gopher and seventh tight end inducted in Canton.

A gentleman's gentleman, Sanders died of cancer in 2015 after spending 43 years with the Lions as coach, scout, radio broadcaster, and player personnel director—longer than anyone in the franchise outside late owner William Clay Ford.

But Sanders never forgot his formative years in Minnesota or the impact the progressive campus had on his outlook.

His mother, Parteacher, died when he was two. His father, Nathaniel, enlisted in the Army. Sanders and his brothers were raised by an aunt. His father left the Army and reunited the family in Greensboro when Sanders was 8.

He became roommates at Minnesota with fellow North Carolinian McKinley Boston.

"I always say to people that the University of Minnesota was probably the difference maker in terms of who I am and how I interact with people," Sanders said. "Because it basically opened my eyes and educated me in a sense that there was another world out there in terms of racial differences."

32 Bud Grant

Harry Peter Grant Jr. was the oldest of three brothers born to Harry and Bernice in Superior, Wisconsin. He quickly earned the nickname that defined him as an NFL coaching icon simply out of convenience.

"My mother didn't care for the confusion of having two Harrys under the same roof," Grant told VikingsUpdate.com. "She took to calling me Buddy Boy. As I grew, the name got shorter."

Before he won 168 games as Minnesota's four-time Super Bowl head coach, before becoming the first person voted into the halls of fame of the NFL and Canadian Football League, before playing for the NBA champion Minneapolis Lakers, Bud Grant was the most resourceful athlete the University of Minnesota had ever seen.

He arrived in 1947 without a scholarship after serving at the Great Lakes Naval Station in Chicago during the waning days of World War II. Nine varsity letters later, Grant forged a legacy as an All-American two-way gridiron stalwart, a starting forward and MVP for the basketball team, and a center fielder who led the baseball club in hitting as a freshman.

In 1950, a panel of sportswriters and broadcasters voted him Minnesota's Athlete of the Half Century.

"As versatile an athlete who has ever played at Minnesota," longtime Gophers broadcaster Ray Christensen wrote.

Athletic prowess came early to Grant but it was not easy.

His father, Harry, was a former quarterback at Minnesota-Duluth and known as a man about town in Superior, across the shipping harbors in northwestern Wisconsin.

Before winning 168 games as the Vikings' four-time Super Bowl head coach, before he was the first person voted hall of fames of the NFL and Canadian Football League, and before he won an NBA championship for the Minneapolis Lakers, Bud Grant was the most resourceful athlete the University of Minnesota had ever seen. University of Minnesota Archives

Despite a bout with polio that left him with a limp, Grant grew to 6'3" as a 14-year-old freshman at Central High School. He won conference and regional honors in basketball and baseball and was named to *Esquire* magazine's all-star baseball game at Chicago's Comiskey Park.

Minnesota, Wisconsin, and Northwestern recruited Grant, but none of the schools offered him a scholarship before the war. So he became a walk-on star with the Gophers.

After graduating in 1949, he became a reserve on the world champion 1949–50 Minneapolis Lakers.

Meanwhile, the Philadelphia Eagles drafted Grant in the first round as a defensive end. In 1952 he switched to receiver and turned his first catch into an 84-yard touchdown against the Steelers.

Grant became embroiled in a contract dispute with the Eagles and jumped to the CFL to play for the Winnipeg Blue Bombers.

"The Eagles offered me $8,000, and I went to Winnipeg for $11,000," Grant told *Sports Illustrated*. "That's not tough arithmetic!"

He still holds the CFL record for most interceptions in a playoff game with five.

In 1957, at age 29, Grant stopped playing and became head coach, leading the Blue Bombers to six Grey Cups, winning four, and amassing 102 regular season victories.

The Vikings hired him in 1967 to succeed Norm Van Brocklin. Grant was an immediate hit in Minnesota with his ramrod-straight posture and perfectly trimmed crew cut, which made him look like a Prussian general.

In 17 seasons with the Vikings, Grant's teams made the play-offs 12 times and won 11 division titles. When he resigned in 1984, only George Halas had won more games in pro football.

Ten years later, Grant was elected to the Pro Football Hall of Fame.

33 The Sun Also Rises

Truth be told, the Gophers had no desire to be in El Paso for another Sun Bowl on New Year's Eve 2003, four years after losing to the same Oregon Ducks in the west Texas outpost.

Pasadena was their decades-long desire until a midseason melt-down against Michigan stuck a thorn in their Rose Bowl balloon.

They should have gone to the Alamo Bowl in San Antonio for a marquee matchup against No. 21 Nebraska. Athletic director

Joel Maturi led a furious public relations blitz, touting Minnesota's No. 20 ranking, its first nine-win season in almost a century, and a high-octane offense that had set nine school records.

Instead the Alamo bid went to marginal Michigan State. The Spartans only had eight wins, but they boasted a 70,000-strong ticket base and promised a large traveling party. Sparty was a more enticing draw for bowl officials than Minnesota, which struggled to draw 40,000 to the dreary Metrodome.

"When you look at the numbers, statistically speaking, there are fewer people attending Minnesota games and fewer people travel to bowl games than Michigan State," Alamo Bowl executive director Derrick Fox told the St. Paul *Pioneer Press*. "It's not the be-all and end-all, but it certainly weighed into it."

Jilted but not jaded, the Gophers packed their bags for El Paso and made history by squeezing out a victory in a nerve-fraying game for the ages.

Rhys Lloyd's 42-yard field goal with 23 seconds remaining edged Oregon 31–30 and secured Minnesota's first 10-win season since 1905.

The go-ahead kick touched off pandemonium on the Gophers' sideline. Players and coaches poured onto the field. Coach Glen Mason yelled and screamed at them to back down lest they draw a penalty. After all, Oregon was getting the ball back with a passing attack that had made mincemeat out of the Gophers' secondary.

Plenty of bad things could happen in 23 seconds. Ducks quarterback Kellen Clemens had already completed 32-of-43 passes for 363 yards and three touchdowns. Wide receiver Samie Parker caught a Sun Bowl–record 16 passes for 200 yards and a score.

But Oregon's comeback hopes died when Clemens' first pass after the kickoff was intercepted by Gophers safety Justin Isom.

The 70th Sun Bowl was a down-to-the-wire thriller that thoroughly entertained the 49,894 in attendance, the fifth-largest crowd in the game's history.

"It was a whale of a football game," said Ducks coach Mike Bellotti.

The teams combined to punt just three times. After a scoreless opening 15 minutes, 31 points were put up in the second quarter. There were five lead changes in the second half.

"We were pretty certain in the second half that we needed to score on every possession," Clemens told reporters afterward.

Laurence Maroney rushed for 135 yards on 15 carries and fullback Thomas Tapeh scored three touchdowns as Minnesota avenged a 24–20 loss to Oregon in the 1999 Sun Bowl.

"I thoroughly enjoyed the '99 game, and we lost," Mason said. "I thoroughly enjoyed the game today, and we won."

Midway through the fourth quarter, Minnesota quarterback Asad Abdul-Khaliq connected with Aaron Hosack on a 34-yard completion. On the next snap, Abdul-Khaliq fumbled—the first turnover of the game.

Oregon matriculated downfield. Clemens dodged a bullet when Gophers safety Eli Ward dropped an interception in the end zone. Minnesota's defense found its resolve, however, holding Clemens and the Ducks to a 47-yard Jared Siegal field goal and a 30–28 lead with 4:16 remaining.

"Your goal is to not give up a score after a turnover, but we made them kick a field goal, and that kept the game in balance," noted Gophers defensive coordinator Greg Hudson.

Minnesota averaged 38.7 points per game, the seventh-highest-scoring offense in the country. It was powered by a rushing attack that averaged 289.2 yards per game and 5.5 yards per carry.

With the game on the line, the Gophers rode their superior ground game on the game-winning drive. They marched 55 yards, converting three third downs and a key fourth down on a 3-yard run by Maroney.

Lloyd was forced to kick from 42 yards out into a swirling wind. On November 8, he buried a 35-yard game-winner against

Wisconsin at the Metrodome to swipe Paul Bunyan's Axe from the Badgers.

Oregon defensive tackle Junior Siavali actually got a piece of Lloyd's kick but could not prevent it from sailing through the uprights.

"It was probably one of the sweetest kicks I've hit all year," Lloyd said. "It went kind of low, because I hit it toward the middle of the ball. But it went through. That's kind of all that counts."

Added Mason: "I was a little shaky when it came down to the last kick, but all I told [Rhys] was to hit it good."

Minnesota's 10th win marked the first time in school history it won consecutive postseason games after vanquishing Arkansas 29–14 in the 2002 Music City Bowl.

Their 2003 season did not come up roses but the stale Sun Bowl provided a sweet ending for the Gophers.

"If someone would've told me five years ago, in my fifth year, we would go 10–3 and we would win our bowl game," senior linebacker Ben West said, "I'd have taken it."

34 Maize and Blues

The eruption was more than just noise. It was a cathartic roar unlike anything the Gophers had generated at the Metrodome, an eardrum-aching, decibel-spiking din typical of postseason Twins games.

There were 58 seconds remaining in the third quarter on October 10, 2003, when Thomas Tapeh rumbled into the end zone from two yards out. Minnesota took a 21-point lead on Michigan and the sellout crowd of 62,374 was delirious with joy.

They were legacy fans old enough to remember the glory days of the 1960s, newly initiated students unaccustomed to dominance of a college football powerhouse, and plenty more crowding the bandwagon.

It was like a giant curtain had parted to reveal the Gophers' manifest destiny after four decades of dormancy.

Undefeated and poised for a seventh win that would boost their No. 17 ranking, tighten their grip on a Rose Bowl bid, and elevate them into the national-championship conversation.

Poof!

Those dreams vanished in 15 nightmarish minutes as Michigan scored 31 fourth-quarter points in the greatest comeback in that school's storied history, an unlikely 38–35 win that haunts Dinkytown to this day.

Instead of being Minnesota's launchpad to Pasadena, the meltdown at the Metrodome was the Wolverines' course correction as they reeled off six straight wins to punch their Rose Bowl ticket. The Gophers sifted through the ashes of what might have been and settled for an unfulfilling Sun Bowl appearance.

"Until this very moment, you look back and say, 'What if?'" quarterback Asad Abdul-Khaliq mused in 2004. "What if we just won that damn game?"

Minnesota was off to its best start since winning the 1960 national title. Michigan had lost two of three, tumbling to No. 21 in the rankings. The Gophers had a national television audience on ESPN to showcase their bona fides, a quirky Friday-night game with a unique backstory.

Six years after arriving in Minnesota, head coach Glen Mason had resurrected the program into a viable Big Ten contender, and the Gophers could not escape the Metrodome fast enough.

The mausoleum in downtown Minneapolis was a soulless fan destination after the team moved indoors in 1982 from cozy on-campus Memorial Stadium. The Gophers were a hot ticket again but marginalized tenants whose occupancy was dictated by whomever and whenever the Twins and Vikings were playing.

In 2003, the Twins won their second straight American League Central Division crown. The Gophers were put on notice that their biggest game ever at the Metrodome, their most consequential game in 40 years, might conflict with Game 3 or 4 of the AL Championship Series. It would have to be rescheduled.

Never mind that the Twins were ultimately swept by the Yankees in a first-round series to make any ALCS conflict moot. Saturday was out. Friday night it was.

One fewer day to prepare only intensified the hype. The Gophers were favored, the stakes obvious.

"It's probably going to be the biggest game for everyone on the team in their career," senior safety Eli Ward told the St. Paul *Pioneer Press*. "I know it's definitely going to be the biggest game in my career. We'll definitely be fired up."

The noise was deafening as the Gophers ran out of the tunnel. They fed off the Metrodome's frenzied energy and manhandled the Wolverines.

Running backs Tapeh, Marion Barber III, and Laurence Maroney averaged more than 10 yards a carry as the trio combined for four rushing touchdowns in three quarters. Defensively the Gophers were clogging running lanes to stymie Michigan's Heisman Trophy candidate Chris Perry.

Their 28 points already were the most the team had scored against Michigan since 1937. Minnesota controlled momentum, the line of scrimmage, and the clock before tumbling down the rabbit hole, where nothing was as it appeared.

The fourth quarter became a kaleidoscope of Wolverines quarterback John Navarre dinking, dunking, and dicing through the Gophers' flat-footed defense in a hurry-up scheme.

Navarre exploited Minnesota with screen plays it was unprepared to defend. He connected with Perry for a 10-yard touchdown just 36 seconds into the fourth quarter to cut the deficit to two touchdowns.

Minnesota was still in command, a 7–0 record firmly in its grasp. Until it wasn't.

Up to that point, Abdul-Khaliq was an efficient steward, completing 7-of-12 passes for 64 yards. Then he committed the ghastly sin of trying to manufacture a play instead of absorbing a sack.

Tumbling to the turf with a defender wrapped around his ankle deep in Minnesota territory, Abdul-Khaliq threw a pass that was intercepted by Jacob Stewart and returned 34 yards for a touchdown.

"You always look back at a play like that and think, 'What the hell was I thinking?'" Abdul-Khaliq recounted. "I just got caught up trying to be something I'm not, trying to always make something happen."

Suddenly, it was a seven-point game. The Metrodome grew eerily quiet as tension squelched joy.

"I was amazed how they went from cold to hot," Mason said afterward. "We gave them life."

Abdul-Khaliq's 52-yard quarterback sneak regained Minnesota's 14-point lead but the drive only burned 2:49 off the clock. The Gophers had nothing left to give on offense and no answer for screen passes on defense, and allowed Michigan to take, take, and take.

The Wolverines racked up 13 first downs in the final 15 minutes.

Fifty-three seconds after Abdul-Khaliq's score Navarre hit Braylon Edwards streaking down the sideline for a 52-yard touchdown. Perry tied the game on a 10-yard run with 5:48 remaining.

The Gophers responded by going three-and-out. Blocking assignments were missed. One receiver ran the wrong route. Disaster was palpable.

Michigan steadily marched down the field during a 12-play drive that exhausted Minnesota's defense and resolve. With 47 seconds remaining, Garrett Rivas nailed a 33-yard field goal to extend Michigan's winning streak in the series to 15 games.

The Gophers lost despite rushing for 424 yards, more than any team had ever accumulated against Michigan.

"Everybody out there left everything they had on the field," a crestfallen Abdul-Khaliq told reporters. "For some reason I can't explain, we didn't get it done."

The repercussions were huge.

The following week the Gophers played host to nationally ranked Michigan State. There were only 38,778 at the Metrodome. The bandwagon was noticeably lighter.

Minnesota fell behind 17–0 in the first quarter and never recovered in a 44–38 loss to the Spartans, the death knell for their Rose Bowl aspirations.

The Gophers also lost to Iowa. But had they defeated Michigan, and the Big Ten conference season played out exactly the way it ultimately did, Minnesota would have gone to Pasadena.

It was more than a lost 15 minutes. It was opportunity lost.

35 Déjà Blue

No, not again. Not another season-wrecking, soul-crushing loss to Michigan. Not another blown fourth-quarter lead. Not another year for the Little Brown Jug to remain bolted down in Ann Arbor.

Yes, again, as usual.

It was not a costly interception by a renegade quarterback or defensive collapse that doomed the Gophers on October 9, 2004. The lightning bolt this time was thrown by a true freshman quarterback named Chad Henne, whose late-game heroics at Michigan Stadium crushed Minnesota's resolve once again.

Henne needed just 67 seconds to complete 5-of-6 passes on the final drive. He hit Tyler Ecker in stride on a crossing route. The tight end shook off two would-be tacklers and rumbled 31 yards for the go-ahead touchdown in a wild 27–24 victory.

The Wolverines scored 10 unanswered points after Rhys Lloyd's 27-yard field goal gave Minnesota a 24–17 lead with 13:14 remaining in the fourth quarter.

The collapse was not as egregious as the 21-point fourth-quarter meltdown at the Metrodome 365 days earlier. But try arguing that technicality in another somber Gophers locker room after another undefeated season was tainted, their Rose Bowl express derailed again.

"It is hard to swallow, really," senior cornerback Ukee Dozier told reporters afterward. "We just knew coming into this game that we were going to win. Just like last year. We didn't think the plays were going to go the way they went."

It was another missed opportunity to climb the ladder of national respect and clear-cut a path to Pasadena, where the

Gophers have not played since 1962. The narrative was identical to the teams' 2003 clash at the Metrodome, with similar ramifications in the Big Ten.

Minnesota was ranked No. 13, Michigan No. 14. The Gophers were 5–0 and 2–0 in the Big Ten. The Wolverines also were 2–0 in conference but had been nicked by an early-season loss at Notre Dame.

Despite playing at home, Michigan was an underdog. For the first time since the 1960s, Minnesota arguably had as much if not more talent on its roster than its old rival. Hail to the victors who controlled their Rose Bowl destiny.

The stakes could not have been higher, although Gophers coach Glen Mason tried hard to lower expectations before the game, recalling how his 2003 team bought into the hype and was overwhelmed by it.

"I've been doing this a long time; I know what happens," Mason said. "All of a sudden, you get in a game, and when people aren't used to being in that big game, they make it a bigger thing. The teams that have been there before, they don't make it a bigger thing."

The rematch was played more tightly. Neither team led by more than 10 points as Michigan took a 17–14 halftime lead. Running backs Laurence Maroney and Marion Barber III accounted for Minnesota's first-half touchdowns with scoring runs of 80 and 19 yards, respectively.

However, the Wolverines were committed to stopping the run a year after the Gophers gashed them for 424 yards on the ground. Minnesota finished with a respectable 189 rushing yards, but it was only the second time in two seasons it failed to eclipse 200.

Quarterback Bryan Cupito's 26-yard touchdown pass to Jared Allerson in the third quarter gave the Gophers a four-point lead. But they squandered a golden opportunity to deliver a knockout blow when Michigan's Leon Hall fumbled a punt and Minnesota's Amir Pinnix recovered at the 9-yard line.

The Gophers settled for Lloyd's kick. Michigan countered with a field goal and Henne's gut punch.

"You 'what-if' yourself and you look at a number of situations, especially late in the game, that could've turned the tide our way," said Mason. "It became a one-series football game. Michigan had to go the distance as time was running down. Credit them—they made the plays. And criticize us—we didn't."

Michigan tailback Mike Hart set a school freshman record with 160 yards rushing after scoring the game's initial touchdown. Henne finished with 328 yards on 33-of-49 passing.

Afterward, Mason struggled to put on another brave face.

"Hey, I'm hurting right now. I might be putting on a good facade, but I hurt inside," he said. "But we'll get back up. We'll show up at East Lansing this week. I don't know if we'll win or lose, but we'll show up."

The Gophers showed up at Michigan State, all right, but were smoked 51–17 by the Spartans to tumble out of the top 25. They never recovered from their 16th straight defeat to Michigan, losing five of their final seven games.

Minnesota had to settle for a New Year's Eve date with unranked Alabama in the Music City Bowl in Nashville, where the Gophers won 20–16.

Vengeance against Michigan would have to wait for another year. The longest Rose Bowl drought in the Big Ten endures.

36 Baggage Unloaded

Glen Mason resuscitated Gophers football from a 30-year slumber, yet nine seasons into his coaching tenure the Little Brown Jug remained an elusive bauble.

Not only did Michigan dominate the lopsided rivalry with 16 consecutive victories entering a 2005 clash in Ann Arbor, but the Wolverines had shattered Minnesota's hearts the previous two seasons with fierce fourth-quarter comebacks.

Twice the ranked Gophers were undefeated at midseason with visions of a Big Ten championship dancing in their heads only to be cold-cocked by storied Michigan.

Mason had defeated every conference foe, including perennial powerhouses Ohio State, Penn State, Iowa, and Wisconsin—every team except the Wolverines. Forget the Maize-and-Blue. Michigan was Mason's great white whale.

He built a consistent winner and managed to upset several top-10 teams but never the program responsible in 2003 and 2004 for extending Minnesota's Big Ten title drought to 43 years.

"When I decided to come up here to the University of Minnesota, it was with the idea of being able to stand up here in front of you and say, 'We're champions of the Big Ten,'" Mason said before the 2005 game. "There are a lot of people doing that in this league, every single team. If it was easy, someone would do it every year."

Next year finally came for the Gophers on October 8, 2005.

Jason Giannini's last-second, 30-yard field goal let them strut out of the Big House with a 23–20 victory and the Little Brown Jug, the traveling trophy that had been in Ann Arbor since 1987.

A week earlier, the Gophers were 4–0 and ranked No. 18, but a 30-point blowout loss at Penn State knocked them out of the top 25. The Wolverines were ranked No. 21 but struggling at 2–2. They desperately needed a victory to keep their Big Ten title hopes alive.

On a sun-splashed afternoon, Michigan took leads of 3–0, 6–3, 13–3, and 20–13.

Running back Mike Hart ran 28 times for 109 yards and a touchdown. Wide receiver Jason Avant had six catches for 73 yards. Kicker Garrett Rivas converted field goals of 47 and 23 yards. But he also missed two kicks.

Michigan never trailed until Giannini's heroics, an unexpected turnabout given how conservatively Minnesota was moving on offense. Mason was playing for overtime.

After forcing the Wolverines' sixth punt of the game, the Gophers took possession at their 13-yard line with 2:49 remaining and the score at 20–20.

Starting quarterback Bryan Cupito had been knocked out of the game with a shoulder injury and concussion with seven minutes remaining. Backup Tony Mortensen was instructed to hand off to running backs Laurence Maroney and Gary Russell.

On third-and-long, Russell ran off tackle right and outran the edge of Michigan's defense. Sixty-one yards later Russell was hauled down at Michigan's 13.

"I was kind of hoping we wouldn't go to overtime, but I was willing to do that," Mason told reporters afterward. "I was going to conserve the time. I didn't want to give the ball back to Michigan and have Avant go down there and make a great catch on us. So I was trying to take as much time off the clock as I could."

Mason got that and more.

Two running plays centered the ball for Gianni with six seconds left, and he buried the kick.

"It's a heartbreaker," said Avant. "Since I've been here, there hasn't ever been anything like this."

The Gophers certainly could feel Avant's pain.

In 2003 at the Metrodome, Minnesota surrendered a jaw-dropping 31 fourth-quarter points in a paralyzing 38–35 loss to Michigan. A year later at Michigan Stadium, they yielded the game-winning touchdown with two minutes remaining in a 27–24 loss that was no less devastating.

"Do you know that little hump everyone was talking about? We just made it over," Maroney crowed in the visitors' locker room in 2005.

Michigan and Minnesota have played for the Little Brown Jug since 1903. Before Maroney and his teammates reclaimed it, the Wolverines were in possession for 19 years, longer than some of the 2005 Gophers had been alive.

Ernie Wheelwright, who caught a 20-yard touchdown pass from Cupito in the second quarter, finally got it alone and wandered the field with it thrust over his head.

Senior guard Mark Setterstrom had a color picture of the Jug in his suit coat pocket after the game.

"For the program, I think it's huge," he said. "It's something that, for the last 20 years, we haven't been able to do. It's not just us; it's been a lot of hard work, and it's been really close the last few years."

Alas, the big win at the Big House did not launch the Gophers to greatness in 2005. They lost four of their final six games and were defeated 34–31 by Virginia in the Music City Bowl.

A year later Michigan reclaimed the Jug with a 28–14 victory at the Metrodome. Mason was fired at the end of the 2006 season, with a 1–7 record against the Wolverines.

37 The Little Brown Jug

A pig, an axe, a bell, and a jug sound more like ingredients to an Appalachian jubilee of pulled pork sandwiches and moonshine than spoils among the Big Ten's oldest adversaries.

The Floyd of Rosedale, Paul Bunyan's Axe, and the Little Brown Jug are the prizes in Minnesota's long-running rivalries with Iowa, Wisconsin, and Michigan, respectively. The Governor's Victory Bell widened the trophy chase in 1993 when Penn State joined the conference.

Michigan considers its annual border battles with southern neighbor Ohio State the mother of all rivalries but its oldest and most mythical is Minnesota, which started in 1892.

Ironically, the Little Brown Jug is not brown at all. One side is blue, the other maroon, representing the colors of each school.

In 1902, Michigan thumped the Gophers 23–6 in Ann Arbor. A year later, the underdog Gophers sought vengeance, and the campus was electric for the October 31 rematch. The *Minneapolis Tribune* reported two men were arrested at 2:00 AM for waking up neighbors with "Gopher yells."

More than 30,000 fans packed Northrop Field, where attendance had typically averaged between 3,000 and 4,000. The Wolverines nursed a 6–0 lead until the final minute, when Minnesota mounted a late touchdown drive to pull within a point (before 1912 touchdowns were valued at 5 points, plus the extra-point conversion).

With Halloween darkness descending, Ed Rogers made the kick. Fans stormed the field. With 60 seconds still on the clock, team captains agreed to call the game a tie.

Gophers in the Pro Football Hall of Fame

Player	Year inducted
Bronko Nagurski	1963
Leo Nomellini	1969
Bobby Bell	1983
Bud Grant	1994
Carl Eller	2004
Charlie Sanders	2007
Tony Dungy	2016

The next day, janitor Oscar Munson was cleaning the faculty room in the armory where Michigan players dressed. He found a five-gallon glazed jug.

Apparently, Wolverines coach Fielding Yost did not trust visiting teams to hydrate his players so he hauled water from Ann Arbor. But in their haste to escape the chaos on the field and catch a train to Chicago, Michigan forgot its jug.

Munson took the jug to Minnesota athletic director L.J. "Doc" Cooke, and the pair decided to turn it into a trophy.

They painted it the school colors, writing "Michigan Jug—Captured by Oscar, October 31, 1903" on one side, and spelled out the score, "Minnesota 6, Michigan 6," enlarging the Minnesota point total.

Cooke kept the jug in his office for years until Michigan visited Minnesota again in 1909.

"What's that?" Yost asked Cooke when the Wolverines prepared to dress for the game.

Cooke told him it was the 30-cent water jug Yost had left behind six years earlier.

"That's the first time I heard about that!" Yost laughed.

Cooke told Yost he would have to win back the jug. Michigan did just that the following day, defeating the Gophers 15–6. It took 10 years for the Gophers to reclaim the jug.

Gophers in the College Football Hall of Fame

Player	Year inducted
Bronko Nagurski	1951
Henry Williams	1951
Herb Joesting	1954
Bert Baston	1954
Ed Widseth	1954
Bernie Bierman	1955
Dick Wildung	1957
Pug Lund	1958
John McGovern	1966
Eddie Rogers	1968
Bobby Marshall	1971
Bruce Smith	1972
Paul Giel	1975
Leo Nomellini	1977
Clayton Tonnemaker	1980
Bobby Bell	1991
George Franck	2002
Tom Brown	2003
Carl Eller	2006
Sandy Stephens	2011

In September 1931, the Little Brown Jug vanished from the Michigan trophy case. Two months later four men wearing dark goggles dropped off an imitation at an Ann Arbor gas station, according to Mgoblue.com.

Yost argued the jug was authentic, but nobody was buying it. Michigan defeated the Gophers the next two years. In August 1933, another jug randomly surfaced in some bushes outside a medical building on Michigan's campus.

Yost came clean and acknowledged this was, indeed, the Little Brown Jug, the one that has been maintained ever since by the football equipment managers at each school.

The Little Brown Jug practically has an Ann Arbor address. Michigan has won 55 of the last 67 games in the series, including 23 of the last 25.

The NCAA Football Bowl Subdivision includes 75 regular season trophy games. They have Michigan and Minnesota to thank for the tradition.

38 Tony Dungy

Tony Dungy had just turned five years old when his father, Wilbur, brought the youngster from their home in Jackson, Michigan, to his first football game at nearby Michigan Stadium, home of the storied Wolverines.

It was October 1960 and the Gophers were the dominant Big Ten team. They defeated Michigan 10–0 that Saturday afternoon en route to a Rose Bowl berth.

Thirteen years later, Tony Dungy was the Gophers' freshman starting quarterback in Cal Stoll's Veer-T offense. The future Super Bowl–winning coach whose defensive acumen transformed NFL pass coverages initially was drawn to Minnesota because of its radical offensive scheme.

"It was a fun, no-huddle approach where the quarterback controlled the offense," Dungy recalled. "I wanted to be good at the position and do the job well."

Recruited primarily as a running quarterback, Dungy started his first game in 1973 against Nebraska and finished his freshman year with 156 yards rushing and 97 yards passing. He also earned a varsity basketball letter before forgoing the sport to concentrate on football.

Knee and shoulder injuries hampered Dungy as a sophomore, but he finally broke through as a junior in 1975, when Stoll switched to a pro-style offense.

He set a then–school and Big Ten record with 15 touchdown passes and finished No. 5 in the country in both total offense and passing. As a senior, Dungy captained the Gophers and finished in 1976 as Minnesota's all-time leader in pass attempts (586), completions (274), passing yards (3,515), and touchdown passes (25)—records that have since been surpassed.

Dungy was elected class president as a 14-year-old at Frost Junior High School in Jackson and was a two-time Academic All–Big Ten selection for Minnesota, graduating with a degree in business administration.

His father was a physiology professor and his mother, Cleomae, taught high school English. His two sisters worked in the medical field as an obstetrician and nurse, while his brother became a dentist.

"We were very fortunate to have grown up in that environment," Dungy said. "My dad had a doctorate in biology and my mom had a master's in English. I understood very early the importance of academics."

Dungy was an undrafted safety for the NFL's Steelers and won a Super Bowl ring in 1979 with Pittsburgh before returning to Minnesota to coach defensive backs under Stoll.

In 1981, Dungy's former head coach in Pittsburgh, Chuck Noll, hired him to coach the Steelers' secondary, making the 28-year-old the youngest assistant coach in NFL history.

Dungy became the league's first black defensive coordinator in 1984 and was hired by Vikings coach Dennis Green in 1992 for the same job in Minnesota. In 1996 the Tampa Bay Buccaneers hired him to be their head coach. Dungy compiled a 54–42 record in six seasons and led the Bucs to four playoff berths.

He also created the so-called "Tampa-2" zone coverage scheme that proved successful in defending the NFL's increasingly sophisticated passing attacks.

After Tampa Bay fired Dungy, he promptly was hired by the Indianapolis Colts. He and quarterback Peyton Manning won five consecutive division titles and led the Colts to a Super Bowl XLI victory in 2007, when Dungy and Bears coach Lovie Smith became the first two African American coaches to face each other in the title game.

39 Carl Eller

There might not have been a more punishing defensive combination in college football during the early 1960s than Carl Eller and Bobby Bell.

Coach Murray Warmath recruited the North Carolinians from the Jim Crow South and they powerfully bracketed the Gophers' interior line, helping lead Minnesota to its last Rose Bowl victory in 1961.

"Moose," as Eller was called, played his entire sophomore season with a broken hand, practicing during the week with a plaster cast before ditching it on game days.

In 1962, Eller was part of a defense that held their opponents to only 52.2 rushing yards per game, a school record that still stands. He was a two-way starter during his junior and senior years, handling left-tackle duties on the offensive line and earning All-America honors both years.

In 1963, the 6'6", 260-pounder was runner-up for the Outland Trophy as the country's best defensive lineman.

In 1984, the Gophers football program renamed its Outstanding Defensive Player of the Year Award the "Carl Eller Award."

Eller in 2006 was inducted into the College Football Hall of Fame.

"I think it means more just simply because I'm older and can appreciate it more and understand the significance of it," he said that year. "I realize this is quite an honor and achievement and not something I've taken lightly. I'm very appreciative of it."

Eller was the sixth overall pick in the 1964 NFL draft by the Vikings. He played 225 games over 15 seasons, earning six Pro Bowl berths while playing in four Super Bowls.

In 2004, Eller was elected to the Pro Football Hall of Fame.

40 Darrell Thompson

Reflecting on the greatest Gophers running backs of all time, there is Darrell Thompson—and everyone else.

Almost 30 years after graduating, Minnesota's all-time leading rusher stands tall with 4,654 yards and 40 touchdowns. Moreover, Thompson's 98-yard scoring run against Michigan on November 7, 1987, remains a Big Ten record.

Thompson arrived in 1986 after a standout three-sport career at Rochester John Marshall High School and was an immediate force. Chiseled at 6'1", 200 pounds, Thompson was a beast who boasted 4.4-second speed in the 40-yard dash—size and determination that made him elusive and difficult to tackle.

He is the only Big Ten running back to eclipse 1,000 yards as a freshman and sophomore.

Recruited intensely by Iowa, Nebraska, and UCLA, Thompson was lured to Minnesota by coach John Gutekunst, who made the ball carrier his top priority after replacing Lou Holtz in 1986.

"The day after I was named head coach, I was on a plane to Rochester to recruit him," Gutekunst recalled.

Thompson set a then–Division I-A record with 205 yards in his debut and was team MVP every season from 1986 to '89. He also holds Gophers career records for rushing touchdowns (40), 100-yard games (23), and attempts (936).

"I think I made the right decision," Thompson told the Minneapolis *Star Tribune* in 2016. "The friends, the relationships, and the community—I'd do it all over again.

"I wanted to play and I wanted an education. An education was important for me because I didn't know anyone who was playing professional football or Division I football at the time," he said in another interview with Gophersports.com.

"I knew I was the best player in Rochester, but that didn't mean a lot because Rochester isn't that big. I came out and was able to earn a spot at Minnesota and ended up being lucky enough to play in the pros, but the important thing in the beginning was finding a good school and a good football program."

A first-round pick by Green Bay in 1990, Thompson played five seasons for the Packers, rushing for 1,641 yards and eight touchdowns behind Brett Favre before retiring in 1995.

Today he is a color analyst for Gophers radio broadcasts. The father of four lives in suburban Minneapolis and is director of Bolder Options, a nonprofit that coordinates mentors for troubled youth in the Twin Cities.

41 Bob Stein

Bob Stein might be more renowned for what he accomplished off the field than on it as a two-time All-American and Academic All-American defensive end at Minnesota.

He graduated in the top 10 percent of the University of Missouri–Kansas City Law School, which he attended full-time while playing for the Kansas City Chiefs, having turned down postgraduate scholarships to Harvard, Michigan, and Stanford law schools.

As the first president of the NBA's Minnesota Timberwolves, Stein shepherded construction of Target Center, the club's downtown Minneapolis arena.

More recently the sports attorney represented a class action on behalf of retired NFL players against the league. *Dryer v. NFL* fought for royalties for the NFL's use of players' likenesses, especially in NFL Films productions.

Stein's rookie season with the Chiefs during the final year of the American Football League was memorable. The 21-year-old linebacker was part of the defense that shut down the heavily favored Minnesota Vikings for a 23–7 victory in Super Bowl IV.

He played six more seasons in the NFL for the Chiefs, Los Angeles Rams, Vikings, and San Diego Chargers.

Stein was recruited out of suburban St. Louis Park by legendary Gophers coach Murray Warmath and starred on the 1967 team that shared the Big Ten championship with Indiana. He also kicked for the Gophers, and in 1968 became the first to convert a 40-yard field goal.

"It was really a big deal for me to play football at the University of Minnesota," Stein told author Jim Bruton.

Stein was asked in 2011 how rare it is for modern athletes to earn two-time academic All-American honors like he did.

"It's harder now for guys to do both at a high level more so because of the time dedication needed for both school and football," Stein told Gopherhole.com. "When I played guys came in expecting to need a job after college and now most think they are going to the NFL so that has changed the mentality.

"There are plenty of excellent scholars that play football, but it is harder now to compete against the person who is in school with a main focus on school. You have to be smarter to play today as the game is more complicated. The fundamentals aren't different but the details are."

42 Juice on the Loose

The Gophers entered the 1968 football season with a chip on their collective shoulders and lingering thirst for the "Juice."

Despite a 9–1 record the previous year Minnesota was denied its third Rose Bowl berth of the decade because of the bureaucratic snafu that spun out of a three-way tie for the 1967 Big Ten championship.

Indiana and Purdue also finished 9–1. The three teams each had defeated and lost to one another. The "no-repeat" league rule at the time prohibited Purdue from returning to the Rose Bowl.

In 1961 and '62 the Gophers went as an at-large team. The Hoosiers had never played in the Rose Bowl (and have not since).

So the Big Ten's athletic directors, over Minnesota's objections, voted to send Indiana west to play Southern California and Trojans superstar running back O.J. Simpson.

Simpson earned game MVP honors, running 25 times for 128 yards and both touchdowns as the Trojans nailed down their national championship with a 14–3 win over Indiana.

Fast forward eight months. Minnesota's season-opening opponent in 1968 was Southern California, the No. 1 team in the country.

Simpson, the Heisman Trophy runner-up, was the biggest attraction in the sport. The epicenter of college football on September 21, 1968, was Memorial Stadium.

USC's O.J. SIMPSON—THE BEST RUNNER EVER TO FACE GOPHERS? read one headline that week in the *Minneapolis Tribune*.

The 6'2", 207-pound speedster had rocketed to prominence in 1967 after two years of junior college in his native San Francisco. Simpson's 1,543 yards and 13 touchdowns included averages of 26 carries and 140 yards.

Gophers coach Murray Warmath mused that Orenthal James Simpson had earned his nickname during a 24–7 win over Notre Dame: "Every time Simpson got the ball against the Irish the priests on the sidelines must have muttered, "Oh, Jesus! Oh, Jesus!"

Simpson was fast and powerful. Earlier that year he helped the USC 44-yard relay team set a world record at the NCAA track and field championships.

"Every time he gets the ball we're going to try to have 11 men try to stop him," Warmath told reporters. "If they give the ball to someone else we're not going to be concerned about him. If they try to pass the ball to him we're going to be concerned—very concerned."

The Gophers were underdogs but confident. Not only were they playing at home but they had the edge in experience. Only 25 of the 46 Trojans who traveled to Minnesota had ever played in a college game. Nineteen national champions had graduated, including 10 who were drafted by the NFL—five in the first round.

The Gophers even caught a break with the weather as rain muddied Simpson's running track in the first quarter and pounded the 60,820 fans in attendance, including Governor Harold LeVander, who was wrapped in a homemade plastic baggie.

Simpson fumbled on USC's initial drive, giving Minnesota great field position. Phil Hagen quickly connected with Ray Parson for a 10-yard touchdown pass. Bob Stein followed with a 40-yard field goal to give Minnesota a quick 10–0 lead.

However, Trojans safety Mike Battle turned the momentum dramatically when he intercepted Hagen to set up Simpson's 36-yard touchdown run.

It was 13–13 at halftime. The rain stopped and sun broke through in the third quarter. And the Trojans rode their horse.

John Wintermute's 83-yard kickoff return for a touchdown gave the Gophers a brief 20–16 lead. But Simpson single-handedly took over the game with a series of clock-controlling dashes that made "Simpson Run" the official announcement on the public-address system.

Simpson finished with 365 yards total—236 rushing and 57 receiving on six catches, as well as three kickoff returns for 72 yards. He scored four touchdowns and accounted for 24 of USC's points in a 29–20 victory. Simpson ran eight straight times for his final score.

"No, I wasn't tired," he told reporters afterward. "Before the game we didn't think we could run wide because of Minnesota's outstanding defensive ends. But they were coming in hard, hitting our fullback head-to-head, and leaving the outside for me to run."

Simpson said he had no trouble running on the wet turf.

"My problem early in the game was that I was stuttering and hesitating too much," he said. "They were putting it to me, and instead of me trying to run over them I was sidestepping. I got hit a couple times on the ball and fumbled. This was my fault because I didn't have the ball covered."

Warmath lauded his team's effort against the No. 1 team in the country just as Gophers defenders lavished praise on the nation's most powerful and elusive runner.

"He is a great player and ran as well as anybody I've ever faced," said Stein, an All-American defensive end. "When he got past the linebackers, he'd turn it on."

The Gophers slipped a spot in the national polls to No. 16. They stumbled the next week against Nebraska, losing 17–14 to the Cornhuskers and falling out of the national rankings. They never regained their standing in 1968 and finished 6–4.

The Trojans, meanwhile, finished 9–1–1 and ranked No. 4 after losing 27–16 in the Rose Bowl to eventual national champion Ohio State.

Simpson won the Heisman Trophy and was the No. 1 overall pick in the 1969 NFL draft by the Buffalo Bills. In 1973 he became the first NFL player to eclipse 2,000 rushing yards in a season and finished his 11-year Hall of Fame career with San Francisco in 1979.

Simpson's fame grew exponentially after football. He transcended race as one of the most visible African American corporate pitchmen, actors, and broadcasters of the 1970s, '80s, and '90s before his name became synonymous with one of the most notorious crimes of the 20th century.

Simpson was charged with the June 1994 murders of his ex-wife Nicole Brown Simpson and her acquaintance Ron Goldman. He was acquitted the following year after a sensational trial that captivated the country, although Simpson became a pariah who never reclaimed his revered stature in sports or pop culture.

In 2008 Simpson was convicted for orchestrating an armed robbery in Las Vegas that schemed to reclaim sports memorabilia he had sold or auctioned during his cultural exile.

He is serving his 33-year prison sentence at Lovelock Correctional Center in Nevada. Simpson is eligible for parole in October 2017—five decades after his dominant performance at Memorial Stadium.

A day after Simpson ran wild in Minnesota, longtime *Minneapolis Tribune* columnist Dick Cullum lavished praise on the young football star for his otherworldly talents on the field and his composure off it—words that ring eerily prescient almost 50 years later.

"This is a young man of genuine, not feigned modesty. Strong character and keen intelligence are shown in every word he utters," Cullum wrote September 23, 1968. "He has strength of mind and urges to excel, which drives him to draw everything out of his physical gifts.

"O.J. will be an important person long after he has finished with football."

43 Bert Baston

Albert Preston Baston was the first Gophers player to receive a forward pass as the game evolved early in the 20th century. The was end also the school's first two-time All-American, forming a triple-threat backfield with quarterback Pudge Wyman and running back Bernie Bierman.

Baston's true heroism emerged on the World War I battlefield when he earned the Navy Cross for valor as a wounded Marine lieutenant leading a platoon in France.

The dynamic Gophers averaged 50 points per game in racking up a 12–1–1 record during Baston's junior and senior seasons in 1915 and '16. Their only loss was a 14–9 defeat to Illinois.

A year after graduating from Minnesota, the St. Louis Park native enlisted in the U.S. Marine Corps and served in the 17th Company. During the Battle of Belleau Wood on June 6, 1918, as the Allies counterattacked advancing German forces in the forests of eastern France, Baston was shot in both legs.

He suffered one wound "big enough to stick a broom handle through," his family told the St. Louis Park Historical Society.

The Navy Cross, the second-highest military decoration for valor behind the Medal of Honor, was presented to Baston. His official citation read:

"The Navy Cross is presented to Albert P. Baston, First Lieutenant, U.S. Marine Corps, for extraordinary heroism while serving with the 5th Regiment (Marines), 2d Division, A.E.F. in action near Château-Thierry, France.

"Although shot in both legs while leading his platoon through the woods at Hill 142, Lt. Baston refused treatment until he had personally assured himself that every man in his platoon was under cover and in good firing position."

Baston was hospitalized almost a year recovering from his wounds. He operated a bakery in Detroit before returning to Minneapolis in 1920 to open a Chevrolet dealership.

In 1932, Bierman, his former teammate, hired him to coach ends for the Gophers, a position he held for 18 years as the duo guided Minnesota to five national championships.

Baston was called back into service during World War II, this time as a Marine colonel. He commanded a battalion in the European and North African theaters that repaired Jeeps and rocket launchers, according to the St. Louis Park Historical Society.

He was indicted into the College Football Hall of Fame in 1954 and died in St. Cloud, Minnesota, in 1979.

44 Glen Mason

Glen Mason's 10-year run at Minnesota helped restore swagger in Dinkytown as the program's 24th football coach led the Gophers to seven bowl appearances, reintroducing a power running game while producing several NFL players.

There were stirring upsets of Penn State and Michigan on the road and three straight bowl victories from 2002 to '04. Mason elevated the Gophers to No. 13 nationally in 1999, their highest ranking in 37 years. And there were epic collapses, including a 24-point lead in the fourth quarter of a 44–41 overtime loss to Texas Tech in the 2006 Insight Bowl that led to Mason's firing.

Mason went 64–57 and launched a run of seven bowl appearances in eight years. But he was only 32–48 in the Big Ten. He produced the first eight-win season in 32 years in 1999 but started 0–5 in the Big Ten in 2006.

Mason groused about playing in the soulless Metrodome and struggled to build a loyal fan base and recruit competitively. He championed an open-air campus stadium but was let go only months after the Minnesota legislature approved funding to help build TCF Bank Stadium.

In other words, his reign was complicated.

Mason was hired in 1996 to succeed Jim Wacker, whose tenure spanned five straight losing seasons. A Woody Hayes protégé as an Ohio State player in the late 1960s, Mason was head coach at Kent State and Kansas. He interviewed for the Minnesota job in 1991 to succeed John Gutekunst but withdrew after meeting with the search committee.

Mason's third season in Minnesota was his breakout. The Gophers upset No. 2 Penn State in Happy Valley on a Dan

Nystrom field goal as time expired. He was named Big Ten coach of the year and signed a seven-year, $9.2 million contract, doubling his salary to average more than $1 million per year.

In January 2001, Mason interviewed with Ohio State after coach Jon Cooper was fired. He was one of three finalists for the job that would go to Jim Tressel.

In 2003, the Gophers went 10–3 and defeated Oregon 31–30 in the Sun Bowl, capping Mason's finest season in Minnesota. A year later Marion Barber III and Laurence Maroney became the first running-back tandem to eclipse 1,000 yards rushing in consecutive seasons.

Mason coached 11 All-Americans and also had four national award winners, including Matt Spaeth, the 2006 John Mackey Award recipient, and Greg Eslinger, the 2005 Outland Award beneficiary.

45 Thunder and Lightning

The Gophers' greatest running-back tandem ever was inseparable off the field, though Marion Barber III and Laurence Maroney were hardly two peas in a pod.

Barber was an unheralded prospect and legacy from the lily-white Minneapolis suburb of Wayzata, where his father, former Gopher Marion Barber Jr., had settled after a seven-year NFL career with the New York Jets. Maroney was a blue-chip recruit from the inner city of St. Louis who rose above his downtrodden high school team.

Together they made history as the first teammates to rush for more than 1,000 yards apiece in consecutive seasons.

Barber (1,196 and 1,269 yards) and Maroney (1,121 and 1,348 yards) combined for 4,934 yards and 50 rushing touchdowns in 2003 and '04.

Barber was nicknamed the "walking muscle" for his brute strength, while Maroney was known as the "fastest kid on the block." Competition brought out the best in both unselfish backs, who completely bought in to coach Glen Mason's rotation to Minnesota's benefit.

The Gophers went 17–8 those two seasons and extended their bowl winning streak to a team-record three games.

"It's never a rivalry between us," Maroney said at the time. "I'm never a person to get jealous and go to the coaches to say that Marion's getting more carries than me or Marion's got more yards than me. There's no one bigger than the team. You can't win by yourself. All we want is a win. When we win, we're happy."

Barber practically finished Maroney's sentences.

"I don't see it as a competition between us," he said. "I see it as both of us bettering ourselves. I never feel like I need to do something to look better than the next person. We're just looking to get that 'W' at the end. There's a bunch of pluses between us; never anything negative."

Maroney was the 2003 Big Ten Freshman of the Year and a 2006 first-round (21st overall) pick of the New England Patriots. He rushed for 2,430 yards in four seasons for the Pats and played in Super Bowl XLII, when the Giants upset undefeated New England.

Barber was the 2004 Music City Bowl MVP before being drafted in the fourth round (109th) by the Dallas Cowboys. He played six seasons with the Cowboys and was a 2007 Pro Bowler before finishing his career in 2011 with the Chicago Bears.

46 Dan Nystrom

Dan Nystrom was the most productive kicker in Minnesota history, but the success of his four-year career can be distilled into one shining moment at Happy Valley in 1999.

The image of Nystrom in his white No. 28 road jersey, leaping into the air with both arms outstretched in triumph after vanquishing heavily favored Penn State with a 32-yard game-winning field goal, was seared into the memories of Gophers fans starving for catharsis.

There was third-year coach Glen Mason, in shirtsleeves and tie, leaping into the arms of an assistant coach as the Gophers rushed the field at Beaver Stadium. And athletic director Mark Dienhardt anchored in place, eliminating all dread before he could bring himself to celebrate.

"I wanted to make sure there weren't any flags," he would say.

Minnesota's improbable 23–21 victory was a watershed for a dead program. It propelled the Gophers to an 8–3 record and their first winning season since 1990. The eight wins and 4–0 Big Ten road record were benchmarks not reached in 38 years.

All this was punctuated by a freshman kicker who was three months shy of his 19th birthday when he stared down one of the best teams in the country and emerged from the Nittany Lions' den as the day's unlikely hero.

On November 6, 1999, the Gophers came to Penn State as two-touchdown underdogs to No. 2–ranked Penn State. They were 0–4 against the Nittany Lions. Two years earlier Minnesota led 15–10 with five minutes remaining, possession, and Penn State out of timeouts.

However, running back Thomas Hamner fumbled, and Penn State rallied for a 16–15 win.

The Gophers opened the 1999 season 4–0 but lost three of four heading to Happy Valley. They had not defeated a top-five opponent since upsetting Michigan in 1986. Moreover, they had only won four of 33 Big Ten road games.

Early in the game, Nystrom missed his first extra point of the season. Penn State led 17–9 in the third quarter but the Gophers rallied for a pair of scores.

Billy Cockerham hit Hamner—the goat of 1997—for a 49-yard touchdown pass and a 21–20 lead. They failed on the two-point conversion. Penn State added a late field goal for a 23–21 lead.

The Gophers caught a break on their final drive, a break they had coming for the better part of a decade. On fourth-and-6 from the Nittany Lions' 40, Cockerham heaved a desperation pass that bounced off Ron Johnson's chest. Alert receiver Arland Bruce snatched the ball before it fell to the turf, extending the drive.

Three plays and one timeout later, Nystrom was summoned for a 32-yarder with four seconds remaining.

With Beaver Stadium in a fury, Nystrom calmly shrugged off Penn State coach Joe Paterno's timeout to ice him and buried the kick.

Field-goal execution relies on synchronized timing among snapper, holder, and kicker. Here, imperfection led to an improbable finish.

Snapper Derek Rackley's low snap forced holder Ryan Rindels to take an extra beat putting the ball down and spinning the laces out for Nystrom.

That split-second delay allowed All-American linebacker and kick-blocking expert LaVar Arrington to descend from the apex of his leap and miss Nystrom's attempt.

"I wanted a chance to make it up to my team by kicking the [winning] field goal," Nystrom said. "I was nervous. You're always nervous in that situation. But I think I was prepared."

Although the Gophers lost 24–20 to Oregon in the Sun Bowl, the program had been resurrected, and Nystrom was the pied piper of that resurgence.

His 71 field goals from 1999 through 2002 are 14 more than the 57 Chip Lohmiller bagged in the late 1980s. And he holds the top two rankings for field goals in a season—25 and 20, respectively, in 2000 and 2002.

Kicking was not Nystrom's only talent. The New Hope, Minnesota, native was a member of the Metropolitan Boys' Choir. He sang as a youngster for President George Bush and later in college for President George W. Bush.

He also performed regularly with teammate Ben Utecht, an accomplished singer in his own right.

"One of the best things is to go somewhere to sing with Ben, have our names introduced as Gopher football players and everyone sits back and thinks, 'Oh, this is probably going to be terrible,' and afterward for everyone to be pretty impressed with how we sang and ask us to come back," Nystrom recalled.

47 Rhys Lloyd

Rhys Lloyd's mother once joked that the kicker was so laid-back he could fall over. But there was nothing carefree about his journey from English soccer prodigy to clutch college kicker.

Lloyd is remembered for his grace under pressure and burying a pair of game-winning kicks with one second remaining in 2003, vanquishing rival Wisconsin at the Metrodome to reclaim Paul Bunyan's Axe and later clinching a wild Sun Bowl victory over Oregon.

Soccer was Lloyd's first love. His father, Bryn, was a professional player in the United Kingdom. Lloyd, at 15, earned a spot on Chelsea's prestigious youth professional team.

Bryn spent two summers as a soccer instructor in Minnesota before landing a full-time gig and moving his family to Apple Valley, a St. Paul suburb. Rhys (pronounced REES) joined Eastview High's soccer team but his strong leg caught the eye of the football coach.

The Gophers recruited Lloyd; however, his failure to take the ACT exam forced him to play two years at Rochester Community College. Faced with a 40-yarder to win the 2002 state championship against St. Cloud, Lloyd missed the kick.

In 2003, Lloyd was academically cleared to play for Minnesota and beat out two competitors during the preseason. The 220-pound natural sidewinder immediately impressed by routinely booming 60-yard field goals in practice and stymieing opponents with touchbacks.

In the season's penultimate game, the Gophers and Badgers were tied at 34 when Minnesota drove into Wisconsin territory and called timeout with one tick left, setting Lloyd up for a 35-yard attempt.

"I said the snap's going to be good. The hold is going to be good. The protection is going to be good. And the kick is going to be good," coach Glen Mason said postgame. "Now don't forget to go get the Axe."

Wisconsin called a timeout to ice Lloyd, who walked to the sideline with a smile as Mason tried to calm his unflappable kicker.

"He was just saying, if you make this, all the pizza you can eat," Lloyd said. "I was like, fair enough."

Lloyd converted, and the Gophers stormed Wisconsin's bench to seize the rivalry trophy.

Six weeks later, the Gophers put their fate on Lloyd's right leg again at the Sun Bowl in El Paso, Texas.

Minnesota and Oregon traded offensive haymakers for 59-plus minutes as Oregon clung to a 30–28 lead in another down-to-the-wire thriller.

The outcome hinged on Lloyd's 42-yard attempt. He nailed the historic kick as time expired. It was the first time Minnesota had won bowl games in consecutive years and the victory secured its first 10-win season in 98 years.

"It was one of the sweetest kicks I've hit all year," Lloyd said.

The Vikings signed Lloyd as a kickoff specialist in 2010 but he was cut during training camp. He had spent three years with the Carolina Panthers and led the NFL in touchbacks in 2008.

48 Eric Decker

The most prolific wide receiver in Gophers history never received a sniff from Division I or II programs coming out of Rocori High in tiny Cold Spring, Minnesota. Those kinds of skilled players just didn't come from central Minnesota.

However, in the summer of 2006, with Eric Decker planning to attend in-state Division III St. John's University, he crashed a recruiting camp at Minnesota and spent the afternoon burning the state's best cornerbacks.

Then-coach Glen Mason took notice, offering Decker a scholarship on the spot.

"You start thinking, 'What are we seeing in this guy that other people don't?'" Mason, now an analyst for the Big Ten Network, told the *New York Times*.

John Gagliardi, the longtime coach at St. John's, called Mason the next day.

"Gosh darnit," Gagliardi said, according to the *Times*. "You found him."

Despite several injuries, Decker caught 227 passes for 3,119 yards in four seasons at Minnesota, mostly as the featured offensive weapon with quarterback Adam Weber. As a senior, Decker was named a National Football Foundation Scholar-Athlete as one of the country's top student-athletes.

The two-sport star played center field for the Gophers baseball team and was drafted by the hometown Minnesota Twins in the 27th round of the 2009 MLB draft.

However, Decker's Velcro hands made football his destiny. Originally drafted in the third round by the Denver Broncos in

2010, Decker became a favorite target for quarterback Peyton Manning.

He signed with the New York Jets as a free agent in 2014. The following season Decker scored 12 touchdowns to go with 1,027 yards—teaming with Brandon Marshall (14 touchdowns) to break the NFL record for most touchdowns by a receiving tandem. The previous record was held by the Vikings' Cris Carter and Randy Moss.

Off the field, Decker became a reality TV star after marrying country-music singer Jessie James.

49 Adam Weber

Minnesota's all-time leading passer shrugs off the school records he shattered during a five-year career in which he overcame skepticism, injuries, and a parade of offensive coordinators.

No quarterback completed more passes (909) or threw for more yards (10,917) and touchdowns (72) than Adam Weber, one of just five Big Ten signal-callers to eclipse 10,000 yards.

He ended his Gophers tenure in 2010 ranked third in Big Ten history behind former Purdue quarterbacks Curtis Painter (11,163) and Drew Brees (11,792).

"To get into that elite group of guys in the Big Ten, where there have been a lot of great quarterbacks, means a lot and goes to show that as a team and as a player we were able to accomplish a lot of great things even though our record may not show that," Weber said.

Weber grew up in suburban Shoreview, Minnesota. His father, Bob, was a Gophers special teams player from 1974 to '77.

He won the starting job in 2007 as a redshirt freshman and never looked back.

Weber started a record 50 games at Minnesota and passed for 250 yards or more 14 times. He also had six 300-yard passing games and one 400-yarder. Weber's 258 completions and 24 touchdowns in 2007 are school records as well.

Weber teamed with All-American wide receiver Eric Decker to become Minnesota's most prolific quarterback-receiver tandem.

Gophers Athletic Directors

Men	Years
Mark Coyle	2016 to present
Beth Goetz (interim)	2015 to '16
Norwood Teague	2012 to '15
Joel Maturi	2002 to '12
Tom Moe	1999 to 2002
Mark Dienhart	1995 to '99
McKinley Boston	1992 to '95
Dan Meinert (interim)	1991 to '92
Rick Bay	1989 to '91
Holger Christiansen (interim)	1988 to '89
Paul Giel	1971 to '88
Marshall J. Ryman	1963 to '71
Ike J. Armstrong	1950 to '63
Frank G. McCormick	1945 to '50
Lou Keller	1941 to '45
Frank McCormick	1932 to '41
H.O. Crisler	1930 to '32
Fred Leuhring	1922 to '30

Women	Years
Chris Voelz	1988 to 2002
Merrily Dean Baker	1982 to '88
M. Catherine Mathison (interim)	1981 to '82
Vivian M. Barfield	1976 to '81
Belmar Gunderson	1974 to '76

"The records here at the U, I take a lot of pride in those," he said. "But a lot of those have come over time. I've been very fortunate to have started four years. With that many games those records will add up."

He is the only three-time captain in program history.

In 2008, despite surgery to repair a torn meniscus, Weber returned five days later and led Minnesota to an emotional 27–20 victory at Illinois that made the Gophers bowl eligible for the first time under second-year coach Tim Brewster.

Weber led the Gophers to a pair of Insight Bowls in Phoenix but lost both games.

In his final game, Weber was carried off the field after leading the Gophers to a game-winning, fourth-quarter drive that vanquished No. 24 Iowa, giving him a chance to clutch the Floyd of Rosedale trophy in his swan song.

Weber was also the winning quarterback in Minnesota's 2009 victory over Air Force that christened TCF Bank Stadium.

"What I'll cherish the most were those moments inside games when you realize how lucky you are to look around and see 70,000 people and realize you're playing football for the Gophers," he recalled. "It's been an amazing ride."

Weber signed with the Denver Broncos as an undrafted free agent in 2011. He also had brief stints with the Tampa Bay Buccaneers and the CFL's Saskatchewan Roughriders.

In 2015, he rejoined the Gophers as an assistant offensive coach. Weber aspires to be a college head coach.

"That is my goal," he said. "I love the sport, I love the idea of leadership, of being a leader of a program and of being the face of a program, things like that. Being able to mold it the way you want to."

50 Bud Wilkinson

He was a guard-turned-quarterback and three-time national champion Gophers football star in the 1930s when he wasn't earning All-America honors as their hockey goalie.

Became a coaching legend for the Oklahoma Sooners and later Keith Jackson's sidekick on college football telecasts.

Counseled two presidents.

The one thing Charles "Bud" Wilkinson never did was become Gophers head football coach, despite mid-1950s headlines that touted him as Minnesota's unanimous choice to succeed Bernie Bierman and a myth that never died.

"No one ever asked me to coach there," Wilkinson told the St. Paul *Pioneer Press* in 1978. "I have no regrets, none at all. Life is life."

What a life.

Born in Minneapolis, Wilkinson graduated in 1933 from Shattuck Military Academy. He thrived as a guard on the undefeated 1934 and 1935 Gophers before switching to quarterback at Bierman's request in 1936 and carried the winning streak all the way to a third straight national title.

Besides hockey, Wilkinson also found time and energy to letter in golf.

"I was very average in both," he recalled. "I'm not positive I could have beaten Patty Berg in golf but maybe. She grew up five houses from me in south Minneapolis and she was damn good."

A founding member of the LPGA Tour, Berg won 15 major titles, most ever by a female golfer.

Wilkinson served as an assistant coach for Bierman, but instead of succeeding the Minnesota legend he was hired by Oklahoma and built a legacy there.

Wilkinson's Sooners won 13 straight conference championships, three national titles, four Orange Bowls, two Sugar Bowls,
and 47 straight games from 1953 to '57—the longest winning
streak in Division I football.

He retired in 1963 as the winningest coach in college football
with a record of 145–29–4.

President Kennedy tapped Wilkinson in 1961 to serve as the
director of the Council on Physical Fitness, and he also served as a
special consultant for President Nixon.

After an unsuccessful bid for the U.S. Senate in 1964,
Wilkinson joined ABC Sports and worked as a color analyst for
12 seasons on the network's top-rated college football broadcasts.

Wilkinson coached the NFL's St. Louis Cardinals for two
seasons in 1978 and '79.

51 P.J. Fleck

P.J. Fleck crushed his introductory news conference with verbal
revelry and theatrical flourish as predictable as Minnesota perma-
frost, microphone not included.

Turned out amplification was wholly unnecessary as Fleck
thundered away with lyrical truisms while chopping his hands back
and forth across the packed room of reporters and boosters like a
union delegate whipping votes.

The 36-year-old upstart was hired January 6, 2017, to salvage a
football program mired in crisis and an administration under siege
in the wake of a sexual assault investigation that resulted in the
suspension of 10 players and led to the firing of head coach Tracy
Claeys.

In January 2017, Gophers athletic director Mark Coyle (right) made P.J. Fleck, 36, the Big Ten's youngest coach and second-youngest FBS head coach. Fleck transformed a 1–11 Western Michigan team into a 13–1 Mid-American Conference powerhouse and Cotton Bowl participant in 2016. AP Images

Fleck radiated energy and confidence as he referenced Big Ten championships, Rose Bowls, and national titles—feats not accomplished in Minnesota for a half century. His head coaching journey started in 2013 at Western Michigan, where he transformed a 1–11 team to a 13–1 Mid-American Conference powerhouse and Cotton Bowl participant.

Healing, growing, and winning were his Gopher goals, commitment and passion his pledges, collectivism his answer—all delivered with full-throated gusto.

He vowed his players would wear collared shirts, sit in the front row of class, and serve the community. *Elite* was the introductory buzzword. Fleck said it 13 times from the podium.

"I'm the solution guy," Fleck told players in his initial meeting. "I'm going to find a solution to make your life elite—your personal life, your social life, your spiritual life, your academic life. Our players will have incredible, elite actions every single day."

He meshed his "Row the Boat" mantra from Western Michigan with the aquatic origins of "Ski-U-Mah," Minnesota's cheer and one of the state's most endearing pieces of folklore.

"There's a canoe, which is a boat," Fleck explained. "You got a paddle, which is an oar, and we've got the Northern Star here, which is our compass. I am not here to change tradition. What I am here to do is change a culture."

With less than a month until national signing day, Fleck went to work salvaging his 2017 recruiting class. Nine players he had recruited to Western Michigan flipped their commitments to Minnesota.

Fleck also brought with him offensive coordinator Kirk Ciarrocca from Western Michigan, which averaged 41.6 points per game and scored 75 touchdowns in 2016. And he hired Robb Smith from Arkansas as his defensive coordinator.

Philip John Fleck became the Big Ten's youngest coach and second-youngest FBS head coach to Memphis' Mike Norvell. He was given a five-year, $18 million contract following a lightning-fast search by athletic director Mark Coyle.

Shortly after firing Claeys on January 3, Coyle was scorned by Claeys sympathizers. Aw-shucks Jerry Kill even vowed never to set foot into TCF Bank Stadium again because his close friend and successor was purged in a cultural housecleaning.

Coyle pivoted quickly from the fallout. He identified Fleck as the country's hottest coaching prospect and reeled him in with clinical precision. Within 48 hours, a deal had been struck and Fleck was flying to Minnesota.

"The very first thing that stood out to me was his authentic energy and passion; he's a leader," Coyle said of Fleck. "I talked this week about a vision that we wanted to compete at the highest level with great integrity and character academically, athletically, and socially. I feel like his teams have done that."

Coyle also stiff-armed former Louisiana State coach Les Miles, who flew to Minnesota from Baton Rouge to chase a Big Ten job. Miles won the 2007 national championship and a pair of SEC championships with Louisiana State but was fired in September 2016 after the Tigers' uninspiring 2–2 start.

Minnesota wasn't interested.

"I don't talk about specific candidates," Coyle said about Miles' interest. "It's an attractive job, and we did receive a lot of phone calls from different candidates. I'm always amazed when you do these searches the people that reach out and contact you about these opportunities. We felt prepared about the search and are excited about the outcome."

Fleck and Coyle succeeded in changing the football-program narrative. However, winter bona fides do not guarantee autumn success.

Fleck inherited a 2016 team that won nine games for the first time in 13 years and upset Washington State 17–12 in the Holiday

Bowl. But his greatest challenge was to heal a locker room and fan base fractured by scandal.

A Title IX investigation tainted 10 players suspended for varying levels of suspected involvement in an alleged sexual assault in September 2016. The Hennepin County attorney's office twice declined to press charges based on insufficient evidence.

Coyle was criticized for failing to communicate his reasoning for the suspensions before the Holiday Bowl when grilled by players, whose unfulfilled demands for clarity sowed mistrust and inflamed passions, spawning a brief boycott. Claeys and most of his staff were fired, in part, for their support of the player-led boycott over Coyle's suspensions.

"We talked about it and we moved on," Fleck said of his initial players meeting. "But I did tell them the same thing...that my focus is on them now, not them back when, it's them now. That's why I'm here. I'm a solution-driven guy, and that's what I want to continue to do as we move forward through Gopher football.

"The first thing I told them was very simple," he added. "I said, 'Guys. You did not pick me. But I picked you.'"

Linebacker Carter Coughlin, one of the most vocal players on the team about Claeys' firing, told the St. Paul *Pioneer Press* he was "very excited" to play for Fleck and that he "absolutely does" seem like someone he wanted to play for.

Coughlin also tweeted: "We can't change what has happened because it's in the past. We can only focus on the future. I'm excited to be led by Coach Fleck! Ski-U-Mah!"

Fleck played wide receiver at Northern Illinois and was named all-MAC during his senior season in 2003. Undrafted, he signed with the San Francisco 49ers and spent two years on the roster and returned one punt for 10 yards in his only NFL game in 2004.

He spent one season as a graduate assistant for Jim Tressel at Ohio State and returned to coach wide receivers at Northern

Illinois, where he worked two seasons under Kill before Kill left for Minnesota in 2010. Fleck also coached receivers at Rutgers (2010–11) and the Tampa Bay Buccaneers (2012) before taking over Western Michigan.

"I know there's going to be a lot of challenges ahead," Fleck said. "I know there's going to be people that fit with the change, that don't fit with the change, that like the change, that don't like the change.

"Everybody wants change until you get change. Well, I got news for everybody. Change has arrived!"

52 Pug Lund

Pugnacious aptly summarized Francis Lund's battering-ram running style, but it also represented a state of mind for the hard-nosed halfback, whose football career started and stopped on his terms.

Lund became an anomaly long before the recruiting wars commenced between border rivals Minnesota and Wisconsin. The Rice Lake, Wisconsin, native eschewed overtures in 1930 from his home-state Badgers and crossed over to sell himself to the hated Gophers.

"I just decided I wanted to go to Minnesota because during my sports-loving years in high school the legend of Bronko Nagurski and Biggie Munn had been built up to tremendous heights in my mind," Lund told the *Minneapolis Tribune* in 1955.

"I was never certain that I could play football. In fact, I remember telling my high school coach that I probably won't make it, but I told him that I would at least go out for the team."

"Pug" stuck as a nickname after a reporter said during a team photo shoot, "Francis Lund, that's a helluva name for a football player." Teammate Al Pappas overheard the exchange and said, 'Call him Pug.'

"The picture came out with my name as Pug and that was it," Lund said.

Lund played three years for Minnesota, earning All-America honors in 1933 and '34, when he was also named Big Ten Most Valuable Player. He captained the 1934 national championship team, the first under coach Bernie Bierman.

Lund averaged almost six yards per carry that season. Against Pittsburgh he took a lateral and threw the game-winning touchdown pass to Robert Tenner late in the fourth quarter of a 13–7 victory, preserving Minnesota's undefeated season.

Underclassmen rarely played during that era, let alone starred. However, when quarterback Myron Uhl was hospitalized with pneumonia and almost died early in the 1932 season, Lund paired with Jerry Manders to form a potent one-two backfield punch in Minnesota's single-wing offense.

Lund played more than 50 minutes as a two-way sophomore. He rushed for 813 yards in eight games, passed for 407 and combined for seven touchdowns for more than 1,220 yards of total offense.

Lund was also a three-year letter winner in track and field at Minnesota.

"Lund was our spark plug," Bierman said. "He was battered and broken up; teeth knocked out; finger amputated and thumb broken, and through all that he carried on."

A month before the start of 1934 fall practice, Lund had the pinkie finger of his left hand amputated after it was mangled during spring drills.

"The finger had stiffened so it stood straight out, so I had it cut off," he recalled to the St. Paul *Pioneer Press* in 1961.

Rejecting several offers to play pro football, Lund settled into a career selling insurance for New England Mutual Life in Minneapolis.

He was inducted into the College Football Hall of Fame in 1958 and was feted alongside President Eisenhower, who played football as an undergraduate at West Point and received the National Football Foundation's first gold-medal award during his second term in the White House.

"After 24 years or so a person gets a singular pleasure from something such as this," said Lund, who died in 1994 at age 81.

53 Mr. Patriot

Gino Cappelletti is the all-time leading scorer for the defunct American Football League. How fitting.

One of the original Patriots started the clock on the renegade league by kicking off against the Denver Broncos in the AFL's inaugural game September 9, 1960, at Boston's Nickerson Field. Cappelletti also scored the first points in league history with a 35-yard field goal in the Patriots' 13–10 loss.

Cappelletti played 10 seasons with the Patriots before the 1970 AFL–NFL merger and retired as the club's all-time leading scorer with 1,130 points, surpassed only by the great Adam Vinatieri's 1,158.

Not bad for an undersized kid from tiny Keewatin, Minnesota, to whom the Gophers struggled to assign a position when he arrived in 1952.

In Minnesota, Cappelletti had the bad timing of playing quarterback in a single-wing formation that flowed from All-American

Gophers NFL First-Round Draft Picks

Player	Team	Year
Laurence Maroney	New England Patriots	2006
Willie Middlebrooks	Denver Broncos	2001
Darrell Thompson	Green Bay Packers	1990
Brian Williams	New York Giants	1989
John Williams	Baltimore Colts	1968
Gale Gillingham	Green Bay Packers	1966
Carl Eller	Minnesota Vikings	1964
Bud Grant	Philadelphia Eagles	1950
Clayton Tonnemaker	Green Bay Packers	1950
Leo Nomellini	San Francisco 49ers	1950
Dick Wildung	Green Bay Packers	1943
Urban Odson	Green Bay Packers	1942
George Franck	New York Giants	1941
Hal Van Every	Green Bay Packers	1940
Larry Buhler	Green Bay Packers	1939
Ed Widseth	New York Giants	1937

tailback Paul Giel. So he focused his efforts on kicking, a marginalized position in those days.

Coaches rarely attempted field goals. However, Cappelletti persuaded coach Wes Fesler to let him attempt a 43-yarder against Iowa on November 1, 1952, and he buried it, helping the Gophers secure a 17–7 victory at Memorial Stadium.

During the 1953 and '54 seasons Cappelletti converted a team-record 31 straight point-after attempts.

The following year, Cappelletti tried out for the Detroit Lions as a quarterback.

"They had Bobby Layne and Earl Morrall," he told the *Providence Journal* in 2012. "And I didn't have a big arm. I didn't get to stick around long enough to show them what I could do as a kicker."

The NFL remained elusive, however, as Cappelletti served in the Army, knocked around the Canadian Football League, and tended bar in Minneapolis before the summer of 1960.

A new professional football league was formed to compete against the NFL. Cappelletti was invited to the first training camp of the then-called Boston Patriots. He appeared in every one of Boston's AFL games from 1960 to '69 and spent more than 50 years with the franchise, bracketing stints as a popular radio analyst around a brief tenure as special teams coach (1979–81).

"Kicking was my pride and joy," he said. "I loved doing it."

54 Yell "Yay...Gophers!"

Minnesota played its first football game in 1892, the year the university marching band was founded.

The school already had its "Ski-U-Mah" cheer but needed a brassy fight song to stir fans after they moved in 1899 from the wooden chairs that surrounded a vacant field adjacent to the Armory to Greater Northrop Field, which had grandstands to seat 20,000.

"Hail! Minnesota" was a sentimental class song that surfaced in 1904 and included a cheeky reference to university president Cyrus Northrop's nickname, "Prexy," in the second verse. But the hymn was considered too stately for bringing football fans to their feet.

So, in 1909, The *Minneapolis Tribune* sponsored a songwriting contest and crowdsourced the answer a century before social media made the practice chic.

Among the judges were Minnesota Governor A.O. Eberhart; Northrop; the university's music professor, Carlyle M. Scott; marching band leader J.A. Sende; and Arthur Allen, president of the glee club.

Floyd M. Hutsell, organist, choir director, and voice teacher at First Methodist Episcopal Church in Minneapolis, won the $100 contest with his original title, "Minnesota, Hats Off to Thee!" His lyrics were printed in the November 21, 1909, *Tribune*:

Rah, rah,
Honor to our college Minnesota U.
Loyal to thy standards We'll never be untrue.
Underneath thy pennant Pulses beat with pride
And victory e'er shall be our aim O'er the nation wide,
(YELL)
Minnesota, hats off to thee!
To thy colors true we shall ever be,
Firm and strong, united are we.
Rah, rah, rah, for Ski-U-Mah,
Rah! Rah! Rah! Rah!
Rah for the U of M.

M-I-N-N-E-S-O-T-A!
Minnesota, Minnesota!
Yay, Gophers! Rah!

The university changed the title to "The Minnesota Rouser" after the *Tribune* divested itself of the copyright in 1929.

Hutsell was an eccentric by the buttoned-up standards of the Victorian Era.

Shortly after writing Minnesota's most popular fight song, he separated from his wife and left his two children to "set out upon a career as a glamorous and romantic," according to an April 1962 profile in *Minnesota Alumni* magazine.

Hutsell legally changed his name to Robert LaMar. He found work as a Vaudeville singer and was traveling companion to a young Eddie Cantor, who later became one of radio and film's first comedic stars.

LaMar played in Gilbert and Sullivan operettas on Broadway and toured the country directing and producing light opera. He married a pianist, Estelle Hill, and the couple settled in Medill, Oklahoma, in 1951 to teach music to church choirs.

By then, the "Rouser" was baked in as a cultural phenomenon in Dinkytown. It outlasted several competing fight songs, including "The Minnesota March," composed in 1928 by the "March King," John Philip Sousa, whose roiling "The Stars and Stripes Forever" and "Semper Fidelis" are the official marches of the United States and U.S. Marine Corps, respectively.

Gophers fans immediately took to the "Rouser," adopting a ritual by thrusting their fists in the air when Minnesota is spelled out and making a circular motion with their fists during the "Yay, Gophers!" yell.

LaMar died of a heart attack October 23, 1961, at age 79. His wife, Estelle, decided to have both of her late husband's names on his tombstone.

"LaMar" is engraved on one side of the granite slab, recognizing his life's work in show business. On the other side is "Hutsell," accompanied by the musical notes of what became "The Minnesota Rouser."

55 Paul Bunyan's Axe

College football's longest-running Division 1A rivalry is Minnesota–Wisconsin at 126 games and counting, plus two iconic prizes.

How fierce was this border battle after it started with a 63–0 Gophers victory in 1890? The 1906 game was canceled by President Theodore Roosevelt, who was horrified by injuries and deaths on football fields during the sport's bawdy early years.

In 1948 the Wisconsin "W" club created Paul Bunyan's Axe, a majestically sculpted award with the results of the team's clashes emblazoned on a six-foot-long handle and Minnesota's initial victory printed on the blade. The original axe handle ran out of room in 2000 and was replaced.

Its predecessor was less blunt in substance and more metaphorical in style.

To replicate the fervor of the Little Brown Jug, Dr. R.B. Fouch of Minneapolis designed the Slab of Bacon in 1930 to reward the winning team that would, ahem, bring home the bacon.

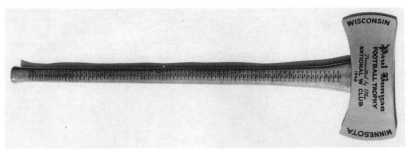

College football's longest-running Division 1A rivalry is Minnesota–Wisconsin at 126 games. In 1948 the Wisconsin "W" club created Paul Bunyan's Axe, a majestically sculpted award with the results of the team's clashes emblazoned on a six-foot-long handle and Minnesota's initial victory printed on the blade.
University of Minnesota Archives

The replica slice of meat was carved out of black walnut. Raised in the center was a football with the letter "M" in maroon and gold or "W" in cardinal and white, depending on which way the slab was hung. "M" up signified a Gophers win, "W" up for a Badgers victory.

In the early 1940s, the Slab disappeared from one of the stadiums during a postgame crowd-rush. Unseen for five decades, the Slab of Bacon suddenly reappeared in the summer of 1994 while workers cleaned out a storage room at Camp Randall Stadium.

Wisconsin officials assumed it had been missing since 1945. However, the scores of every Wisconsin–Minnesota game until 1970 were printed on the slab.

Somebody was still bringing home the bacon.

56 Floyd of Rosedale

Only 300 miles separate the universities of Minnesota and Iowa, a distance so close and a football rivalry so fierce that it has pitted players, coaches, students, and citizens against each other—and even governors.

All for the right to hug a 15½-inch-high, 21-inch-long bronze statue of a hog. The first game played for the Floyd of Rosedale in 1935 might have been the most bloodthirsty.

The undefeated Gophers (5–0) were the defending national champions and en route to winning their second consecutive title when they visited Iowa City.

The undefeated Hawkeyes (4–0–1) had just been reinstated following a slush-fund scandal. A year earlier, the Gophers knocked

Gophers Men's Basketball Scoring Leaders

Player	Seasons	Points
Mychal Thompson	1975–78	1,992
Willie Burton	1987–90	1,800
Randy Breuer	1980–83	1,777
Andre Hollins	2011–15	1,765
Sam Jacobson	1995–98	1,709
Kevin McHale	1977–80	1,704
Quincy Lewis	1996–99	1,614
Tommy Davis	1982–85	1,481
Trent Tucker	1979–82	1,445
Charley Mencel	1952–55	1,391

out Iowa's star player, Ozzie Simmons, with various injuries, infuriating Iowa fans and Governor Clyde Herring.

"If the officials stand for any rough tactics like Minnesota used last year, I'm sure the crowd won't," Herring bellowed to reporters.

This wasn't merely bulletin board material for the Gophers' locker room. Herring was practically inciting a riot.

To take the edge off, Minnesota Governor Floyd Olson reached out to Herring with a wager: "I will bet you a Minnesota prize hog against an Iowa prize hog that Minnesota wins."

The Gophers won 13–6. Nobody rioted. Olson collected his namesake hog from Herring, who had received it from Rosedale Farms in Fort Dodge, Iowa.

Olson commissioned an artist friend, Charles Brioschi of St. Paul, to create a bronze sculpture of the hog. An essay contest was held for rights to the real pig. A 14-year-old boy won it and later sold the hog to the University of Minnesota, which sold it to a breeder.

Turns out, the hog was the brother of Boy Blue from the Will Rogers movie *State Fair*.

Minnesota has won Floyd 42 times; Iowa, 38. There have been two ties in the series.

57 Trent Tucker

Imagine Trent Tucker's scoring production with a three-point line.

"It would have been a blast, and I think Darryl Mitchell and I could have been two of the top scoring guards in the nation," Tucker once said. "That sure changed the game when they put it in."

Alas, the sharp-shooting, 6'5" guard from Flint, Michigan, was finished three years before the NCAA evolved. Nonetheless, Tucker was among the most versatile players in Gophers history.

He and Mitchell combined on a backcourt under coach Jim Dutcher that helped propel Minnesota to the 1982 Big Ten championship, the year Tucker became an All-American as a senior.

"He shot threes before they were in the rules," said late Gophers radio broadcaster Ray Christensen.

Tucker finished his career ranked in the school's top eight in points (1,445), steals (164), field goals (631), and free throw percentage (.772). But it took him 22 years to finish school.

Drafted sixth overall in 1982 by the Knicks, Tucker played 11 seasons in the NBA with New York, San Antonio, and Chicago. He retired after winning the 1993 league title, playing 69 games at guard behind Bulls legend Michael Jordan.

Remembered as a selfless and productive winner, Tucker also earned a place in NBA infamy during a split-second play that changed how the league measures time.

Tucker was playing for the Knicks against the Bulls on January 15, 1990, at Madison Square Garden. With the score tied at 106 and one-tenth of a second remaining, New York guard Mark Jackson planned to inbound to Patrick Ewing for an alley-oop.

However, Jordan choked off Ewing's path to the basket. Desperate to get the ball in play, Jackson flung it to Tucker, who launched a wild three-pointer that went in before the buzzer went off. The Knicks won. The Bulls howled in protest.

"That was the first year the NBA added tenths of seconds to the [game] clock, so there were some kinks that needed to be worked out," Tucker recalled to GopherHole.com. "I guess what happened that game was a perfect storm of kinks. I just flung it up there and it went in and we won!"

Replays showed that the hometown clock operator did not start it until Tucker's shot was halfway to the basket. The following off-season the NBA crafted what became known as the "Trent Tucker Rule," stating that at least 0.3 seconds must remain on the clock for a player to complete a shot.

After retiring, Tucker returned to Minnesota and spent five years as radio color analyst for the Timberwolves. In the early 2000s, he threw his name in contention for a men's basketball assistant coaching position at his alma mater but was rejected.

He did not have a college degree.

"Without a degree, I knew the opportunity level was diminished," he told Gophersports.com. "I knew that if I ever went back, it would open doors to more opportunities. It most certainly has."

Tucker re-enrolled in 2004 and graduated two years later with an undergraduate degree in psychology and communications.

"My counselors at that time said, 'You know you can take your time, you don't have to rush through this,'" Tucker said during an interview with MinnPost.com. "I said, 'No, I don't want to take a class here and a class there, because it's going to take me 10 years to finish. If I'm going to finish, let's do it now.'"

Tucker went on to start his own clothing line, worked as an athletic director coordinator for Minneapolis Public Schools, and continues to help underprivileged kids and at-risk children stay in school through his namesake foundation.

His fondest memory at the U was clinching the Big Ten title by defeating Ohio State in a winner-take-all showdown in March 1982 at Williams Arena.

"We knew we had the potential to be a very good team and certainly our main goal was to win the Big Ten title," he said. "It's really an incredible feeling to progress through a program with a core group of guys and accomplish the goal we set out for ourselves. We had the pieces that season and it all came together."

58 Randy Breuer

"Big Man U" got even taller in 1979 when 7'3" Randy Breuer came to Dinkytown, following the monster footprints left by Mychal Thompson and Kevin McHale.

Breuer was a two-time All–Big Ten first-team center who led the Gophers in scoring, rebounding, and blocks three straight seasons from 1980 to '83, guiding Minnesota to the 1982 Big Ten title before playing 11 NBA seasons.

He grew up in Lake City along the Mississippi River in the southeastern corner of the state. The town's high school basketball coach was painting a house one summer day when he noticed a towering fifth-grader walking by with a group of friends.

Jerry Snyder climbed down the ladder, chased down the posse and asked Breuer, "Do you play basketball, young man?" according to the Minneapolis *Star Tribune*.

Breuer shrugged but Snyder, realizing he had a prodigy to mold, told the boy he would on the grade-school basketball court that winter.

"Best thing I ever did as a coach—getting down off that ladder," Snyder recalled.

Breuer's finest moment came in March 1982 when the Gophers clinched the Big Ten title—their first in a decade—against Ohio State at Williams Arena. He scored 32 points, including 10-of-10 from the free-throw line, while pulling down 12 rebounds.

Breuer scored the game-winning basket with 55 seconds remaining against Tennessee-Chattanooga in the second round of the NCAA tournament as the Gophers advanced to the Sweet 16.

"Randy played his best in big games," said former Gophers coach Jim Dutcher.

Minnesota has only won one Big Ten basketball championship since, in 1996–97, a title that was vacated because of an academic fraud scandal.

Drafted 18th overall in the 1983 NBA Draft by the Bucks, Breuer played in Milwaukee for six and a half seasons. He also played for the Timberwolves, Atlanta Hawks, and Sacramento Kings before retiring in 1994.

59 Jim Brewer

It only took one game for Jim Brewer to script his destiny.

"I ain't satisfied," Brewer wrote on a locker-room blackboard after scoring 20 points in his freshman debut for the Gophers in 1970.

He never was.

Freshmen were not allowed to play varsity ball in that bygone era so "Papa" had to wait until his sophomore season for his true breakout. Brewer led Minnesota in rebounding each of his three seasons and was a key cog of coach Bill Musselman's "Muscle Men."

Brewer captained the 1971–72 Big Ten champions as Williams Arena became the hottest sports venue in town. Cheers of "Brew!" rained down whenever he grabbed a rebound or blocked another shot.

Brewer's 6'9", 225-pound frame and hard-nosed style betrayed deft passing and ball-handling acumen that made him one of the country's best centers and hardest big men to defend.

"He does so many things that just don't show in the box scores," recalled Musselman. "How many big players can bring the ball up the court against the press the way Jim can? He was tremendous on the boards and took the center jumps for us."

Brewer averaged 13.5 points per game and his 1,009 career points rank 36th in school history. But his hallmarks were defense and a determination to win.

He is the only player in school history to be voted team MVP three straight years, and his resume flows from there:

First-team All–NCAA Tournament; Big Ten MVP; First-team All–Big Ten; All-American; the "M" award to the best student-athlete from each conference school.

After his sophomore season, Brewer was selected to represent the United States at the 1972 Munich Olympics, becoming the starting center on the team's silver medalists.

The Americans lost the gold-medal game to the Soviet Union, a match tainted by controversial officiating in the waning seconds that harkened their defeat.

Brewer and his teammates voted not to accept their medal.

"We hadn't earned the silver medal," Brewer said afterward. "We had won the gold medal. That's the medal we had earned, so why accept something else?"

Brewer was so revered by Minnesota his No. 52 was retired after he graduated in 1973.

The second overall pick that year by the Cavaliers, Brewer played nine NBA seasons with Cleveland, Detroit, Portland, and Los Angeles. He won the 1982 title with the Lakers before retiring.

60 Kevin McHale

Williams Arena was not only the building where Kevin McHale transformed himself into one of the Big Ten's all-time big men, it was his sanctuary.

As a player from 1976 to '80, he often visited after hours when nobody was there, and let the silence of the typically deafening venue wash over him as he shot basket after solitary basket.

"I spent many hours by myself in Williams Arena just shooting and loved it," he once said. "It is funny how you can get a peaceful feeling in a huge building like that all by yourself. There is nothing else like it. It feels like home."

McHale grew up in a mining family in Hibbing, Minnesota, and came to U of M in the fall of 1976. He was a two-time team MVP. The physical, confident power forward led the Gophers to the 1980 NIT finals and became the school's all-time leader in blocked shots (235) and finished second in rebounds (950) and sixth in career points (1,704).

However, success was fleeting.

The Gophers "won" 24 games McHale's freshman season—more than any previous team, including signature road victories over powerhouse Detroit and Marquette.

However, their record was unofficial because of NCAA sanctions levied against former coach Bill Musselman. Following a two-year postseason ban, Minnesota had a nice NIT run when McHale was a senior but never qualified for the NCAA tournament.

"Playing at the 'U' was the first time I ever went through losing in my life and it was frustrating," McHale told Gophersports.com. "But through that losing I learned a lot and I would do it all over again if I had to."

The Celtics drafted McHale third overall in 1980, and the seven-time NBA All-Star won three world championships in Boston during a 13-year career. He became the first Gopher to be inducted into the Basketball Hall of Fame in 1999, when he was vice president of basketball operations for the Minnesota Timberwolves.

He also coached the Houston Rockets from 2011 to '15. McHale is one of six members of Boston's 1985–86 championship team who have been an NBA head coach, including Larry Bird, Sam Vincent, Dennis Johnson, Danny Ainge, and Rick Carlisle.

"I have been lucky to have the opportunities I have had," he said. "I look at myself as a kid who came from a mining family up in northern Minnesota and was fortunate to be a student at the University of Minnesota. I have always strived to get better."

61 John Kundla

John Kundla was the original Zen master of NBA coaching before cigar-chomping Red Auerbach won multiple championships with the Boston Celtics and Phil Jackson crafted dynasties with the Chicago Bulls and L.A. Lakers.

He won a Big Ten championship as a Gophers forward in 1937, won six pro titles as Minneapolis' coach before the Lakers went Hollywood in the late '50s, and in 1963 integrated Minnesota's college basketball program during the height of the civil rights movement.

In July 2016, Kundla celebrated his greatest statistic. Surrounded by family and former players, the oldest living Hall of Famer in the four major North American professional sports raised his arms from the rests on his black wheelchair.

"I made it!" Kundla yelled as he celebrated his 100th birthday at his assisted-living apartment in northeast Minneapolis.

Bingo and fishing take up Kundla's leisure time but basketball still occupies his heart. He listens to Timberwolves games on the radio and marvels at the size and skill of LeBron James, according to a St. Paul *Pioneer Press* profile.

When James' Cleveland Cavaliers dethroned Golden State and Warriors coach Steve Kerr in the 2016 NBA Finals, Kundla retained his stature as the only NBA coach to have won championships in his first two seasons.

Kundla won the 1949 championship of the Basketball Association of America, the NBA's predecessor, and then led the Minneapolis Lakers to the inaugural NBA title in 1950. He became the first coach to win three straight NBA championships from 1952 to '54, christening the three-peat club later joined by Auerbach, Jackson, and Pat Riley.

Kundla was born July 3, 1916, outside Pittsburgh, the son of a coal miner and steel worker from Slovakia. When he was 5, Kundla moved to Minneapolis with his mother while his father stayed behind in Pennsylvania.

He was a three-year letter winner at Minnesota before breaking into coaching at St. Thomas University in St. Paul. Then World War II interrupted Kundla's career. After serving with the Navy in the South Pacific, he returned to Minnesota.

In 1947, the 31-year-old Kundla was hired to coach the Minneapolis Lakers, who reigned over the nascent NBA.

Over 12 seasons Kundla compiled a record of 466–319, including 70–38 in the postseason. He coached future Hall of Famers George Mikan, Vern Mikkelsen, Jim Pollard, Slater Martin, Elgin Baylor, and Clyde Lovellette.

"I had a great experience, but I thank the players," Kundla said. "I had good ballplayers and they adjusted real well and played as a team."

Kundla refused to follow the Lakers to Los Angeles, returning in 1959 to his alma mater, where he led the Gophers to a 110–105 mark in 10 seasons.

No black player had ever played at Minnesota before Kundla recruited Lou Hudson, Don Yates, and Archie Clark in 1963.

"The nasty letters I got...." Kundla recalled to the *Pioneer Press*.

Kundla exuded class and dignity on and off the court. He never screamed at his players or stomped his feet at officials. Okay— maybe once he spiked his bow tie in disgust.

"He had respect without having to demand it," said former Gophers player Paul Presthus. "He always treated people fairly. He's accomplished a lot, but he's a better person because of the way he treats people."

As his 100th birthday party wound down, Kundla's players shook hands with their former coach and paid their respects.

"See you next year," one of them said.

"Ski-U-Mah!" Kundla replied.

62 Flip Saunders

Phil "Flip" Saunders was half player, half coach with the Gophers in the mid-1970s before he fully formed his basketball legacy as one of the NBA's most respected head coaches of the new millennium.

Saunders, named Philip Daniel after his two grandfathers, only weighed 4 pounds, 14 ounces, when he was born in Cleveland. His mother, Kay, a former hairdresser, bestowed upon him the nickname "Flip," which would remain synonymous with Saunders his entire life.

He arrived at Minnesota in 1974 and finished his Gophers career ranking third in career free throw shooting (.809 percent) and ninth in assists (295). The point guard started all but two games in four seasons and helped lead Minnesota to 70 victories, including a 24–3 record as a senior in 1976-77.

"He was the one guy we felt we could not play without," Jim Dutcher, Saunders' coach at Minnesota, told the Minneapolis *Star Tribune*. "You couldn't get him out of the gym. He was just a very, very intelligent player. And as a coach, he was really good at relaying information to the players."

After graduation, Saunders was hired to coach Golden Valley Lutheran College in suburban Minneapolis, where he won 92 of 105 games over four seasons. He returned to Dinkytown in 1981 as an assistant to Dutcher, helping guide the Gophers to their last Big Ten championship in 1982.

A brief stint as an assistant at Tulsa preceded Saunders' jumping to the Continental Basketball Association, where he coached three teams, winning CBA titles with the La Crosse Catbirds in 1990 and '92.

In 1995, Kevin McHale, general manager of the Minnesota Timberwolves and Saunders' former Gophers teammate, hired him as an assistant in the front office.

Six months later, Bill Blair was fired as head coach and McHale tapped Saunders for the job he would hold for 10 seasons, shepherding the emergence of high school star Kevin Garnett into an NBA superstar. The Wolves made the playoffs for the first time in franchise history in 1996, the first of eight consecutive postseason appearances.

Saunders reached the Western Conference finals in 2004 before McHale fired him in January 2005.

After coaching the Detroit Pistons to three straight conference finals, Saunders coached the Washington Wizards before returning to Minnesota in 2013 as president of basketball operations.

A year later, he returned to the bench as Wolves head coach. He remained in both posts until he died of cancer in October 2015.

His career record of 427–392 (.521) in almost 11 full seasons in Minnesota remains the high-water mark for the franchise.

63 Dick Garmaker

The Gophers' greatest Big Ten shot maker became a four-time NBA All-Star with the Minneapolis Lakers. So how did Dick Garmaker fly under the radar of so many college basketball programs in the early 1950s?

Because those radars were completely out of Iron Range.

It took two conspicuous seasons at a junior college in his tiny hometown in northern Minnesota for the 6'3", 200-pound forward to be heard.

Garmaker averaged 30 points per game for Hibbing Junior College and led the school to within one point of the 1953 Junior College Championship when the scholarship offers started pouring in. It was an easy choice.

"I had other offers but I always knew Minnesota was for me. Coach [Ozzie] Cowles put the icing on the cake and I told him when he came to visit, that if he wanted me, I was coming," Garmaker recalled.

With only two years of eligibility remaining, Garmaker quickly established himself as a sharpshooter.

He led the Gophers in scoring in 1953–54 as Minnesota finished 17–5, setting a school record that still stands with 137 free throws in 183 attempts.

That drew interest from the hometown Lakers, who drafted Garmaker in the eighth round of the 1954 NBA Draft. However, he elected to play his senior season for the Gophers, another wise decision.

Garmaker led the Gophers again in scoring in 1954–55, averaging 24.2 points and 8.4 rebounds as a consensus All-American.

In just two seasons at Minnesota, Garmaker scored 1,008 points and still holds the school record for averaging 24.8 points per game in Big Ten play.

"The fact that I still hold that record after almost 60 years is quite unbelievable," Garmaker said. "It is very surprising to me that someone hasn't come along and broken that Big Ten record.

Garmaker played five NBA seasons for the Lakers and one more for the New York Knicks, retiring in 1961 having averaged 13.3 points per game.

The Gophers retired his No. 53 in 2011.

64 Jim McIntyre

Before Mychal Thompson, Kevin McHale, and Randy Breuer made Minnesota "Big Man U," there was big Jim McIntyre, a uniquely talented 6'10" center who toughened up the perennially passive Gophers in the late 1940s.

McIntyre was a consecutive All-American in 1948 and '49 and set Big Ten West Conference records for career points (1,223) and conference points (648).

McIntyre, who won two state championships at Patrick Henry High School in Minneapolis, is best remembered for throttling towering George Mikan, the future NBA Hall of Fame center who was playing for defending NIT champion DePaul in December 1945.

In a memorable comeback victory at the Field House, McIntyre held Mikan to two field goals and three free throws in a head-to-head matchup. Mikan's 11 points were a career low in college.

Gophers NBA First-Round Draft Picks

Player	Team	Year
Kris Humphries	Utah Jazz	2004
Joel Przybilla	Houston Rockets	2000
Quincy Lewis	Utah Jazz	1999
Sam Jacobson	Los Angeles Lakers	1998
John Thomas	New York Knicks	1997
Bobby Jackson	Seattle Supersonics	1997
Willie Burton	Miami Heat	1990
Randy Breuer	Milwaukee Bucks	1983
Trent Tucker	New York Knicks	1982
Kevin McHale	Boston Celtics	1980
Mychal Thompson	Portland Trail Blazers	1978
Ray Williams	New York Knicks	1977
Ron Behagen	Kansas City–Omaha Kings	1973
Jim Brewer	Cleveland Cavaliers	1973
Lou Hudson	St. Louis Hawks	1966
Dick Garmaker	Minneapolis Lakers	1955
Ed Kalafat	Minneapolis Lakers	1954
Whitey Skoog	Minneapolis Lakers	1951

The key to playing defense was footwork, according to then-coach Dave MacMillan, who required all his inside players to take folk-dancing lessons.

The leading rebounder on that 1948 team was Harry "Bud" Grant, of Superior, Wisconsin, who went on to become a Hall of Fame coach for the Minnesota Vikings.

"He was probably the major reason we had as good a team as we had," Grant said about McIntyre.

Reverend McIntyre, who led various Presbyterian congregations in the Twin Cities, died in 2005.

65 Neal Broten

Gordie Howe originated the hat trick legacy. Neal Broten raised the stakes.

Mr. Hockey set the NHL standard for scoring and brawn with the "Gordie Howe Hat Trick," the rare feat of recording a goal, an assist, and a fight in the same game. Broten is unrivaled in his triple crown.

He is the only person to have won the Hobey Baker Award as college hockey's best player, an Olympic gold medal, and the Stanley Cup. Add his NCAA championship with the Gophers and Broten is the most decorated hockey player Minnesota has ever produced.

Broten set the freshman assists record with 50 in 1979, helping lead the Gophers to their third and final national title under coach Herb Brooks.

The Roseau, Minnesota, native bagged the game-winning goal in the championship game against archrival North Dakota with a stomach-sliding chip shot that remains a popular highlight.

Brooks left Minnesota to coach the 1980 U.S. Olympic team, and brought his playmaking center with him. Together, they made history on the "Miracle on Ice" squad that upset the powerhouse Soviet Union en route to winning gold at Lake Placid, New York.

Broten returned to the Gophers the following season, joining younger brother Aaron on the top scoring line. He earned First Team All-America honors in leading Minnesota back to the national championship game, which it lost to Wisconsin. He won the inaugural Hobey Baker Award and finished his college career with 38 goals among 142 points in 76 games.

Within days, the third-round pick of the Minnesota North Stars signed with his home-state team, and Broten found himself at the center of another hockey fairy tale. The upstart North Stars upset their way into the Stanley Cup Finals for the first time in franchise history before the dynastic New York Islanders halted their magic carpet ride in a five-game series victory.

"I felt like, 'This is pretty smooth sailing,'" Broten told NHL.com in 2014. "You just feel how fortunate you are to be involved with the University of Minnesota, which was a great team, and then the Olympic team, which was a Cinderella upset story, then with the North Stars and making it all the way to the Final. It's hard to get to that Final again. It's a tough road."

It was another 10 years before Broten and the North Stars returned to the Finals, where they were vanquished again, this time by the Pittsburgh Penguins.

Broten's charmed career was hardly finished. A decade after he became the first American to eclipse 100 points in a season, Minnesota shipped him to the New Jersey Devils at the 1995 trade deadline, and once again Broten was in the right place at the right time.

The Devils, perennial playoff underachievers, got hot and rolled through the postseason, sweeping the heavily favored Detroit Red Wings to win the Stanley Cup. Broten scored the winning goals in Games 3 and 4 and finished with 20 points in 20 playoff games.

He retired in 1997 after 1,099 NHL regular season games with 289 goals and 923 points—11th among all U.S.-born players. Broten and his wife, Sally, settled in River Falls, Wisconsin, to raise horses on their 75-acre farm.

The Dallas Stars retired his No. 7 and Broten was inducted into the U.S. Hockey Hall of Fame in 2000.

Underappreciated to be sure and unassuming to this day, Broten is not one to measure his unrivaled success.

"I just played the game. I loved playing the game," he said. "I had a passion for playing with my teammates. I'm not big on talking about legacy. I was a decent player; I wasn't a great player. But things worked out. I played with some great players and good teams and won some championships."

66 Thomas Vanek

Thomas Vanek had a freshman hockey season for the ages in 2002–03, and established himself as a game-breaker during his 18 brief but memorable months in Minnesota.

The playmaking winger was the first European-born player to play for the provincial program and single-handedly carried the Gophers to their fifth national championship in 2003 with a star-making postseason performance that made him the No. 5 overall pick later that year by the Buffalo Sabres.

Strong on the puck; dashing with his long, blond locks; and harnessing an insatiable appetite to score, Vanek was unlike any player coach Don Lucia had recruited to Minnesota and quickly dominated the Western Collegiate Hockey Association.

In 83 games he scored 57 goals among 113 points before turning pro.

Born in 1984 in Graz, Austria—Arnold Schwarzenegger's hometown—Vanek came to Minnesota via amateur hockey programs Canada and a two-year stint as a U.S. junior in Sioux Falls, South Dakota.

He played two seasons there for coach Bob Motzko, who recruited Vanek hard after Lucia hired him in 2001 to be an assistant coach. Vanek ultimately chose the Gophers over Michigan and Wisconsin.

Vanek was nicknamed "Teen Wolf" by his teammates after the Michael J. Fox movie character who turned into a werewolf whenever he was heckled or challenged.

"He'd be a good player, and all of a sudden somebody would talk smack to him or whack him, and it was like... *Teen Wolf,*" former teammate Grant Potulny recalled to the Minneapolis *Star Tribune.* "You couldn't stop him. He would just dominate."

Vanek scored 31 goals and 62 points in 2002–03, becoming the first freshman to lead the team in scoring since Mike Antonovich in 1969–70. They were the second most behind John Mayasich's 32 goals in 1951–52.

His credentials as a clutch player were punctuated by 17 goals in the third period or overtime, including his Frozen Four masterpiece in Buffalo.

Against Michigan in the national semifinal, Vanek bagged the OT winner, pirouetting behind the net to fool Al Montoya and tuck the puck between the goaltender's skates at 8:55.

He answered that by scoring the game-winner against New Hampshire, snapping a 1–1 tie eight minutes into the third period. It was the second consecutive national title for the Gophers. At 21 years old, the Austrian was an American champion.

"This championship means so much to me," he told reporters afterward. "When it was tied, I looked at my linemates and said, 'We have to step up.' Most of the time when we do that, it works out."

Added teammate Jordan Leopold: "He's a special player."

Six days later, Carmelo Anthony—Syracuse's freshman basketball superstar—led the Orangemen to the men's national championship. Like Vanek, Anthony was named the tournament's most outstanding player.

His Gophers teammates scrapped the "Teen Wolf" nickname and started calling him "Melo." During a victory rally at Mariucci

Arena, fans chanted "one more year!"—humbling and embarrassing the reserved Vanek.

He played another year in Minnesota before signing with the Sabres and making his NHL debut in 2005.

Vanek played nine years in Buffalo, scoring a career-high 43 goals in 2006–07. He was traded to the New York Islanders and Montreal before returning to Minnesota in 2014 after signing a three-year contract with the Wild.

However, Vanek never was able to rekindle the magic he spun in college. The Wild bought out the 32-year-old's contract after just two seasons. In July 2016, Vanek signed a one-year deal with the Detroit Red Wings.

67 Pat Micheletti

Pat Micheletti never set any personal goals as a skilled winger for the Gophers during the early 1980s despite scoring them by the bucketful.

"The biggest thing for me was being a great teammate and a better friend to my teammates," Micheletti told the Hibbing *Daily Tribune* in 2013. "It was always team first for me, and then everything else fell into place."

Only Minnesota icon John Mayasich has more goals and points than Micheletti, who wrapped his collegiate career with 120 goals among 269 points.

Skating in the shadows of older brothers Joe and Don, who won national championships at Minnesota in the 1970s, Pat was born to be a Gopher. He roamed the locker room as a nine-year-old listening to legendary coach Herb Brooks thundering at his players.

A decade later the former Hibbing High School standout carved out his legacy.

"I lived for Friday and Saturday nights," he said. "I loved to play. There was nothing better."

Despite being only 5'9", 175 pounds, Micheletti played an aggressive style—sometimes too aggressive.

Micheletti racked up 180 penalties and 403 penalty minutes, third most in school history.

"I told people that that was my time to rest during a game," Micheletti joked. "I didn't want to go back to the bench and get yelled at. I wasn't the easiest player to coach, but that's who I was. That's how I made my mark."

Micheletti reigned supreme putting the puck in the net. He was a finalist for the 1985 Hobey Baker Award after scoring 48 goals and 96 points his senior season—second all-time for a single Gophers season.

In his final regular season game at Mariucci Arena, against archrival North Dakota, he bagged four goals and two assists.

The North Stars drafted Micheletti in the ninth round of the NHL Entry Draft in 1982 but he only played 12 games for Minnesota in 1987–88, finishing his pro career in 1990 in Italy.

Micheletti is part of the 1500 ESPN broadcasting crew for Gophers hockey games alongside Wally Shaver and Frank Mazzoco.

68 Glen Sonmor

Glen Sonmor's hockey footprint is wide and deep in Minnesota, where he started shaping a legacy as a player, coach, manager, scout, and broadcaster when Harry Truman occupied the White House.

One of the game's renowned characters was a cultural guidebook for bygone eras of the Gophers, the rebel World Hockey Association, and a rowdier NHL. He played alongside John Mariucci, fought Gordie Howe, introduced the "Hanson Brothers" to Hollywood, and once wore an eye patch as coach of the North Stars to toughen his players.

The recovering alcoholic also counseled addicts and influenced lives for three decades before Sonmor died in December 2015.

"I have never met a man who loves the game of hockey more than Glen Sonmor," said former Wild general manager Doug Risebrough, who gave Sonmor his last NHL job when he hired him to scout for the Wild from 2000 to '09.

John Mariucci, the godfather of college hockey in Dinkytown, was one of the earliest Americans to play in the NHL. He was on the downslope of his career in 1949 when Sonmor joined the minor league Minneapolis Millers. The two shared a passion for the game and pugilism that sealed their bond.

Mariucci also drove Sonmor to the U campus in the spring of 1950 to enroll him.

"He pulled me aside and said, 'Kid, of all my teammates who have been Canadians, you're the first one that ever finished high school. You're going to college,'" Sonmor recalled in 2011.

Sonmor's playing career ended suddenly in 1955 when he lost his left eye after being struck by a wayward puck. Mariucci was there to pick him again, this time spiritually.

Gophers NHL First-Round Draft Picks

Year	Player	Team	Pick
1979	Mike Ramsey	Buffalo	11
1985	Tom Chorske	Montreal	16
1989	Doug Zmolek	Minnesota	7
1996	Erik Rasmussen	Buffalo	7
2000	Jeff Taffe	St. Louis	30
2002	Keith Ballard	Buffalo	11
2003	Thomas Vanek	Buffalo	5
2004	Blake Wheeler	Phoenix	5
2004	Kris Chucko	Calgary	24
2006	Erik Johnson	St. Louis	1
2006	Phil Kessel	Boston	5
2006	Kyle Okposo	NY Islanders	7
2007	Patrick White	Vancouver	25
2007	Jim O'Brien	Ottawa	29
2009	Nick Leddy	Minnesota	16
2009	Jordan Schroeder	Vancouver	22
2010	Nick Bjugstad	Florida	19
2012	Brady Skjei	NY Rangers	28

"He said: 'Don't worry about what you're going to do. I've got you the freshman coaching job at the university,'" Sonmor said. "That's what I needed to hear."

Sonmor never spoke a bitter or self-pitying word about his fate and embarked on the career that would define him. He succeeded Mariucci as head coach of the Gophers in 1966. He won two Western Collegiate Hockey Association championships and led Minnesota to the 1971 Frozen Four before turning pro and handing over the program to Herb Brooks.

Sonmor went on to coach the Minnesota Fighting Saints of the defunct WHA, which included Dave "Killer" Hanson and the Carlson brothers—Jack, Jeff, and Steve from Virginia of Minnesota's Iron Range.

The Carlsons spent the 1974–75 season playing for the Saints' affiliate in the steel town of Johnstown, Pennsylvania, where a young screenwriter named Nancy Dowd had embedded to polish a script about minor league hockey. They were the inspiration for the colorful characters of *Slap Shot*, the 1977 cinematic cult classic that starred Paul Newman as the washed-up player-coach who unleashed his band of brawlers to terrorize the fictitious Federal League.

Sonmor was hired by general manager Lou Nanne in 1978 to coach the North Stars.

During his five years in Minnesota, Sonmor posted a regular season record of 177–161–83, plus a 26–21 mark in the postseason, which included a trip to the 1981 Stanley Cup Finals, where the North Stars lost to the New York Islanders.

In October 2006, Sonmor was awarded the NHL's Lester Patrick Trophy for outstanding service to U.S. hockey. A year later, the University of Minnesota bestowed him with an honorary letter for his service to the school's hockey program, which concluded with him serving as radio analyst for Gophers games.

69 Lou Nanne

There is no more recognizable Gophers cheerleader than Lou Nanne, the Canadian defenseman with the golden fundraising touch who has left fingerprints across the State of Hockey as a player, coach, manager, broadcaster, and ambassador.

"Louie" never runs out of stories to tell and hockey fans across generations have plenty to share.

To old-timers he was one of legendary Gophers coach John Mariucci's rare out-of-state recruits, from Sault Ste. Marie, Ontario. The smooth-skating and productive defenseman earned All-America honors as a senior in 1963 after scoring a then–school record 74 points as a blue liner.

North Stars fans remember him as the expansion team's first true superstar as the NHL All-Star finished with 72 goals among 239 points. The naturalized American captained the 1975 and '77 U.S. national teams.

From player to North Stars coach in 1978, Nanne kept climbing the franchise ladder. From general manager to team president, he acquired franchise legends Don Beaupre, Dino Ciccarelli, and Mike Modano before stepping down in 1990.

During his tenure with the North Stars, Nanne also served as a television analyst for CBS, NBC, and CBC's signature show, *Hockey Night in Canada.*

To local hockey fans Nanne is the voice of the Minnesota State Boys Hockey Tournament, where he has served as commentator since 1964. Nanne was elected to the U.S. Hockey Hall of Fame and received the Lester Patrick award in 1989 for dedication to hockey.

After graduating from Minnesota, Nanne was drafted by the Chicago Blackhawks but rebuffed their contract offers to play with the minor league Rochester Mustangs. He also coached the Gophers' freshman team while honing his business acumen working for Minneapolis businessman and Gophers booster Harvey Mackay's envelope company.

Today Nanne is an executive with Minneapolis-based Voyageur Asset Management Co. and remains one of Minnesota's most dedicated fundraisers, leading the effort to subsidize construction of the $166 million Athletes Village project on campus.

70 Reed Larson

You can talk about his 1976 NCAA championship with the Gophers, NHL first-round pedigree, three All-Star appearances, 685 points as a defenseman, and election to the U.S. Hockey Hall of Fame.

But any conversation about Reed Larson's hockey credentials begins and ends with "the Shot."

In the wooden-stick era, before hybrid models made snipers out of fourth-line grinders, Larson boasted one of the most intimidating slap shots in hockey—a heavy, right-handed blast that shattered defenders' sticks, shin guards, and bones, not to mention the courage of many a goaltender.

Larson, who was born in south Minneapolis and starred for Roosevelt High School, honed his skills on the outdoor rink at Sibley Park and perfected his shot in his parents' garage after plunging new stick blades into pots of boiling water to bend them to his liking.

The bottom of an old toboggan was his launching pad.

"I helped my dad clean out one side of it, and we found an old wrestling mat that we hung up to shoot at," Larson once told the Minneapolis *Star Tribune*. "I loved to shoot. I was always experimenting with different sticks and shafts and curves."

Larson spent summers waterskiing at his parents' lake cabin and also wrestled and participated in gymnastics—rings and high bar were his preferred disciplines.

"That had a lot to do with my muscle development," he recalled.

Larson won the WCHA title in 1975 and a national championship the following year under Gophers coach Herb Brooks. In

1976, the Red Wings drafted Larson 22nd overall. He left Minnesota after his junior year and debuted for Detroit in 1977, when he was runner-up for the Calder Trophy as the NHL's top rookie.

The steady blue liner was named Red Wings captain in 1981. In 10 seasons in Motown, Larson recorded five 20-goal seasons and eight seasons of at least 60 points. He was traded to Boston in 1986 and played in the '88 Stanley Cup Finals, where the Bruins were swept by the Edmonton Oilers.

The first American-born player with 200 goals, Larson also played for the Oilers, New York Islanders, Minnesota North Stars, and Buffalo Sabres before retiring from the NHL in 1990 with 222 goals and 463 assists in 904 games.

In 1996 he was elected to the U.S. Hockey Hall of Fame.

71 Jordan Leopold

Jordan Leopold endured a losing season and dramatic coaching change from Doug Woog to Don Lucia before the NHL's Calgary Flames offered him a chance to turn pro after his junior year in 2001.

Nagging at one of the best defensemen in Gophers history was a sense he would leave before something special happened.

How clairvoyant.

Leopold returned in 2001–02 for an unforgettable senior season. The captain punctuated his college career by winning Minnesota's first national championship in 23 years after sweeping most of the sport's individual honors—the Hobey Baker Award as the country's best player, two-time All-American, and two-time WCHA Defensive Player of the Year.

"I've won individual awards, but I've never won any team awards," he said after picking up his Hobey Baker trophy the night before the Gophers played Maine in the NCAA championship game. "So if we win tomorrow, it will be the best day of my life."

Minnesota defeated the Black Bears in overtime at Xcel Energy Center in St. Paul. Leopold's dream came true.

Leopold joined Neal Broten (1981), Robb Stauber (1988), and Brian Bonin (1996) as Hobey Baker winners. Broten won a national title in 1979, the last time the Gophers tasted that level of success before 2002.

"I came back because there were some things left to be done and because we had the team to do it," Leopold said.

The Golden Valley, Minnesota, native played 695 games over 13 NHL seasons with the Calgary Flames, Colorado Avalanche, Florida Panthers, Columbus Blue Jackets, Pittsburgh Penguins, Buffalo Sabres, St. Louis Blues, and Minnesota Wild before retiring in 2015.

72 Mike Crowley

No Gophers player dominated the puck, opponents, and headlines like Mike Crowley in the late 1990s.

Crowley owns the two highest-scoring seasons by a defenseman with 63 points as a sophomore in 1996 and 56 more as a 1997 junior. His 46 and 47 assists in those respective seasons rank first and second among defensemen in school history. Lou Nanne is the only other Gophers defenseman to lead the team in season scoring.

The two-time Hobey Baker Award winner came from a winning pedigree. Crowley won three straight Minnesota State High School hockey championships at Bloomington Jefferson—including a perfect 28–0 season in 1992–93—before cracking the Gophers' lineup as a freshman in 1994–95.

Crowley was among five Jefferson players from that era who went on to play in the NHL, including his former Gophers teammates Ben Clymer and Mark Parrish.

"That was a great time to be a young adult," said Crowley. "We had a lot of players who enjoyed individual success in both high school and college, but the most fun is having team success, and that's what those records are all about."

Crowley was the fourth two-time All-American in Gophers history and was the 1997 WCHA Player of the Year.

Drafted in the sixth round by the Philadelphia Flyers in 1993, Crowley helped lead the Gophers to the 1995 NCAA Frozen Four and the 1997 WCHA regular season title.

He played in 67 regular season games during parts of three seasons for the Anaheim Ducks during a five-year pro career.

73 Jack McCartan

Two decades before the 1980 "Miracle on Ice," there was another unheralded group of American kids who shocked the Olympics by vanquishing hockey powerhouses en route to an unlikely gold medal.

And before Jim Craig, there was Jack McCartan, the accidental goaltender from St. Paul who was a two-sport star and baseball phenom at Minnesota.

McCartan was the most outstanding goalie of the 1960 Winter Olympics in Squaw Valley, California, backstopping Team USA's upsets of Canada, the Soviet Union, and Czechoslovakia to win gold.

It was the start of a 45-year hockey odyssey that included a brief moment in the NHL, a long career in the minors, and a successful scouting career for the Vancouver Canucks.

McCartan inherited the goaltending job as a freshman at Marshall High School when the senior starter quit. He also played baseball—very well, it turned out.

He hit .436 and belted eight home runs as an All-American third baseman in 1956, helping lead the Gophers to their first College World Series title. He won a bronze medal for Team USA at the 1959 Pan American Games.

Meanwhile, McCartan was a two-time All-American goaltender and team captain, compiling a 2.80 career goals-against average for the Gophers.

"Baseball was my No. 1 sport," McCartan told New York hockey author Stan Fischler. "If I had concentrated on baseball, I could have turned pro."

After his Olympic heroics, McCartan signed with the New York Rangers and debuted in March 1960 against the Detroit Red Wings at Madison Square Garden.

His first save was denying Gordie Howe on a breakaway.

"I hugged the near post, and he faked a shot to the far corner while still holding the puck," McCartan told Fischler. "Gordie wanted to pull me out of the net and put it behind me. But I was ready for him, and when he took a wrist shot low, I dove at the puck and got my body in front of it for my big first save."

McCartan earned a 3–1 victory and posted a 1.75 goals-against average in four games. He played eight more games for the Rangers in 1960–61 but failed to gain traction in the NHL.

McCartan played for nine teams in nine different minor leagues before retiring in 1974 with his hometown Minnesota Fighting Saints of the World Hockey Association.

74 Robb Stauber

For decades the Gophers routinely produced playmaking centers, sharp-shooting wingers, and smooth-skating defensemen, making Minnesota a destination for highly skilled hockey players.

Goaltending was mostly an afterthought, a position that had to be filled. The crease did not bring much individual glory beyond Jack McCartan until Robb Stauber arrived from Duluth in the late 1980s.

Stauber had a season to remember in 1987–88, becoming the first goalie to win the Hobey Baker Memorial Award as college hockey's best player.

"It's the type of award that seems to become more and more significant as time goes on," Stauber said in 2004. "I see how hard the guys work to achieve their goals, and while I never had this as a specific goal, to receive such an honor is very special. I think there will always be a little bond between the Gophers Hobey winners."

Stauber's 44 games, 2,621 minutes, and 1,243 saves that season earned him WCHA Player of the Year honors. Those marks remain team records. His five shutouts rank second behind Kent Patterson's seven in 2011–12.

Stauber backstopped Minnesota to consecutive WCHA championships and three straight Frozen Four appearances, losing a heartbreaker in overtime to Harvard in the 1989 title game at the St. Paul Civic Center.

He finished with a sterling career record of 73–23–0. Drafted by the Los Angeles Kings, Stauber played 17 professional seasons, including five in the NHL.

During the Kings' 1993 run to the Stanley Cup Finals, Stauber won three of four starts in L.A.'s first-round victory over Calgary, which he considered his career highlight.

That year Stauber started running goaltending camps. In 2002, he opened Goalcrease Inc., which grew into an internationally renowned goaltending school in Edina. He also spent several seasons as Gophers men's goaltending coach and was an assistant for the U.S. women's Olympic team that won a silver medal at the 2014 Sochi Games.

"I'm not sure if I am a big part of the tradition of Gopher hockey because there are some legendary names that have passed through the program," he said. "It's a great feeling to know that along the way I have hopefully made contributions to this program that have had a positive impact. But I don't think I could ever impact the program the way the program has impacted me."

75 Brian Bonin

If Brian Bonin stacked his college hockey accolades they might surpass his 5'9" frame.

Over his four seasons in Minnesota, Bonin won three WCHA championships, played in two Frozen Fours, and won 102 of 170 games.

His 216 points were sixth most in program history when he graduated in 1996. Bonin was one of only five Gophers to

Gophers Men's Hockey Scoring Leaders

Player	Seasons	G	A	Pts.
John Mayasich	1951–55	144	154	298
Pat Micheletti	1982–86	120	149	269
Corey Millen	1982–87	119	122	241
Butsy Erickson	1979–83	109	129	238
Larry Olimb	1988–92	59	159	218
Brian Bonin	1992–96	100	116	216
Steve Ulseth	1977–81	84	118	202
Tim Harrer	1976–80	117	84	201
Johnny Pohl	1998–2002	71	129	200
Dick Dougherty	1951–54	109	78	187

eclipse 100 goals and 200 points and just the second behind John Mayasich to twice be named first-team All-American.

What is more, the 1996 Hobey Baker Memorial Award winner is one of only two players to win back-to-back WCHA Most Valuable Player awards.

Still…

"I'd trade everything for a national championship," Bonin said. "We won three playoff titles, and those were the best feelings, celebrating with your teammates. I didn't think much about the Hobey because I didn't want any individual things to separate me from my teammates."

As a senior in 1995–96, Bonin led the country in scoring with 34 goals and 47 assists, averaging almost two points per game. The chemistry major also finished with a 4.0 grade-point average before winning a bronze medal for the United States at the 1996 World Ice Hockey Championships—the first American medal in the tournament since 1952.

The White Bear Lake native was the 1992 Minnesota Mr. Hockey.

Best in state. Best in country. Best in class. However, Bonin's amateur stardom never translated into professional success.

He was drafted by Pittsburgh and played briefly for the Penguins and the hometown Minnesota Wild but spent most of his eight-year professional career in the minors.

76 Salute Lindsay Whalen

"Before Lindsay" and "After Lindsay" is the demarcation that distinguishes Minnesota women's basketball from its humble growth as a niche sideshow to a must-see revenue juggernaut.

Lindsay Marie Whalen was, according to her coach, Pam Borton, a "once-in-a-lifetime player" who transcended gender while elevating the program to national prominence in the early 2000s.

"Her contributions have been unbelievable; she has kind of put the program on the map," Borton said.

The slashing playmaker was the first Gophers athlete to have a bobblehead doll, which quickly sold out. Her No. 13 jersey was the most popular at the school store and eventually was retired.

Whalen led Minnesota to its only women's Final Four in 2004, when gross ticket sales soared past $1 million and almost matched the program's operating budget of $1.5 million. Only football, men's basketball, and men's hockey could boast that.

Whalen's first Big Ten home game on January 4, 2001, was a 79–76 loss to Indiana. There were 1,107 fans at the tiny Sports Pavilion. When she graduated three years later, the Gophers were regularly selling out 14,000-seat Williams Arena.

"The feeling of running out to that many people in The Barn was almost surreal," Whalen recounted. "We were just looking at each other in awe, running up the steps and onto the court. We couldn't believe that many people were there to watch us play."

The Hutchinson, Minnesota, native was a three-time All-American, an Academic All-American, and 2002 Big Ten Player of the Year.

Whalen finished her career with 2,285 points, more than any male or female Gophers basketball player before Rachel Banham surpassed her in 2015–16.

Those are the cold, hard facts. But Whalen's impact is measured in the emotional connection she forged with the campus and fans captivated by her on-court combination of hard-nosed play and pure joy as a creative and productive guard.

She paired with center Janel McCarville to form a potent scoring tandem that in 2002 sparked Minnesota to its first NCAA tournament appearance in a decade. A year later they won 25 games and, for the first time in school history, advanced to the Sweet 16.

The Gophers were poised for another deep postseason run in February 2004 when ice water was dumped on the parade.

Whalen broke two bones in her shooting hand against Ohio State in Columbus when she tumbled over the back of Kim Wilburn and crashed hard on the floor.

"I remember sitting in a hotel room with my mom and brother after I broke it…and my mom and I both broke down crying," Whalen recalled. "Afterward, I told her that there wasn't going to be any more crying about my hand. I reminded her that it could have been much worse and we will get through this. So, we moved on from there and things worked out okay."

The Gophers lost three of their last five games with Whalen sidelined. She returned in time for the first round of the NCAA tournament against UCLA at packed Williams Arena.

Fearless and confident, Whalen bagged 31 points in a convincing 92–81 victory, and the Gophers were on their way.

Double-digit wins over Kansas State, Boston College, and Duke propelled Minnesota to the Final Four in New Orleans.

"Getting a police escort around the city of New Orleans when we were there for the Final Four, that was really cool," she said. "We felt like we were with the president or something."

The fairy tale ended when the Gophers lost 67–58 to dynastic Connecticut, which went on to win its third straight national championship and fifth overall.

Whalen was drafted fourth overall in the 2004 WNBA Draft by Connecticut and helped lead the Sun to the WNBA Finals her first two seasons, finishing runner-up to league MVP Candace Parker in 2008.

In 2010 the Minnesota Lynx traded for Whalen, bringing the prodigal daughter back to the state, where she helped transform a mediocre franchise into a dynasty.

Three WNBA championships in five years highlighted a Lynx career that also saw her reunite with McCarville in 2013. One is hard pressed to identify a more mutually fulfilling bond between a community and professional athlete than that of Whalen with Minnesota basketball fans.

"So many people have thanked me for many great memories, but I also want to say thank you to everyone that has touched me," she said. "Thanks!"

77 Janel McCarville

The rim cost $2 at a garage sale. The backboard was two-by-fours and part of a tree trunk nailed to the side of a barn. The floor was a 10-by-20-foot concrete slab. The crowd was dad, cows, and some chickens.

That was how basketball started for 13-year-old Janel McCarville, the Wisconsin farm girl who transformed herself into a powerful post player and helped make her sport relevant again at Minnesota.

From tiny Stevens Point, Wisconsin, McCarville left an indelible mark on college basketball, the WNBA as the No. 1 overall pick in 2005, and international basketball. Her career took her from Charlotte to New York, Russia, Slovakia, Italy, Spain, Turkey, and back to Minnesota, where she reteamed with Lindsey Whalen in 2013 to help the Lynx win their first WNBA championship.

"Not once in my wildest dreams did I think basketball would take me where it has taken me and allow the opportunities I have gotten," McCarville said in 2008. "I don't take it for granted and I enjoy every moment of it."

Her parents, Terry and Bonnie, owned a 160-acre farm. McCarville slept in a tiny bedroom with no door off the kitchen, according to a 2013 *Star Tribune* story. Her days consisted of a 6:00 AM bus ride to school, chores, and shooting hoops off the barn.

"Her house didn't have cable, so she would hang out at the houses of her good friends on the team, so she could watch NBA games," her high school coach, Kraig Terpstra, told the newspaper.

"She's not only the most talented player I ever coached, she was hands-down the smartest."

Williams Arena was a ghost town for women's basketball before the 6'2" McCarville and Whalen, her playmaking sidekick, arrived in the early 2000s. The unlikely tandem lifted the Gophers from Big Ten bottom feeders to the Final Four in 2004 and set the standard by which the program will be forever measured.

McCarville was unlike any center the Big Ten had ever seen. Brute strength and soft hands made her impractical to defend. Her bleached-blonde hair, arm tattoos, swashbuckling style, and magnetic personality made her impossible to overlook.

Opponents dreaded matching up against her. Teammates gravitated to her spirit like bees to honey.

"She has a swagger about her," teammate Shannon Schonrock once said. "We feed off that. She's a spark."

McCarville was a four-year starter who finished her career as the Gophers' all-time leader in field goal percentage (.582) and second in rebounds (1,206). Her 1,835 points rank sixth.

The Gophers finished 1–15 in the Big Ten in 2000–01 before McCarville debuted the following season for coach Cheryl Littlejohn.

There were only 1,103 fans at Williams Arena for her first game. McCarville made a layup 40 seconds into the game and sank another field goal a minute later. She finished 7-for-7 with nine rebounds, five assists, and 21 points. A star was born.

A year later, Littlejohn was fired and replaced by Brenda Olfield, who led Minnesota to 20 wins and just its second NCAA tournament berth.

In 2002, Pam Borton took over and guided the Gophers to the Sweet Sixteen. In 2003–04, McCarville and Whalen became Batman and Robin, Williams Arena was sold out for women's games, and the Gophers roared into the national semifinals, taking the state of Minnesota on a wild ride with them.

"I get a lot of credit for that run, but Janel was our anchor," Whalen recalled.

McCarville set the NCAA record for most rebounds in the national tournament with 75 in five games, setting another record for tournament rebound average with 15 per game.

"Lindsay taught Janel how to play as an All-American," Borton said.

Clashes between McCarville and Borton defined their relationship as much as their shared success. Borton benched McCarville for a period during her junior season. The conflicts steeled both to their demands and expectations, which they eventually realized were never mutually exclusive.

"I think it took a whole year for Janel to grasp our system," said Borton. "She realized we were only trying to make her better and that we weren't going anywhere. Yes, we butted heads but there's not many times you get to coach a kid like Janel. She made us better as coaches."

After signing with the Lynx in 2013, McCarville relocated back to Stevens Point, where the farm had turned into a family compound. The original $2 rim was taken down from the barn and attached to a smaller chicken coop, where it was easier for her nieces and nephews to reach.

The global basketball star had come full circle

"This is what I work for," she said. "So I can sit here the rest of my life."

78 Rachel Banham

Rachel Banham was haunted by doubts entering her senior basketball season.

The Gophers' multidimensional shot maker knew her surgically reconstructed right knee was prepared for hardwood pounding and that her anterior cruciate and medial collateral ligaments had fully healed from the devastating tear that short-circuited her first attempt at senior year and required a medical hardship waiver to return.

But an athlete must trust her body to perform, let alone excel. Banham was not sure what to expect when she returned for the 2015–16 season.

"I know in the beginning of the year, I felt really awkward. I said, 'This just doesn't feel right. Am I going to get back to where I was?'" Banham recalled. "When Big Ten [season] hit, I started to feel really good. I think as I had some bigger games, I started to really surprise myself and realize the sky's the limit. And I still have a lot more that I can reach."

Banham reached for the stars and became one virtually overnight.

She scored 30 points in her second game back against Maine, shattered former All-American and Lynx point guard Lindsay Whalen's school scoring record after five games, and heated up in a stretch drive for the ages.

On February 7, 2016, at Northwestern, Banham set Minnesota and Big Ten single-game scoring records with 60 points during a 112–108 double-overtime victory over the Wildcats. Her magnificence tied the NCAA single-game scoring record set by Cindy Brown in 1987.

Gophers Women's Basketball Scoring Leaders

Player	Seasons	Points
Rachel Banham	2011–16	3,093
Lindsay Whalen	2000–04	2,285
Carol Ann Shudlick	1990–94	2,097
Laura Coenen	1981–85	2,044
Linda Roberts	1977–81	1,856
Janel McCarville	2001–05	1,835
Molly Tadich	1983–87	1,706
Kiara Buford	2008–12	1,532
Emily Fox	2005–09	1,449
Carol Peterka	1982–86	1,441

By the first overtime, she had broken Carol Ann Shudlick's Minnesota record of 44 points before quickly surpassing the Big Ten record of 49 points shared by Penn State's Kelly Mazzante and Illinois' Kendra Gantt.

Banham finished 19-for-32 from the floor and 8-for-15 from three-point range and converted 14-of-16 free throws.

"I had no idea," she confessed afterward. "I knew I was around the 30-point range. But after that, I didn't see any of it. I could hear a few girls on the bench after I got 60. You don't think about it. It just happens."

A week later, Banham punctuated a 35-point game with a buzzer-beating three-pointer to vanquish Iowa at Williams Arena. She also racked up games of 48 and 52 points.

Suddenly, her favorite NBA player, retiring L.A. Lakers superstar Kobe Bryant, was congratulating her on Twitter and drawing comparisons to his slashing style of play.

Banham, dressed in Bryant gear, later met her idol courtside at Staples Center during Lakers warm-ups in Los Angeles.

"We made eye contact and he was like, 'Hey!'" Banham told NBA.com. "He was like, 'I gotta get you a jersey so you can come out and play. We kind of need you right now.'"

After the game, Bryant signed Banham's jersey with a note: "To Rachel: Be the greatest."

There was no one greater than Banham in 2015–16.

Banham rewrote every scoring record in Minnesota women's basketball history. The Big Ten player of the year averaged a league-record 30.5 points per game and graduated as the conference's career scoring leader with 3,093 points.

She ranks seventh all-time in the NCAA ahead of such luminaries as Cheryl Miller, Chamique Holdsclaw, Maya Moore, and Elena Della Donne.

"I don't think it really hits me fully right now," Banham said after the season. "I think down the road, I'll really, really appreciate. It's crazy when you hear those names because it's people I really look up to and I've watched when I was growing up."

The Connecticut Sun drafted Banham fourth overall in the 2016 WNBA Draft, but she reinjured her right knee after just 15 pro games and faced another difficult rehabilitation.

In July 2016, Banham had microfracture surgery, and the Sun announced she would be sidelined four to six months.

79 Jerry Kindall

The only person to win NCAA baseball championships as a player and head coach, Jerry Kindall played behind Hall of Fame shortstop Ernie Banks with the Chicago Cubs and was a forgotten contributor to the Minnesota Twins' 1965 American League pennant-winning club.

He was a two-sport star at St. Paul's Washington High on the city's east side. He grew up idolizing the old St. Paul Saints of the

American Association and watched future Brooklyn Dodgers stars Duke Snider, Roy Campanella, and Clem Labine hone their skills at Lexington Park.

"Old Lexington Park in St. Paul was like the Holy City to me, the Taj Mahal," Kindall recalled.

Kindall helped christen a golden era of Gophers baseball under head coach Dick Siebert. He also earned a pair of varsity letters in basketball.

In 1956, the All-American shortstop hit a then–program record 18 home runs with 48 RBI as Minnesota won the first of its three national championships in eight years.

In Big Ten play that year, Kindall batted .440 with six home runs as the Gophers won 30 of their last 34 games. He was the first and last player to hit for the cycle in the College World Series. Minnesota, which boasted 16 of 18 home-state players, roared past Arizona 12–1 in the NCAA title game.

Kindall's performance earned him a $50,000 bonus when he signed with the Chicago Cubs. The 6'2", 175-pound infielder—nicknamed "Slim"—struggled at the plate his first two seasons, hitting just .162 in spot duty.

After the 1961 season, rumors swirled that Kindall might replace Ernie Banks at shortstop, but instead the Cubs traded him the following year to the Cleveland Indians. He played a career-high 154 games in 1962, hitting 13 home runs with 55 RBI for the Indians.

A three-way trade in 1964 landed Kindall with the hometown Twins. In 1965, he earned the second-base job in spring training and played 125 games. However, a midseason hamstring injury sidelined Kindall. He lost his job to rookie Frank Quilici, who played every inning of the Twins' seven-game World Series loss to the Los Angeles Dodgers.

Released by Minnesota the following spring, Kindall's playing career was finished. He was only 30.

Kindall returned to his alma mater and mentored as an assistant coach under Siebert for five years. In 1972, he was hired by the University of Arizona, where Kimball built a college baseball dynasty.

He won national titles in 1976, 1980 and 1986, winning 860 games in 24 seasons. Three times he was named national coach of the year.

Kindall's program produced 34 All-Americans and graduated 209 players into the professional ranks, including Scott Erickson, Terry Francona, J.T. Snow, and Craig Lefferts.

"I've coached or played all my life," the 72-year-old Kindall said in 2007 when he was inducted into the College Baseball Hall of Fame, "and I have been surrounded by terrific people."

80 Jim Rantz

Jim Rantz had never started a game for the Gophers when the St. Paul native was summoned to pitch the rubber match of the 1960 College World Series and finished his career with an extra-inning victory of a lifetime.

Then again, Rantz often found himself at the intersection of chance and history.

Before he became a baseball hero for the Gophers, he was a hockey linemate of Herb Brooks, who famously won gold in 1980 as Team USA's men's hockey coach.

The longtime Twins scout was also in central Illinois one night during the summer of 1981 to see his son, Mike, play college ball only to watch an anonymous outfielder named Kirby Puckett put on a show.

Rantz was a two-sport star at St. Paul's Washington High School and walked on to Minnesota's baseball and hockey teams in 1956, playing for coaching legends Dick Siebert and John Mariucci, respectively. As a sophomore he earned a hockey scholarship.

Four years after Siebert won his first national title in 1956, the Gophers were back in the College World Series. Rantz was a reliever who earned the win in Minnesota's come-from-behind victory over Arizona in its second game.

The best-of-three final against Southern California featured three extra-inning thrillers. For the deciding game against the Trojans, Siebert turned to his senior right-hander.

Rantz took a 1–0 lead into the top of the ninth and was one out away from clinching the championship with a shutout. However, a walk, stolen base, and single allowed the Trojans to tie the game.

Rantz escaped the ninth without further damage and retired USC in the 10th. In the bottom of the frame, the Gophers scored the winning run on a bases-loaded walk.

Rantz signed with the Washington Senators after his college career ended and was in the minors when the franchise moved to Minnesota in 1961 and became the Twins. It was the start of a fruitful 53-year relationship.

He spent five seasons in the minors, but arm injuries prevented Rantz from pitching in the majors. He joined the Twins' front office and worked in public relations for five years before becoming assistant farm director.

With major league players out on strike in 1981, Rantz visited his son to watch him play for Peoria in the Collegiate League. Mike Rantz's opponent that night was Quincy, which featured Puckett in center field.

There was not a single scout in attendance besides Rantz.

"He had something like four hits and made a great throw from center field to throw out a runner at the plate," Rantz recalled in an interview.

Based on the report of scout Ellsworth Brown, who followed up on Rantz's recommendation, the Twins drafted Puckett, who went on to a Hall of Fame career in Minnesota.

In 1986, Rantz was named director of minor league operations. Twenty-one years later, he was inducted into the Twins Hall of Fame. The annual award for the best pitcher in the Twins' minor league system is named after Rantz, who retired in 2012.

"One of the things I'm most proud of is the fact I did it all in one place," Rantz told the St. Paul *Pioneer Press* upon his retirement. "I was born and raised in St. Paul, married my high school sweetheart [Pearl], played at the University of Minnesota, signed with the Senators in 1960, and (have) been with the organization ever since.

"It's time for me to see what else goes on in the summer besides baseball."

81 Terry Steinbach

Another multisport infielder-turned-catcher was Terry Steinbach, one of three New Ulm brothers (Tim and Tom) who played Gophers baseball. The Steinbach boys were teammates in 1981.

Steinbach was a star third baseman in American Legion baseball and at New Ulm High School, where he remains hockey's all-time leading scorer.

He considered playing hockey and baseball at a Division II college in Iowa before settling on Minnesota and getting down to business in baseball.

Gophers MLB First-Round Draft Picks

Player	Team	Year
Glen Perkins	Minnesota Twins	2004
Brent Gates	Oakland Athletics	1991
Paul Molitor	Milwaukee Brewers	1977
David Globig	Milwaukee Brewers	1976
Dave Winfield	San Diego Padres	1973
Noel Jenke	Boston Red Sox	1969
Bobby Fenwick	San Francisco Giants	1967
Frank Brosseau	Pittsburgh Pirates	1966

Steinbach was a two-time first-team All-Big Ten third baseman in 1982, when he was named the conference tournament's Most Valuable Player. He also batted .402 and drove in 65 runs that season, breaking the team record set by his older brother, Tom. Steinbach now ranks tied for eighth for most RBI in a season behind Derek McCallum's 86 in 2009.

The 1983 Big Ten Player of the Year also helped head coach John Anderson win his first conference championship. Steinbach was identified as a lunch-bucket player, which was revealed by his mode of transportation.

He tooled around Dinkytown in a 1966 Ford Galaxy, which he bought for the kingly sum of $50 and which was held together by layers of bumper stickers.

Drafted that year by the Oakland Athletics, Steinbach left Minnesota following his junior year and turned pro. He made his major league debut on September 12, 1986, homering off Cleveland's Greg Swindell to become just the 60th player to hit a home run in his first major league at bat.

Steinbach's 14-year career included three World Series appearances with the A's and a championship ring in 1989. He was named the 1988 All-Star Game MVP with a home run and two

RBI and caught two no-hitters, the first by Dave Stewart in 1990 with Oakland and the last by Eric Milton in 1999 for Minnesota at the Metrodome.

After becoming a free agent in 1996, Steinbach took a pay cut to sign with the hometown Twins but never regretted the decision, even though he was part of three consecutive losing seasons to end his career.

"Being born and raised here, to have the opportunity to come back and finish my career here, it's been a dream come true," Steinbach said during his retirement news conference on October 1, 1999.

A three-time All-Star, Steinbach finished with a .271 career batting average, 162 home runs, and 745 RBI.

After retiring, Steinbach was asked how he would like his career to be remembered.

"Not the home runs, not the runners I threw out, not the big plays, but how did you treat the game," Steinbach said. "I always felt honored to put on a major league uniform."

82 Glen Perkins

No Gophers pitcher struck out more hitters in a season than Glen Perkins, who never lost a Big Ten game even though the hard-throwing left-hander almost threw away his college career before it started.

Academically ineligible as a freshman, Perkins took a red shirt but still was muddling through the classrooms in the spring of 2002 when head coach John Anderson sat down Perkins for a pivotal meeting that scared the future MLB All-Star closer straight.

Anderson cross-examined Perkins about whether he was "mentally ready" to compete as a Division I student-athlete and whether Minnesota was the "right place" for the Stillwater, Minnesota, native, suggesting he was better suited for junior college.

"Do you want to be here?" Anderson challenged Perkins, according to a June 2004 story in the St. Paul *Pioneer Press*.

"I told him I wouldn't be here if I didn't want to be," Perkins recalled. "I've spent the last two years making up for that first year, and I think I've done a pretty good job of that."

As a sophomore starter in 2003, Perkins went 10–2 with a 2.91 earned run average and set the single-season record with 117 strikeouts. He fanned 113 more hitters as a junior, posting a 9–3 record as the 2004 Big Ten Pitcher of the Year.

Perkins was 15–0 with 139 strikeouts in 129 innings of Big Ten play, adding two postseason victories to his unblemished conference record. He finished his Minnesota career with a 19–5 mark, 2.87 ERA, 13 complete games, two shutouts, and 230 strikeouts in 216⅔ innings.

Out of the academic wilderness, Perkins transformed himself into a two-time second-team All American, joining C.J. Woodrow as the only two Minnesota pitchers to earn the honor, and one of the nation's top pitching prospects of 2004.

"I learned so much from that first year," he said. "It's really made me a better person. I know there's more to college than baseball. You have to take care of business in the classroom. I have no regrets about the way things have turned out."

Said Anderson: "You hope eventually they figure it out and get it, but you don't know. I was surprised to some degree that [Perkins] stuck it out."

The hometown Twins drafted Perkins 22nd overall, the highest-drafted Gopher since Dan Wilson went seventh in the first round in 1990. Only Wilson, Paul Molitor (third overall—1977), and Dave Winfield (fourth overall—1973) were taken higher.

Perkins debuted with the Twins in 2006, but his big-league career failed to launch. He had a 4.81 ERA over his first 303 innings as a starter and was demoted to the minors in 2010.

The Twins converted Perkins to a reliever in 2011 and he flourished. He became their full-time closer in 2012, earned the save in the 2014 All-Star Game at Target Field (the second of three straight All-Star appearances), and set a team record with 28 consecutive saves to start the 2015 season.

He entered the 2016 season third on the Twins' all-time saves list with 120, trailing Joe Nathan (260) and Rick Aguilera (254), but only made two appearances before having season-ending elbow surgery in June.

Perkins has cultivated a philanthropic bond with the Gophers baseball program, donating $500,000 to help renovate Siebert Field.

"They're still a big part of my life," he said about Gophers athletics. "The guys there mean as much to me as anyone else in my life."

Perkins' enduring love for his former pitching coach, Todd Oakes, was evident when "T.O." died in May 2016 following a four-year battle with leukemia. He was just 55.

"There is not a single person more responsible for the career I've had than Todd Oakes," Perkins said. "He has impacted me on the field more than anyone could have imagined or than would have expected from a college pitching coach. That said, what T.O. taught me extended beyond the field. He taught me that a bad day at the field is a better day than sitting in a cubicle.

"He taught me that baseball is just a game and should be treated as such. He taught me that a faith in God is more important than any of the above. And for that, I am eternally grateful. I will miss you every day of my life T.O. and I will do my best to live through your words."

83 Greg Olson

Greg Olson was recruited out of Edina-East High School as an infielder and quarterback. He left Minnesota as a pro catching prospect who would spend 8½ seasons in the minors before becoming an all-star rookie and hometown participant in one of the greatest World Series ever played.

Olson was a first-team All–Big Ten catcher as a sophomore in 1981, when he hit .391 with 39 RBI in 49 games and helped lead the Gophers to the inaugural West Division championship.

As a junior in 1982 he was a key cog in head coach John Anderson's debut season. Olson finished with a .375 average over three seasons in Minnesota—fourth all-time behind Mark Merila's .393. His .464 on-base percentage ranks fifth behind Merila (.517).

He was the trendsetter in a 10-year span during which the Gophers produced three All-Star big-league catchers, including Terry Steinbach and Dan Wilson. Olson, who played third base during his first fall practice in 1979, never expected to don the so-called tools of ignorance.

But head coach George Thomas took a longer look at the strong-armed quarterback and made it so.

"Ole was a great athlete and had great flexibility," Anderson told SABR biographer Joel Rippel in 2008. "Becoming a catcher made his career."

Later, during 1980 spring football practice, a junior quarterback was lost to injury and Gophers football head coach Joe Salem convinced Olson to fill the spot.

"I said, 'What the heck,'" Olson recalled to Rippel.

Although he did not letter in football, the weight training increased Olson's strength and durability, and his baseball career flourished.

The Mets drafted Olson in the seventh round in 1982, but his only highlight for New York was catching an 18-year-old Dwight Gooden in the low minors. He eventually signed with the Twins and played a handful of games for Minnesota before being released and signed by the Braves in 1990.

Olson's career had stalled and he contemplated retiring to become an insurance salesman back in Minnesota before the 29-year-old rookie hit .300 and was selected to represent last-place Atlanta at the All-Star Game.

In 1991, Olson caught starters Steve Avery, Tom Glavine, and John Smoltz as the Braves built a decade-long pitching dynasty that later included Greg Maddux and became the gold standard in baseball.

The Braves flipped the script that season, winning the National League West. Olson became an unlikely hitting star in the NLCS, hitting a two-run homer in a Game 3 victory over Pittsburgh and delivering the game-winning double in Atlanta's Game 6 win. The Braves won the series in seven games.

Olson's reward was a World Series matchup against his home-town Twins, who also went last-to-first in 1991. Every game of that thrilling series was decided by one run, with Minnesota winning Game 7 at the Metrodome 1–0 in 10 innings.

Among the enduring images of the '91 World Series was Olson on the cover of *Sports Illustrated*, photographed during a backward somersault hanging onto the ball after tagging Dan Gladden, the Twins outfielder who had bulldozed the catcher at the plate in Game 1.

Olson played two more playoff seasons with the Braves before ceding the position to Javier Lopez. He managed the Minneapolis

Loons of the independent North Central League, and even followed the franchise to the Prairie League, before quitting baseball in 1996 and earning his real estate license.

84 Dan Wilson

Dan Wilson came to Minnesota from Barrington, Illinois, with a rocket launcher of an arm that made him a dual threat as a catcher and right-handed pitcher.

He went 6–1 as a freshman starter in 1988 and was named Big Ten Freshman of the Year as a catcher. But something had to give. Wilson risked diluting his talent. He agonized about giving up pitching, but agreed with coach John Anderson that the Gophers were better served with him behind the plate.

"It was a very pivotal time for me," Wilson recalled when he was inducted into the "M" Club Hall of Fame. "I had to make a decision. I liked pitching, but I enjoyed catching a little bit more. I enjoyed playing every day and getting a chance to hit. I really wanted to pursue catching."

It was the best decision the renowned game-caller ever made.

Wilson was a 1990 All-American and two-time All–Big Ten catcher, finishing with a .336 batting average in three seasons at Minnesota. Cincinnati drafted him seventh overall in 1990, the third-highest-drafted Gopher behind Paul Molitor and Dave Winfield.

Wilson was traded with Bobby Ayala to Seattle in 1993 in exchange for Bret Boone and Erik Hanson and played 12 seasons for the Mariners. He was a 1996 All-Star and reached the postseason four times in Seattle, backstopping the Mariners in 2001 during their MLB record-tying 116-win season.

"Being part of that and playing with some great players like Ken Griffey Jr. [and] Randy Johnson were thrills for me that I will always remember," Wilson said. "The University of Minnesota was where I was prepared for all of that."

Wilson retired in 2005 as the best defensive catcher in baseball history with a career fielding percentage of .995. In 2016, he ranked tenth behind Chris Snyder (.998).

Two decades after leaving Minnesota following his junior season, Wilson returned in 2010 to collect his degree from the College of Continuing Education. He had earned almost $30 million playing pro ball but spent five years after he retired earning credits to graduate.

His wife, Annie, also received an elementary education degree from Minnesota.

"We have four kids, and for them to see the importance of education and to have them share in the moment with me is very special," Wilson told the *Star Tribune* after graduation. "That's something I thought they needed to see; for me to show them that I needed to finish school myself."

85 Bobby Marshall

One of Minnesota's first three-sport icons, Bobby Marshall thrived for the Gophers in the shadows of Jim Crow America at the dawn of the 20th century.

His father was black, his mother white. His paternal grandparents were Virginia slaves. Born in Minneapolis in 1880, Marshall starred in football, baseball, and track and field at Central High School and worked with his father as a janitor to help raise his two sisters after his mother died.

In 1901, he enrolled at Minnesota to study law, according to author Steven R. Hoffbeck, who chronicled Marshall's college and professional baseball career in his 2005 book *Swinging for the Fences: Black Baseball in Minnesota.*

"He became a Minnesota hero who fit well into the university partly because he was so fair-skinned he could get by in white society," Hoffbeck wrote.

Marshall was an All-American end known for his fierce blocking skills and flying tackles. From 1904 to '06, Marshall helped lead the Gophers to a 27–2 record as they outscored overwhelmed opponents by a whopping 1,314–63.

He earned All–Western Conference honors all three years in football. As a senior in 1906, he kicked a 60-yard field goal through the mud and rain to vanquish Chicago.

Marshall lettered in track as a sprinter and was baseball all-conference as a first baseman.

After graduation he opened a law office in Minneapolis but flourished playing segregated baseball for the St. Paul Colored Gophers, who barnstormed against the best Negro League teams in the United States.

From 1912 to '30 Marshall played, managed, or coached black and white baseball teams throughout Minnesota.

The Minneapolis Millers awarded him a lifetime pass to their games, and he watched future major league stars Roy Campanella and Willie Mays.

Marshall died in 1958 at age 72. In 1971, he was posthumously inducted into the College Football Hall of Fame.

86 Hannah Brandt

What's in a name? For Hannah Brandt, it was the twist of fate that launched a storied hockey career.

Minnesota's all-time women's hockey scoring leader grew up in Vadnais Heights, Minnesota, not exactly a rink rat.

"Hockey did not run in my family at all," she recalled in a 2015 interview with Fox Sports North. "My mom had me in dancing, gymnastics—anything you can think of."

Brandt was preschool classmates with a girl named Hannah Brodt, niece of former Gophers hockey players Winny and Chelsea Brodt. Their similar surnames caused a mixup among preschool staff, which ended up giving one Hannah the other's medication.

"So our parents ended up meeting each other through that and they got me into [hockey]," Hannah Brandt said.

At seven years old, Brandt was already skating with the Minnesota Wild. Sort of.

Her father, Greg, was a Wild season-ticket holder. In March 2001, he was the one millionth patron to enter the new arena and was honored during a pregame ceremony. Hannah donned a

Marian Gaborik No. 10 jersey and planted the Wild flag at center ice before the national anthem.

She debuted in 2012 as the reigning Ms. Minnesota Hockey and scored a hat trick in her first game. The freshman tallied 33 goals among 82 points as Minnesota went 41–0 to win the NCAA championship.

Brandt never stopped racking up points.

Midway through her senior season Brandt surpassed childhood idol Natalie Darwitz's 246 points with a flourish, scoring a career-high five goals to establish a new Minnesota record.

"I remember watching Natalie Darwitz play here; she was unbelievable," Brandt said. "To break one of her records is crazy to me. For that to become reality is pretty special to me."

Added coach Brad Frost: "What an accomplishment. We've had incredible players coming through our program and for her to be at that milestone is really great."

The two-time WCHA player of the year is one of just four three-time All-Americans in Minnesota history and the only three-time All-American in Gophers women's hockey history. She graduated with 115 goals, 170 assists, and 285 points, second most in NCAA Division I history.

Brandt also won three national championships for the Gophers, captaining the team to its second straight title in 2016. She rejoined the U.S. National team in 2016–17 and is gunning for a spot at the 2018 Olympics.

"When I was a little kid I always dreamed of being a Gopher, so it's crazy that I was able to live out that dream," she said.

Just to name one.

87 Amanda Kessel

Amanda Kessel skated into that familiar dog pile of Maroon-and-Gold–clad teammates, a yard sale's worth of hockey sticks, gloves, and helmets littering the goal crease after the Gophers won the 2016 NCAA women's hockey championship.

Was this really happening? Did Kessel just score the title-clinching goal against previously undefeated Boston College, or was she dreaming her storybook ending to a remarkable career almost ruined by concussion?

"I never could have imagined this happening. I'm just so grateful. I'm still waiting to wake up," Kessel said, still absorbing the magnitude of the moment at New Hampshire's Whittemore Center.

It was Kessel's third NCAA championship with Minnesota and definitely the most fulfilling.

Kessel dominated the national tournament, bagging a hat trick in Minnesota's first-round victory over Princeton and the game-tying goal in the semifinals against archrival Wisconsin.

Boston College was gunning for the first perfect season in women's hockey since the Gophers went 41–0 in 2012–13—Kessel's last season at Minnesota. She won the Patty Kazmaier Award that year as the top player in the country, scoring 46 goals and 55 assists.

The national championship game had Minnesota ahead 1–0 in the third period when Kessel buried a slap shot to put the Gophers in the lead for good.

Coach Brad Frost likened Kessel's comeback to a major league baseball team acquiring a slugger or closer at the trade deadline.

Just six weeks earlier, on February 5, 2016, Kessel returned to the ice at Ridder Arena to a thundering ovation three years after she had last skated for the Gophers. Sidelined by concussion symptoms after suffering a head injury practicing for Team USA leading up to the 2014 Sochi Olympics, Kessel was unsure whether she would ever play competitive hockey again.

She thrived during the Olympic tournament, scoring three goals among a team-high six points as Team USA won a silver medal. But Kessel's symptoms worsened after returning home.

She had redshirted from Minnesota to compete in the Olympics and had a year left of eligibility. But it took two years for her concussion symptoms to subside enough to gain medical clearance.

"Sometimes difficult things happen in life, and they only make you stronger," she said. "It was extremely challenging, but I did everything I could to get healthy."

Kessel's determination was rooted in her family's competitiveness growing up in Madison, Wisconsin, the younger sister of two hockey-playing brothers.

Her name was familiar to Gophers fans before Kessel arrived in Minnesota. Brother Phil played one season for men's coach Don Lucia before jumping to the NHL. Blake Wheeler played college hockey at New Hampshire.

Amanda played high school hockey at Shattuck–St. Mary's, the renowned boarding school in Faribault, Minnesota, where NHL stars Sidney Crosby and Zach Parise starred. As a senior there she scored 122 points in 46 games.

Football, not hockey, is in the Kessel genes. Their father, Phil, played nine games at quarterback in 1982 for the Calgary Stampeders of the Canadian Football League after a stellar career at Northern Michigan University.

During summer in Madison, the Wheelers would round up friends, including Ryan and Garrett Suter, to play pickup games at

Capital Ice Arena, which was operated by Suter's father and 1980 Olympian Bob Suter.

"As far as I can remember I was pretty much at the rink almost every night whether it was for my practices or just going there to watch my brothers' practices," Kessel told NHL.com in 2016.

The Wheeler and Suter brothers would split up and pick the teams.

"It was always kind of a race to see who would get her, and make sure she was on their team," Ryan Suter, defenseman for the Minnesota Wild, recalled in 2016. "She was good, man; she was really good. Just like she is now."

Kessel finished her Gophers career ranked second all-time in scoring behind Hannah Brandt with 108 goals and 248 points.

She signed with the New York Riveters of the National Women's Hockey League, reportedly for a record $26,000 contract. Kessel plans to play in the 2018 Olympics and hopes to end what would be a 20-year gold-medal drought for the United States.

"I think I'd regret it if I didn't get back to this point," Kessel said upon her return to Minnesota. "Playing for the Gophers has been some of the best memories of my life, so it was devastating to think that I wasn't going to be able to finish out a year. I guess it's pretty much a dream come true to come back and really be out there."

88 Natalie Darwitz

Two decades after graduating from a suburban pee wee boys' team, Natalie Darwitz continues to carry the flag for women's hockey in Minnesota.

Darwitz was 15 when she debuted for the U.S. women's national team. She wrapped 13 IIHF seasons around a sterling career at Minnesota before retiring after the 2010 Olympics. The Eagan, Minnesota, native helped the Gophers win back-to-back national championships in 2004 and 2005, and her 246 points were a school record for 11 years.

Darwitz had the cachet and coaching chops to land a Division I job but opted instead to perform an off-campus makeover on a downtrodden Division III team.

Decrepit Oscar Johnson Arena in St. Paul is Mars compared with the posh Olympic venues in Salt Lake City; Turin, Italy; and Vancouver, British Columbia, where Darwitz earned two silver medals and a bronze, or Ridder Arena, where the three-time All-American starred for the Gophers.

Yet there was no place Darwitz would rather be than shepherding tiny Hamline University after spending two seasons at her alma mater as an assistant women's coach under Brad Frost and four as head coach at Lakeville South High School.

In July 2015, only three months after accepting the Pipers job, Darwitz gave birth to her son, Joseph. She and husband Chris Arseneau welcomed the flexible schedule, which allows Darwitz to recruit and organize team activities from home.

"Everything we do in life, there's a bridge. I see our home life getting more hectic," she told the *Pioneer Press* in 2016. "Right

Gophers Women's Hockey Scoring Leaders

Player	Seasons	G	A	Pts.
Hannah Brandt	2012–16	115	170	286
Amanda Kessel	2010–13, '16	108	140	248
Natalie Darwitz	2002–05	102	144	246
Krissy Wendell	2002–05	106	131	237
Nadine Muzerall	1997–2001	139	96	235
Kelly Stephens	2001–05	97	122	219
Ambria Thomas	1997–01	89	112	201
Gigi Marvin	2005–09	87	108	195
Dani Cameranesi	2013–	75	94	169
Ronda Curtin	1999–2003	60	107	167

now, if I could call this place a home and I've proven myself and I can build this into a championship-caliber team—and have the same arrangement—five years down the road, if I'm still here, I'd say that's a pretty blessed life."

As a player, Darwitz was unrivaled in her ability to see the ice and develop plays before her opponents could react. A three-time world champion for Team USA, Darwitz won silver medals at the 2002 and 2010 Olympics and bronze in 2006.

At Minnesota she centered a dynamic scoring line with Krissy Wendell and Kelly Stephens as the Gophers roared to back-to-back national titles.

"That's the difference, playing with Krissy and Kelly, more stuff happens on the ice," Darwitz once said. "To me, it's like a Kobe–Shaq thing. Shaq's gone so Kobe's not going to do as well anymore. Without my teammates, I wouldn't be able to do what I have."

In only 99 games, Darwitz tallied 102 goals and 144 assists, scoring 42 goals and 114 points in her senior season—an NCAA record. Her 246 career points were surpassed in 2016 by Hannah Brandt (285) and Amanda Kessel (248).

She scored the game-winning goal against Harvard in the 2005 national championship game and was named the tournament's Most Outstanding Player. Those are the memories she cherishes most.

"Growing up, besides a youth tournament here or there, I never got to throw the gloves up in air and hog pile on the goalie," Darwitz recalled. "To say you're No. 1 is pretty special. To do that with such a special group, and to piggyback that and do it the following year and with our target on our backs the whole season, that's what athletics are all about. That's why you grind away through the season is for those national championships."

89 Krissy Wendell-Pohl

Krissy Wendell knocked down barriers and built up scoring records aplenty in women's hockey, but she blazed her first athletic trail on the baseball diamond.

Wendell hit .487 in 12 tournament games to become the first girl to start at catcher in the Little League World Series in 1994, when the 12-year-old represented her hometown of Brooklyn Park, Minnesota, in Williamsport, Pennsylvania. She played 18 innings that year at catcher and committed two errors while batting third in the lineup.

However, it was on the ice where Wendell thrived, especially at Ridder Arena. She was paired with Natalie Darwitz and the potent playmakers emerged as the most prolific scorers in women's hockey in the mid-2000s.

A three-time All-American, Wendell scored 106 goals among 237 points in 101 games for Minnesota, ranking fourth all-time in points.

She was twice the WCHA Player of the Year as the Gophers won consecutive national championships in 2004 and 2005. Wendell, whose older brother Erik played men's hockey for the Gophers, capped her college career by becoming the first Minnesota player to win the Patty Kazmaier Award as the country's best women's hockey player.

"She's one of the most gifted athletes I've ever seen," said Joel Johnson, an assistant coach during Wendell's tenure. "She enjoyed scoring goals more than anybody I've ever seen."

Wendell also was a two-time U.S. Olympian who won a silver medal in 2002 and captained Team USA to bronze in 2006.

"Being from Minnesota and being able to represent the U of M was a great honor, especially after watching my older brother who had represented the U the four years prior," she said. "I was excited to be a part of the tradition."

At Minnesota, Wendell met her future husband, Johnny Pohl, who was Erik's roommate while both played for the Gophers. The couple has three daughters and work as a coaching tandem in the Twin Cities.

In 2015–16, the Pohls coached their oldest daughter's under-8 team and the girl's hockey program at Cretin Derham-Hall High School.

90 Noora Räty

Noora Räty made ample history at Minnesota and the NCAA, but the world's pre eminent female goaltender was not satisfied.

In October 2014, she became the first woman to play in Finland's second-tier Mestis League, making 31 saves in a 5–2 loss for team Kiekko Vantaa.

"I still need a little bit more quickness," Räty told Finnish media. "It still takes a little bit too long before I react, so I just have to train some more."

No women's hockey goalie comes close to matching Räty's success at Minnesota.

She concluded her four-year career with the Gophers in March 2013 as a two-time national champion and the NCAA's all-time leader in wins (114) and shutouts (43). Räty earned Most Outstanding Player honors at the 2013 Frozen Four for stopping 47 of 52 shots in two national tournament games.

The Patty Kazmaier Award finalist finished her senior season with a 38–0 record, 0.96 goals-against average, and .956 save percentage.

However, citing a lack of true competition in women's professional hockey, Räty, at age 24, stunned her native Finland when she retired after the 2014 Sochi Olympics.

It was her third Winter Games. Räty won a bronze medal in 2010, four years after debuting for Finland as a 16-year-old at the 2006 Torino Olympics.

Räty said she could not live a proper lifestyle continually training for world championships and Olympics without suitable funding.

"I don't feel that women's hockey can grow or get any better in the future if the USA or Canada don't get a professional league started soon," Räty tweeted after her retirement. "That is the next critical step that our sport needs to take or our sport will never be respected like it should be. Asking players to work full-time and then training like a pro athlete at the same time is just too much and unfair."

A year later Kiekko-Vantaa signed her to a one-year contract. She was demoted to the third-tier league before earning her call-up on October 22, 2014.

"The challenge will be big," Räty said. "Now I need to work hard and change words into deeds."

91 Laura Halldorson

Laura Halldorson fell in love with hockey as a young girl in suburban Minneapolis taping Al Shaver's North Stars play-by-play on the radio and emulating his "He shoots, he scores!" calls.

She played at Princeton alongside the late Patty Kazmaier, whose name adorns the trophy awarded annually to the best women's college hockey player in the United States. But Halldorson made her name as the pioneering coach who established Minnesota as a national powerhouse.

"Laura put Minnesota women's hockey on the map," said former Gophers athletic director Joel Maturi. "She started with a blank slate and built a national championship program."

Three national titles, five consecutive Frozen Four appearances, and eight NCAA tournament berths defined Halldorson's 11-year run at Minnesota, which concluded with a remarkable 278–67–22 (.787) record.

Her teams won 20 or more games every season, including 152 in the Western Collegiate Hockey Association. A three-time American Hockey Coaches Association National Coach of the year, Halldorson led the Gophers to back-to-back NCAA titles in 2004 and '05.

"She has built the foundation and is the core for why the Gophers women's hockey program is as successful as it is now," said former player Nadine Muzerall, who scored the winning goal in the 2000 national championship game.

Halldorson was coaching high school volleyball, basketball, and softball for Wayzata schools and working at a mail-order comb company in 1987 when her college coach, Bob Ewell, offered her an assistant's job at Princeton.

"I had just bought my first car and had a car payment, so I was interested but didn't think I could afford to do it," Halldorson recalled to Wild.com. "He helped me with a part-time job and housing, and so I did that for a couple years. I actually had to save up in the offseason in order to get back, but that's what you do when you have an interest and a passion in doing something."

Halldorson took her first head-coaching job at tiny Colby College in Maine. Minnesota hired her in 1997 before the program was even sanctioned.

She coached five Olympians (Natalie Darwitz, Courtney Kennedy, Kelly Stephens, Lyndsay Wall, and Krissy Wendell) and eight All-Americans.

"We had some special groups of young women who came together as teams and got the job done on the ice," Halldorson recalled.

Citing time demands and a desire to spend more time with her family, Halldorson retired from coaching in 2007.

"You know what? I'm going to have to figure out something else at some point, why not now?" she said then. "I am proud of where the program is now. My goal was to lay a firm foundation doing things the right way but also by being successful on the ice and winning."

92 Brad Frost

He inherited a championship program and elevated it to a dynasty.

Brad Frost entered his 10th season coaching the Gophers' women's hockey program in 2016–17 having won four of the last five national championships, including back-to-back titles in 2012 and 2013 and again in 2015 and '16.

In January 2016, with little fanfare, Frost surpassed Laura Halldorson for career coaching wins at Minnesota, pushing his record to 293–45–22 after running the table again.

"It's a great honor," Frost told the *Pioneer Press* in March 2016. "All the coaches here put their heart and soul into their jobs and teams. Fortunately, we've been able to have great success the last four or five years.

"For us, it's just trying to do the right things every day. No question, the players we have had are pretty special, and that's allowed us to do some very special things."

Like their perfect 41–0 championship season in 2012–13. It was part of a 62-game winning streak that elevated the Gophers to almost mythical status.

Frost had never wanted for talent since Halldorson's former assistant succeeded her in 2007. A shrewd hockey tactician driven to win, Frost also preaches to his players about "the journey."

It is cherishing the fleeting relationships that coalesce in the dressing room, buses, and hotel rooms, bonding for a common purpose and appreciating the memories.

In 2010 the Gophers lost the championship game to Minnesota-Duluth, and Frost remembers how that failure soured an otherwise enjoyable season.

"My first couple years were all about winning national championships; I was focused on the wrong thing," he said.

"If we base our experience on whether we win or lose our last game, that's completely hollow. It's about creating great memories and friendships. I don't think about wins and losses from when I played. I think about the funny things that happened, sometimes away from the ice."

Minnesota's five dynamic seniors of 2015–16—Hannah Brandt, Amanda Kessel, Brook Garzone, Milica McMillen, and goaltender Amanda Leveille—composed the most prolific class in program history, their 148–9–6 record good for a .926 winning percentage. To be sure, a tough act to follow.

Yet the banners hanging at Ridder Arena—seven national championships, 10 consecutive NCAA tournament appearances—are powerful recruiting props. That has kept the talent train running through Dinkytown for two decades.

"He's an amazing coach, and we're surrounded by such great staff," said Dani Cameranesi, a senior entering the 2016–17 season. "They complement us, and we complement them very well."

The Canadian import is the humble steward of a perennial powerhouse among marquee programs that perpetually vex fans, a beacon of stability whose abiding Christian faith has guided him since he arrived in Minnesota as captain of the Bethel University hockey team back in 1992.

Frost has no desire to migrate to another coaching tree and hopes to retire from Minnesota.

"That's certainly a goal of mine," he said. "I have no aspirations to coach anywhere else or move to the men's side. I'm at the premier program in the country on the women's side, with plenty of talent we can attract. There's no need to go anywhere else."

93 "From the Graveyard to the Champion's Circle"

Contraction was an ugly buzzword in Minnesota in early 2002.

Major League Baseball threatened to fold the Twins and Montreal Expos instead of subsidizing their skimpy stadium revenues as the sport's warring owners and players dug in for another labor standoff. A Hennepin County judge saved the franchise by issuing a temporary restraining order that blocked baseball from snuffing the Twins.

From the brink of extinction to 2002 American League Central Division champions, the Twins and their forsaken fans reveled in their back-from-the-dead tale. Actually, the Gophers men's golf team had already written the script.

Facing a $21 million athletic-budget shortfall, university President Mark Yudof on April 11, 2002, recommended eliminating three teams—men's and women's golf and men's gymnastics—after the spring season in a cost cutting and restructuring aimed at trimming the deficit by $8.5 million over five years.

The timing could not have been worse for the men's golf program, which was rocked in September 2001 by the sudden resignation of longtime coach John Means. One of the most successful golf coaches in school history, Means led Minnesota to four straight NCAA finals and three consecutive top-12 finishes.

251

However, an audit revealed that $2,852 worth of airline tickets billed to the university were used by Means' relatives to travel with the team to tournaments. Assistant coach Brad James, an Australian and member of the 1993–95 Gophers teams, was promoted to interim coach. Seven months later, Yudof dropped his bomb.

Alumni and golf supporters were furious the 88-year-old program was suddenly on the chopping block. The public backlash compelled Yudof to give the men's golf program a one-year reprieve if boosters could raise $900,000 by the end of June. Fundraisers beat the deadline by a month and were securing another $1.8 million to sustain the three programs through 2005.

Meanwhile, back in purgatory, the Gophers were grinding away on the course, building their resume and confidence. They made a major statement May 5 by winning the school's first Big Ten championship in 30 years, soaring into the NCAA tournament at Ohio State as giddy underdogs.

"We've been on a mission," sophomore Simon Nash told the St. Paul *Pioneer Press*. "We've tried to use everything we could that was in our best interest as motivation. But the only thing we could control was our golf games, and we went out and did it."

History and geography were not on their side. No northern school had won an NCAA title since Ohio State in 1979 behind future PGA players John Cook and Joey Sindelar. Purdue was the other one in 1961.

Minnesota's highest finish was second in 1944 when Louis Lick won the individual championship. The Gophers entered the 72-hole tournament ranked 22nd nationally with no individuals in the top 50, while their strength of schedule was ranked 72nd. They finished fourth in the West Regional, three shots behind host New Mexico.

Nash made the task more daunting in the second round after being penalized two strokes for throwing his club as the Gophers tumbled to 16th place. He apologized to his teammates and vowed to make up for his undisciplined temper. Nash did just that, firing a career-best 68 in the third round to help Minnesota vault into fourth place behind No. 1–ranked Georgia Tech.

The cold-weather–hardened Gophers were the only team to shoot under par on another wet, windy day. Weather wreaked havoc the first two rounds. NCAA officials considered trimming the 30-team field in half for the final two rounds, which would have left the Gophers out in the cold.

It was another empty threat for a program left on death's door six weeks earlier.

The Gophers responded by shooting a 6-under 278 in the final round, making them the only team to shoot under par for the second straight day. The gutsy comeback fended off Georgia Tech, Clemson, and Texas—all warm-weather schools with long histories of national success.

Ironically, Yudof had announced the day before he was leaving Minnesota to become president at third-place Texas.

"It's unbelievable what this team just accomplished," James told reporters. "This team's got a bigger heart than any team I've ever been with."

Junior Matt Anderson, a walk-on from Edina who was not allowed to try out for the Gophers in 2000 because there were no spots available, led the charge with a 5-under 66. Justin Smith fired a 69. Wilhelm Schauman shot 71 and David Morgan 72.

"I never would have imagined that the day would ever come that they would threaten to cut our program," said Smith, the only player in the field who shot under par all four rounds. "We all used it as motivation. We just played amazing golf the past two or three weeks."

James ditched the interim tag and proceeded to win Big Ten titles in 2006 and 2007, finishing third and seventh at nationals, respectively. He was promoted to director of golf, overseeing the men's and women's programs through 2010, when James returned to his native land as high performance director for Golf Australia and the Australian Institute of Sport.

Gophers boosters Bob McNamara, Harvey Mackay, and Lou Nanne led the effort to raise $2.7 million to save men's and women's golf and men's gymnastics. McNamara went even further, endowing scholarships to insulate the programs from future budget cuts.

James presented McNamara with a 2002 national championship ring. Men's golf was eventually endowed with four and a half scholarships.

"I feel a debt of gratitude to everyone, and I don't want to pinpoint anyone, but Bob McNamara is the one driving this engine," James said in 2002. "The man is absolutely amazing."

McNamara died July 20, 2014, at age 82. His obituary in the *Star Tribune* referenced McNamara's All-American football prowess in the opening paragraph. His efforts to save golf led the second paragraph.

94 John Harris

John Harris defined golf excellence in Minnesota but made his name as the first Gophers hockey captain to win a national championship under legendary coach Herb Brooks, who was not keen about his leader's dual-sport passion.

Brooks challenged Harris in 1973–74 whether he was focused enough on hockey entering his senior season. After all, Harris had come to Minnesota from hockey hotbed Roseau near the Canadian border, where John and younger brother Robby starred on the renowned Rams' high school team.

"Some of the suggestions or recommendations that I got were to go south, where I could play golf year-round and get rid of hockey," Harris told the *New York Times* in 2007. "But I don't regret it and I don't look back. And I feel really lucky every day."

Harris was originally recruited by Glen Sonmor, who left Minnesota in 1973 to coach the Minnesota Fighting Saints of the World Hockey Association. He became Brooks' first captain, a role he later shared under golf coach Les Bolstad.

"What I was blessed with was mentors—Glen Sonmor, Herb Brooks, and Les Bolstad were great," Harris recalled.

Harris was the Gophers' second-leading scorer with 17 goals among 44 points, helping lead Minnesota to its first national championship.

Two months later, he won the 1974 Big Ten golf title and earned All-America honors in his secondary sport. After playing one season of minor league hockey, Harris earned his PGA Tour card in 1976.

He knocked around for three years before retiring to the private sector, cofounding the Harris-Homeyer Insurance Co. in 1979 with Bill Homeyer—father of future U.S. Women's Open champion Hilary Lunke.

However, the competitive juices never stopped flowing. Harris regained his amateur status in 1983 and embarked on a second career as one of Minnesota's most decorated recreational players.

The five-time Minnesota Golf Association Player of the Year won several State Amateur titles. He also played on four Walker Cup teams—the amateur equivalent of the biannual Ryder Cup competition between the best European and U.S. tour players.

Harris won the 1993 U.S. Amateur title over Danny Ellis in a playoff in Houston, a victory he compared to the Gophers' hockey championship two decades earlier.

"It's funny, the feelings right after each were so eerily similar," Harris told *Let's Play Hockey* magazine in 2015. "I remember sitting in the locker room in Boston in 1974. The complete satisfaction, the camaraderie with our teammates, the respect that every player had for all of the players on the team. The bond among those players is so unique. The feeling when I finished in golf was similar."

Later, Harris returned to professional golf on the Champions Tour. In 2006, he won his only tournament, sinking a six-foot birdie putt on the first playoff hole to defeat Tom Jenkins in the Commerce Bank Championship in East Meadow, New York.

The Minnesota Golf Hall of Famer later coached the women's program at Minnesota, drawing inspiration on the course and in life from his college golf coach.

"I was blessed to spend four years with Les Bolstad," Harris recalled. "He was a brilliant coach and teacher. He was real good for my psyche. When I was playing badly, he was encouraging. When I played well he said, 'Great, now let's take this to the next level.'

"He believed in my fundamentals, and I kept getting a little better each year. The foundation and base he gave me was excellent. I used Les as a coach until the day he died."

95 Tom Lehman

Patience was a valuable virtue for Tom Lehman.

Minnesota's greatest golfer was a professional grinder, a five-time PGA Tour winner who needed 12 years to collect his first winner's check. By 1997, Lehman was the No. 1 player in the world.

Born in Austin and raised in Alexandria, Lehman became a three-time All-American at Minnesota and was the 1981 Minnesota Amateur champion. The right-hander perfected a low draw iron shot that ripped through the cold and chill of Minnesota's prairie-swept courses—a skill that helped him win golf's oldest championship.

Lehman turned pro in 1982 and spent a decade on tour honing his game. In 1993, he finished third at the Masters. A year later he was second at Augusta National and won his first PGA title at the Memorial. He won the 1995 Colonial with a then-record 20-under-par and finished third at the U.S. Open.

Lehman peaked in 1996 when he finished second at the U.S. Open and won the British Open at Royal Lytham & St. Annes, the first American to win at the venerable club since Bobby Jones 70 years earlier. He was named PGA Player of the Year with a tour-leading 69.32 scoring average.

Lehman, with more than $18 million in career earnings, was a three-time Ryder Cup competitor and once a captain. Davis Love III, who captained the 2016 U.S. team, selected him as a vice captain for his knowledge of Minnesota golf conditions at Hazeltine National in Chaska, Minn.

Lehman was moved to tears after the United States defeated Europe for just its third title in the biennial event since 1999.

"I'm just so proud," Lehman said after Ryan Moore sank the winning putt on the 18th green. "It was very emotional for me. I was bawling like a baby. Just to be a part of this, representing this state, trying to be part of the team that was going to bring the victory here back home, and then delivering, that's really something."

96 P.J. Bogart

The diving board became P.J. Bogart's stage at age 11, so perhaps it was inevitable that Minnesota's greatest diver would build a professional career performing on one.

After measuring success in meters and pikes, Bogart performed for the Cirque du Soleil theatrical company in Las Vegas for 13 years.

"I've always considered myself a showman, and Cirque du Soleil gives me an outlet for that," said Bogart, who acted in *O* from 2001 to '14.

After growing up in Mesa, Arizona, Bogart came to Minnesota in 1993 and made an immediate splash winning the Big Ten and NCAA platform diving championships with freshman scoring records in the 1- and 3-meter events.

He was an unprecedented four-time All American and the only Gophers diver to win two NCAA titles. Craig Lincoln won the 3-meter event in 1972.

As a sophomore in 1994, Bogart became Minnesota's first All-American in all three diving events. He repeated the feat in 1995 and was named Big Ten Men's Athlete of the Year.

Bogart's senior season in 1996 was also one for the record books. He won his eighth national title with a 632.97-point performance in the 1-meter event and again swept the All-America honors in all three diving events. That helped lead Minnesota to its first Big Ten diving championship in 70 years.

Bogart finished his career with eight national titles, eight Big Ten championships, and 12 All-America honors.

"I was surprised that I was able to get to that level when I first [arrived at Minnesota]," Bogart told the *Arizona Republic* in 2007. "I was definitely a little cocky. I knew I was good. But I was really shocked to have success as a freshman."

Bogart was a U.S. 1- and 3-meter champion and narrowly missed the 2000 Olympics when he finished third in the 3-meter event—four points shy of making the American team.

"It was devastating," said Bogart.

He retreated to a life as a waiter and bartender, but once he saw a Cirque du Soleil show in Australia, with its acrobatics and athleticism, his performance juices flowed again.

Bogart auditioned for a workshop in Montreal, where he immersed himself in acting lessons and stagecraft. He recounted an exercise in which trainees walked toward a mirror screaming, "Why are you looking at me?" each step.

"Once you do that, you can do anything," Bogart once told *USA Today*.

Bogart was cast in the lead role in the aquatic production of *O* and has performed in several stage shows.

"It's a show," he said. "It's not competitive. I'm going to do it as long as I can until they kick me out."

97 Ray Christensen

Ray Christensen called 510 Gophers football games and 1,309 men's basketball games during a storied Twin Cities radio career that spanned 10 U.S. presidents over a half century.

From Paul Giel, Sandy Stephens, and Dan Nystrom to Mychal Thompson, Trent Tucker, and Bobby Jackson, Christensen marked the time from Williams Arena and Memorial Stadium to the Metrodome and Mariucci Arena.

His excitable baritone entertained listeners during autumn Saturday afternoons and warmed them on cold winter nights. Christensen's audience was exclusive and generational but he never projected his soothing voice past the individual he solely wanted to reach.

"Everybody is not listening; anybody is," he said in 2002. "One person has always been my philosophy. If I can get what I'm doing across to one person then I have completed my objective. If it's multiplied by hundreds, or maybe even thousands, fine. That's gravy. But I'm still aiming at one person and I always have."

Christensen, who died in February 2017 at 92, started his career at University of Minnesota station KUOM in 1946, reading news and sports reports while studying broadcasting. Two years later he was hired to be the Gophers' football play-by-play man.

Christensen's first broadcast was September 29, 1951, when Minnesota lost 25–20 to No. 8 Washington at Memorial Stadium.

"Heading into that first game I was very nervous but excited," he said. "My friends and family all listened, and they told me I did a great job. They probably would have told me that regardless of how I did but it was a lot of fun."

Christensen did not get paid his first season except for $2.50 in meal money on the road. In 1952 he earned $25 per game. When he retired in 2001, the university hung a banner honoring Christensen in the rafters at Williams Arena and established a scholarship in his name.

Among his favorite calls were last-second football wins at Michigan in 1986 and Penn State in 1999, plus the Gophers' 1977 upset over the Wolverines in Minneapolis.

"The Gophers have upset the No. 1 team in the nation, Michigan!" went Christensen's call. "The fans are streaming on the field and the Gophers coming over to the sideline and getting the Little Brown Jug and holding it high! Oh, I hope the jug survives!"

His most-imitated call was in 1997 when the Gophers basketball team defeated UCLA to advance to the Final Four, and Christensen bellowed, "The road to Indianapolis is now paved in Gold!"

"People have asked me a lot about that line over the past few years. Often times I will think of a line or statement in case a big event happens, but this time I did not and it just came to me as the final seconds ticked off the clock," he explained.

In 2000, Christensen received the Chris Schenkel Award from the College Football Hall of Fame. Two years later he was inducted into the Minnesota Broadcasters Hall of Fame.

"It is very special to have my picture hanging from the rafters," Christensen said. "Gopher fans, players, and coaches have been so wonderful to me and my family through the years, and the Maroon and Gold have been an important part of our lives. It has been a very special relationship."

98 The Man with the Golden Voice

The Gopher mascot became synonymous with Minnesota even before it became the country's 32nd state in 1858.

A satirical cartoon was published a year earlier depicting nine gopher bodies with the heads of territorial politicians pulling a locomotive. The story covered a $5 million bill to expand railroads into western Minnesota. Local residents started identifying themselves as Gophers. Shortly thereafter the University of Minnesota adopted the nickname.

It was another 80 years before a lyrical broadcaster with a mischievous nature added the "golden" touch.

Halsey Hall was born to be a newspaperman. His father, Smith B. Hall, was a reporter who covered Minneapolis. His great uncle, Harlan P. Hall, cofounded the evening *St. Paul Dispatch*.

In November 1919, when he was 21, Hall's first byline appeared in the *Minneapolis Tribune*. His writing career straddled the Twin Cities as Hall left for the St. Paul *Pioneer Press* and later returned to Minneapolis to cover sports for the *Journal*.

In the early 1930s, Hall joined WCCO radio just as football coach Bernie Bierman arrived in Minnesota and launched a dynasty. Bierman decided to switch the Gophers' jerseys and pants to all gold.

"They were a dull gold and not particularly attractive, but that only made the powerhouse teams of the '30s seem all the more intimidating," wrote Ray Christensen, Minnesota's radio play-by-play announcer from 1951 to 2000.

At WCCO, and later crosstown rival KSTP, Hall broadcast three consecutive national championship teams in 1934, '35, and

'36 during a 10-year run in which Minnesota won five national titles and seven Big Ten championships while losing only 12 games.

During that era of dominance, Hall coined the term "Golden Gophers" describing stars Bronko Nagurski, Pug Lund, and Bruce Smith dashing up and down the field.

Hall was a cheeky storyteller on the air and an after-hours raconteur known for carrying a satchel full of booze wherever he went. *Pioneer Press* columnist Joe Soucheray once joked that whenever Hall disembarked from an airplane his clinking whiskey bottles sounded like a glockenspiel.

Sports Illustrated described Hall's friendly delivery and jovial nature in the booth as "redolent of happy days at Grandpa's house." He also had an irreverent streak, according to author Stew Thornley, who profiled Hall in 2009 for the Society for American Baseball Research.

One Saturday, as the Michigan Wolverines ran out of the tunnel to play the Gophers, Hall described the scene: "Michigan comes onto the field in blue jerseys and maize pants. And how they got into Mae's pants, I'll never know."

Hall went on to broadcast games for the minor league Minneapolis Millers of the American Association. He was tapped in 1961 to join Herb Carneal and Ray Scott as the original voices of the Twins when the franchise relocated to Minnesota from Washington.

Thornley pointed out that it was Hall in Minnesota who first hollered "Holy Cow!" when describing a big play in a ballgame—not Phil Rizzuto with the New York Yankees or later Harry Caray with the Chicago Cubs.

Hall broadcast Twins games until 1972 but remained on the air at WCCO until his death in 1977. So popular was Hall that in 1979 he was posthumously voted Minnesota's top sportscaster of the 1970s.

In 1985 the Halsey Hall Chapter of the Society for American Baseball Research was named in his honor. Four years later Hall was inducted into the Minnesota Sports Hall of Fame.

"Halsey Hall laughed his way through life," eulogized Dick Cullum, Hall's newspaper colleague and friend. "And he kept the rest of us laughing, too."

99 Cheer "Ski-U-Mah!"

Toss an English sport, a Princeton grad, a young Native American canoe racer, and two rugby roommates into fate's blender and you get "Ski-U-Mah," Minnesota's enduring cheer and one of the state's most endearing pieces of folklore.

The Gophers had been playing football for two years on campus without much fanfare in 1884 when an intramural rugby team was organized into competing practice squads.

Professor Thomas Peebles volunteered to lead one of the squads. Whenever his group scored or defeated the other side, players locked arms and put their heads together in a circle, yelling "Sis-Boom-Ah, Princeton," in honor of the professor's alma mater.

John Adams and Win Sargent were on the losing end. The roommates decided they needed a retaliatory chant. They included "Rah-rah-rah" but also wanted Minnesota in it. Only it had one too many syllables. So Adams and Sargent cut one out and renamed the state "Minn-so-ta."

Adams racked his brain for another three-syllable rhyme. One Sunday he went to Lake Pepin, 70 miles southeast of Minneapolis.

That afternoon several young Native American boys were racing canoes. Their friends cheered them on from shore.

Adams listened intently as one of the winners raised his arms and yelled "Ski-oo!" Adams' writer's block melted. He added "mah" to the Native American's chant and he had his cheer, the second line morphing into shorthand for the University of Minnesota:

Rah, rah, rah.

Ski-U-Mah.

Minn-so-ta!

Adams and Sargent took to the streets and became the first Minnesota students to chant it.

"It was late in the evening, and one of the neighboring windows was opened and a voice invited the boys to 'shut up and go to bed,'" according to a 1928 *Minnesota Alumni* magazine article.

The *Ariel,* Minnesota's original student newspaper, printed Adams and Sargent's cheer in 1885. But it initially failed to rouse much crowd noise.

A committee was formed to promote the cheers. Senior student leader Byron Timberlake, a future insurance executive and state legislator, traveled to Des Moines, Iowa, in the spring of 1891 to an interstate oratorical contest, according to *Minnesota Alumni.* Delegations from colleges across the country demonstrated their cheers and sporting rituals.

"Finally, Mr. Timberlake stood up, climbed up on his chair, and with his hat raised high above his head on a cane, he gave the yell for the first time in a public gathering. The yell was the hit of the evening, and Mr. Timberlake was obliged to respond to several encores," according to *Minnesota Alumni.*

In 1896, the cheer debuted at the Michigan game near the university armory. The yell marshal divided the cheer into sections. After the game, the Ariel declared it a rousing success.

"One had to be there to appreciate the effect of four or five hundred 'Rah, Rah, Rah, Ski-U-Mahs' at once," the paper wrote.

Three years later, cheerleaders amplified "Ski-U-Mah" through megaphones when the Gophers moved to Greater Northrop Field. The popular phrase later was incorporated into both the official school song, "Hail! Minnesota," and more commonly in the "Minnesota Rouser."

"Ski-U-Mah" became a chant of approbation and affection in the grandstands. When the cheer leader wanted to compliment a player, he would yell, "What's the matter with Smith?"

The crowd would answer: "He's all right."

"Who's all right?"

"Smith!"

"Who is Smith?"

"He's a la-la, he's a lu-lu. He's a Ski-U-Mah!"

"Who'd you say?"

"Smith!"

"Ski-U-Mah" has evolved into a universal chant shared by alumni at arenas and stadiums and a phrase belted out by Minnesotans who simply want to revel in success.

100 Governor's Victory Bell

Only Minnesota has four active regular season trophy games, punctuated by its most recent addition, the Governor's Victory Bell.

Created in 1993 by then–acting Pennsylvania Governor Mark Singel and former Governor Arne Carlson of Minnesota, the first Gophers–Penn State game at Beaver Stadium in Happy Valley was also the inaugural Big Ten game for the Nittany Lions.

The brass bell bearing a medallion of the Big Ten Conference is suspended from a wooden frame, the top of which is adorned with the state seals, and a brass plate at the bottom that features game scores.

Penn State won the first four games before the Gophers shocked college football in 1999 by knocking off the No. 2–ranked Nittany Lions 24–23 at Beaver Stadium when Dan Nystrom kicked a 32-yard field goal as time expired.

It was the start of a four-game Gophers winning streak, which Penn State promptly duplicated. Penn State won the most recent game between the teams in 2016, and the Nittany Lions hold an 9–5 advantage in the series.

Sources

The author gratefully acknowledges the following sources used in researching Gophers history for this book.

Books

Bernstein, Ross. *America's Coach*. St. Paul: Bernstein Books, 2006.
———. *The "M" Club Hall of Fame*. St. Paul: Bernstein Books, 2007.
Bruton, Jim. *Gopher Glory: The Pride of the Maroon & Gold*. Stevens Point: KCI Sports Publishing, 2001.
Christensen, Ray. *Ray Christensen's Gopher Tales: Stories from all Eleven University of Minnesota Men's Sports*. New York: Skyhorse Publishing, 2012.
Coffey, Wayne. *Boys of Winter: The Untold Story of a Coach, a Dream, and the 1980 U.S. Olympic Hockey Team*. New York: Crown Publishers, 2005.
Gilbert, John. *Herb Brooks: The Inside Story of a Hockey Mastermind*. Minneapolis: MVP Books, 2008.
Hoftbeck, Steven R. *Swinging for the Fences: Black Baseball in Minnesota*. St. Paul: Minnesota Historical Society Press, 2005.
Kill, Jerry. *Chasing Dreams: Living My Life One Yard at a Time*. Chicago: Triumph Books, 2016.
Rippel, Joel. *75 Memorable Moments in Minnesota Sports*. St. Paul: Minnesota Historical Society Press, 2003.

Newspapers and Magazines

Arizona Republic
Chicago Tribune
Hibbing Daily Tribune

Minnesota Alumni magazine
Minnesota Daily
Minneapolis *Star Tribune*
New York Times
Providence Journal
Sports Illustrated
St. Paul *Pioneer Press*
USA Today
Washington Post

Websites
ESPN.com
GopherHole.com
GopherSports.com
Let's Play Hockey
Minnpost.com
NCAA.com
NHL.com
Society for American Baseball Research (SABR.org)
St. Louis Park Historical Society
VikingsUpdate.com

Television
Fox Sports North
WCCO-TV